Harold Pinter

The Birthday Party
The Caretaker
The Homecoming

A CASEBOOK

EDITED BY

MICHAEL SCOTT

MACMILLAN

First published 1986

Published by
MACMILLAN EDUCATION LTD
Houndmills, Basingstoke, Hampshire RG21 2XS
and London
Companies and representatives
throughout the world

Typeset by Wessex Typesetters
(Division of The Eastern Press Ltd), Frome, Somerset

Printed in Hong Kong

ISBN 0-333-35269-6
ISBN 0-333-35271-8 (Pbk)

To Tess and Moya
and in memory of Sheila

CONTENTS

Part Four: *The Homecoming*

GENERAL EDITOR'S PREFACE

The Casebook series, launched in 1968, has become a well-regarded library of critical studies. The central concern of the series remains the 'single-author' volume, but suggestions from the academic community have led to an extension of the original plan, to include occasional volumes on such general themes as literary 'schools' and genres.

Each volume in the central category deals either with one well-known and influential work by an individual author, or with closely related works by one writer. The main section consists of critical readings, mostly modern, collected from books and journals. A selection of reviews and comments by the author's contemporaries is also included, and sometimes comment from the author himself. The Editor's Introduction charts the reputation of the work or works from the first appearance to the present time.

Volumes in the 'general themes' category are variable in structure but follow the basic purpose of the series in presenting an integrated selection of readings, with an Introduction which explores the theme and discusses the literary and critical issues involved.

A single volume can represent no more than a small selection of critical opinions. Some critics are excluded for reasons of space, and it is hoped that readers will pursue the suggestions for further reading in the Select Bibliography. Other contributions are severed from their original context, to which some readers may wish to turn. Indeed, if they take a hint from the critics represented here, they certainly will.

A. E. DYSON

A NOTE ON TEXTS

References throughout this volume have been standardised according
to the following single-volume editions of the plays:

    The Birthday Party   2nd edition, revised (Methuen, London, 1965);
    The Caretaker   2nd edition, revised (Methuen, London, 1962);
    The Homecoming   2nd edition (Methuen, London, 1966).

INTRODUCTION

Once many years ago, I found myself engaged uneasily in a public discussion on theatre. Someone asked me what my work was 'about'. I replied with no thought at all and merely to frustrate this line of enquiry: 'The weasel under the cocktail cabinet.' That was a great mistake. Over the years I have seen that remark quoted in a number of learned columns. It has now seemingly acquired a profound significance, and is seen to be a highly relevant and meaningful observation about my own work. But for me the remark meant precisely nothing. (Harold Pinter, 1970)[1]

Harold Pinter is the product of a post-war generation that has attempted to reject the evils of the twentieth century and present a new outlook on society. That is not to say that Pinter is consciously didactic. Overtly he states that he is not. Rather, he expresses the experience of man in transition, not in terms of the angry young man in frustration or revolt, nor of the vacuity of man faced with metaphysical absurdity: he expressed man in his fear, joy, humour, stupidity, ambition. He is concerned with the human condition as it is today. We should not ask what his plays 'mean' but rather see them as theatrical experiences engaging and provoking an emotional and intellectual response from his audience. He writes:

I am not concerned with making general statements. I am not interested in theatre used simply as a means of self-expression on the part of people engaged in it. I find in so much group theatre, under the sweat and assault and noise, nothing but valueless generalisations, naive and quite untruthful. I can sum up none of my plays. I can describe none of them, except to say: That is what happened. That is what they say. That is what they did.[2]

Dramatic criticism has often become obsessed with defining the meaning of plays but for a playwright such as Pinter the meaning is the play itself. To theorise the subject of the drama is for him to go against the experiences and the emotions he wishes to communicate. Thus, in an early article (1962) he writes:

If I were to state any moral precept it might be: Beware of the writer who puts forward his concern for you to embrace, who leaves you in no doubt as to his worthiness, his usefulness, his altruism, who declares that his heart is in the right place, and ensures that it can be seen, in full view, a pulsating mass where his characters ought to be. What is presented, so much of the time, as a body of active and positive thought, is in fact a body lost in a prison of empty definition and cliché.[3]

– while in a later interview (1971) he goes on to say:

What I'm interested in is emotion which is contained, and felt very, very deeply. Jesus, I don't really want to make a categorical statement about this. But, perhaps, it is ultimately inexpressible. Because I think we express our emotions in so many small ways, all over the place – or can't express them in any other way.[4]

The plays communicate feelings, emotions, experiences which the playwright sees and which he then mediates for our perception as an audience. His plays in this respect have an affinity with the nature of poetry. When asked in the same interview about other playwrights, he shows his admiration for dramatists of a different school – Edward Bond, Heathcote Williams – and reacts firmly to questions implying a lack of political interests:

I'm very conscious of what's happening in the world. I'm not by any means blind or deaf to the world around me . . . No, no. Politicians just don't understand me. What, if you like, interests me, is the suffering for which they are responsible. It doesn't interest me – it horrifies me! (Pause.) I mean, Jesus Christ. Well, you know, there's so much. What can one say? It's all so evident.[5]

He continues by saying that he is not a prophet, nor is he a theorist but a playwright and that 'A play has to speak for itself'.

In a technological age of proof and counterproof and a sociological climate of analysis and polemic, such attitudes have caused problems for critics and audiences alike. When his first major play, *The Birthday Party*, appeared in 1958 it met almost unanimous critical hostility or dismissal. Writing two years later, Kenneth Tynan admitted that he had failed to detect in it the promise of the dramatist. *The Birthday Party* was for him 'a clever fragment grown dropsical with symbolic content', a 'piece . . . full of those familiar paranoid overtones that seem inseparable from much of *avant garde* drama'.[6] Harold Hobson, the influential critic of the *Sunday Times*, however, had run against the stream of adverse criticism in 1958, proclaiming 'that Mr Pinter, on the evidence of this work, possesses the most original, disturbing and arresting talent in theatrical London'.[7] He continued by drawing comparisons between the play and Henry James's *The Turn of the Screw*: a comparison put into perspective by Irving Wardle's less well known positive review of the play in July of the same year (see Part Two, below). Hobson perceptively noted further that 'one of the greatest merits' of the play is the 'fact that no one can say what precisely it is about, or give the address from which the intruding Goldberg and McCann come, or say precisely why it is that Stanley is so frightened', concluding that it 'is exactly in this vagueness that its spine chilling quality lies'.

It was, however, precisely this vagueness to which Literary London in 1958 took exception. A twin phenomenon of revolt against the dramatic conventions of writers such as Noel Coward and Terence

Rattigan had been accepted. John Osborne with *Look Back in Anger* (1956) and Samuel Beckett with *Waiting for Godot* (produced in London in 1955) had drawn the boundaries of the new theatre, and new dramatists were expected – by the critics at least – to be followers of one of the two styles. It was clear that Pinter's work was not in the vein of Osborne. His language was far to eliptic for that school and his plots far too obscure. He was seen therefore, in comparison with Samuel Beckett (whose works he had read) and Eugene Ionesco (whose works he had not read), as the English exponent of what Martin Esslin termed 'the theatre of the absurd'.

Such a categorisation was acceptable for a time, but critical comparisons between Pinter and Beckett began to show that they seemed to be different from each other. In Pinter, the intensity of the metaphysical theme was not as apparent as in Beckett's work. Man, for Beckett, was being contemplated in relation to a void. He seemed 'a tragic joke in a context of total cosmic absurdity'.[8] In plays such as *Waiting for Godot* and *Endgame* metaphysical concerns seemed to be involved with the dilemma of man's existence. Pinter's vision, however, centred largely on man without reference to the spiritual void. In this respect it was possibly easier to associate Pinter with Ionesco, who had quickly become regarded as the spokesman for absurdist theatre. Menace, fear, the clutter of daily living, the concentration on trivial possessions, the focus on the banality of language were elements which seemed to form a common denominator between these two dramatists. Ionesco held the theatrical limelight for some time, but his decline was imminent. Kenneth Tynan, who had earlier celebrated Ionesco as a major new dramatist, began to have doubts about the absurdist movement and Ionesco in particular. In 1958, in an article in the *Observer*, Tynan declared Ionesco's theatre as a dead-end art form, an interesting experiment but a cul de sac in the progress of contemporary drama:

M. Ionesco . . . offers an 'escape from realism': but an escape into what? A blind alley, perhaps, adorned with *tachiste* murals. Or a self-imposed vacuum, wherein the author ominously bids us observe the absence of air. Or, best of all, a funfair ride on a ghost train, all skulls and hooting waxworks, from which we emerge into the far more intimidating clamour of diurnal reality. M. Ionesco's theatre is pungent and exciting but remains a diversion. It is not on the main road: and we do him no good, nor the drama at large, to pretend that it is . . .[9]

Ionesco defended himself, and the debate between the two over a number of weeks became a part of theatre history known as 'the London Controversy'. To a large extent time proved Tynan correct. The Ionesco phenomenon began to fade, in Britain at least. Pinter, however, continued to flourish into the late seventies and the eighties, with his latest dramatic trilogy *Other Places* playing to packed houses at theatres in London and his play *A Kind Of Alaska* being presented on television.

It seems that most critics of Pinter have to find some label or comparison to explain his work, although as early as 1962 and 1966 Ruby Cohn (see Part One, below) and Richard Schechner[10] were expressing serious doubts about too close a link being drawn between him and Beckett, Ionesco or Genet. Traditionally, too, in dramatic scholarship heavily influenced by the restrictive conventions of English literary criticism, playwrights and plays tended to be evaluated in the sixties according to 'meaning'. Discussions revolved around such topics as 'The moral function of . . . plays'. In following this pattern early accounts of Pinter's work found themselves wanting. Much of this early criticism is reduced to telling the story of the plays – understandably, since many readers would have been ignorant of them – and then offering a speculative commentary on their moral significance. Pinter is de-allegorised and his characters, if not fulfilling naturalistic expectations, are explained in terms of their thematic function to the total allegory. This early work unfortunately laid the foundation for an approach to Pinter which has reached industrial proportions, particularly across the Atlantic.

Some of this work is creditable, but too often fundamental mistakes of dramatic criticism are commonplace in essays and books about his work. Far too often his characters, if not given an allegorical parallel, are seen as 'real people' with backgrounds beyond the information of the play. When we are told (in a discussion of *The Caretaker*) that Aston's preoccupation with electric plugs goes back to a time when his father rebuked him for playing with himself in bed,[11] we are in the realm of 'How Many Children had Lady Macbeth?' and even further from the experience of the plays as dramatic events. This trend in criticism, unfortunately not confined to Pinter, can trap even the most exciting of critics. Was Davies the first visitor to the house? Ronald Knowles suggests in his otherwise excellent discussion of the play (see Part Three, below).

Guido Almansi's challenging essay, 'Harold Pinter's Idiom of Lies' (Part One, below), warns of a related pitfall for Pinter criticism: a tendency towards critical credulity. The belief critics have placed in the characters' words fails to square with the plays in which these characters appear. It is nonsense to say, with Nigel Alexander,[12] that Mick, in *The Caretaker*, believed Davies to be an interior decorator; but it would be just as ridiculous to say that he did not believe him to be so. The question of what Mick does or does not believe is as unanswerable as those A. C. Bradley once asked concerning *Macbeth*. Yet Nigel Alexander in the perceptive opening of his essay (excerpted in Part One, below) is highly instructive in demonstrating how Pinter employs dramatic structure to create theatrical tensions between present words and action in relation to information about the past and predictions for the future. This tension is the experience of time not merely for the actors in character but for the audience watching the play in performance.

It is in terms of how Pinter's plays operate rather than what they signify that the best criticism has developed. Peter Davison, John Russell Brown and Bernard Dukore, in particular, have asked how the plays work as drama. In an original approach and entertaining essay, first delivered as a lecture, Peter Davison (Part Three, below) sees a continuity in Pinter and Beckett from the English Music Hall tradition. Pinter's theatricality is based on the conventions of popular entertainment as much as Shakespeare's theatre was indebted to the popular traditions of medieval drama. Thus parallels can be discerned between speeches in *The Caretaker* and the comic monologues of such entertainers as Dan Leno.

Katharine Worth also sees Pinter within the context of a theatrical convention. Noel Coward, in criticising the development of fifties drama, singled out Pinter as an exception to the trend for novelty. Coward believed Pinter to be furthering the essential continuity of English drama. Worth (Part One, below) goes further, pointing out contrasts and comparisons with Anton Chekhov as well as T. S. Eliot.

It can be convincingly argued that Chekhov is the father of much modern drama. He broke away from nineteenth-century explicit theatre to devise implicit drama depending on the subtext, on what was not said but was implied rather than on the surface meaning of the words themselves. Thus, in plays such as *Uncle Vanya* and *The Cherry Orchard*, the dominant form of communication is made through the absence of direct explanation. This is true also of Pinter's drama. Pinter writes of his characters:

Between my lack of biographical data about them and the ambiguity of what they say there lies a territory which is not only worthy of exploration but which it is compulsory to explore. You and I, the characters which grow on a page, most of the time we're inexpressive, giving little away, unreliable, elusive, evasive, obstructive, unwilling. But it's out of these attributes that a language arises. A language, I repeat, where, under what is said, another thing is being said.[13]

Within the subtext is the strategy of pause and silence which in Pinter's plays are as important as the tense dialogue or the comic repartee or the long monologue. In a penetrating study John Russell Brown has examined the pace of the plays. The silences and pauses are considered in their relation to the spoken word in a manner demanded by anyone rightly interested in the plays as primarily artifacts for performance. His interest is in the spatial and visual dimension of the play as much as in its text. Thus, in his discussion of *The Caretaker* (Part Three, below), he emphasises the gestures and movement of the characters, the stage set, the drip in the hanging bucket, as integral to the experience of the play but something which readers are too often likely to miss.

Not surprisingly it is the subtext, the pause, the silences, the setting, in relation to each other and the text, which Peter Hall, artistic director of the National Theatre, stresses in his interview with Simon Trussler and Catherine Itzin (Part One, below). Hall emphasises, however, that his approach to a Pinter production is only one of a possible variety of differing interpretations. As a theatrical practitioner Hall is subscribing to the view so often neglected by traditional literary criticism, that drama is a corporate creative activity involving writer, actors, directors, designers and audience, and thus allowing various productions and interpretations to be totally different from each other and yet be equally valid. It is a view proved correct by Bernard Dukore in his comparison (Part Four, below) between Peter Hall's production of *The Homecoming* in 1965 and Kevin Billington's 1978 revival. Whereas Hall 'stressed menace and savagery', Billington 'emphasised vulnerability and humanity'. We may ask further to what extent these differences depended on a change of social attitudes and economic climates from the sixties to the seventies.

Cultural and social contexts naturally affect dramatic performance and criticism. Views and interpretations change according to the predilictions, social and linguistic conditioning of the critic or interpreter. Peter Hall tells us that, when in *The Homecoming* Ruth refers to Teddy as Eddie, it is 'obviously the intimate and familiar name'. The implication is that it is friendly, and that decision by the director will influence his interpretation of the play. But what if this use of 'Eddie' was seen as a sign of hostility related in the pattern of the play to Ruth earlier calling Lenny, Leonard? An American critic, Charles Carpenter, comments:

the fact that Ruth calls him Eddie suggests that 'Teddy' is meant as a nickname not for Theodore but for Edward – a suggestion which invites comparisons with the similarly cuckolded stuffed shirt named Edward in *A Slight Ache*. But she may also be symbolically withdrawing from him by muffing his name; or she may be knocking the 'Theo' – the divinity – out of what is left of him; or she may be hinting he is no longer her Teddy bear – or Teddy boy, for that matter.[14]

The perception of the critic or the director depends not merely on Pinter's play but on the cultural context of the reader or audience. Theodore is a more popular name in the United States than in England, and the nickname Teddy (having particular associations perhaps with Theodore Roosevelt) is more readily linked in America with Theodore than with Edward. In England the reverse is true. Edward is associated with royalty and is popularly abbreviated both as Teddy and Eddie. Varieties of interpretations derive from the differing points of view of the reader, director, actors and audience as much as from the fluidity of the text.

Concentration on the language employed is one way favoured by some critics evaluating the work. Both Andrew Kennedy and Austin Quigley make important though contrasting contributions to Pinter criticism in this respect. Andrew Kennedy sees the dramatist's linguistic development within the wider context of a search by twentieth-century playwrights for a new theatrical language (Part One, below). As with Katharine Worth, he considers Pinter in the tradition of T. S. Eliot. Pinter has created a poetic structure. Austin Quigley is more sceptical. In his introduction to *The Pinter Problem*, he bemoans the rut into which Pinter criticism has fallen and in particular questions notions of a 'poetic' or 'metaphoric' Pinter:

. . . when forced to confront the recalcitrant details of the text, critics find it very hard to assimilate them to any precise interpretation. The resort to metaphor and analogy, like that to symbol and subtext, still leaves the problem of synthesising the details unresolved. The very attempt to abstract technical brilliance from some other 'end' of the work is . . . to oppose two things which cannot be usefully opposed.[15]

Quigley therefore holds that it is far too easy to offer vague terms such as the 'Pinter music' in order to avoid the critical problems which Pinter's plays pose. His solution is to break the boundaries of conventional Pinter criticism by providing a detailed linguistic study of the works:

If. . . the significance of the language is pursued in terms of its appropriateness to the situation in which it is used, a whole new set of questions emerges: to what extent is the situation independent of the language uttered? how is a character to decide what is appropriate language for that situation? is the question of appropriateness given or is it open to negotiation? what if two characters disagree over what is appropriate at a given time? what kinds of issues are raised by such events?[16]

Quigley's interest therefore focusses on the linguistic relationship established between characters which must be seen as the essence of the drama. His critique is naturally very detailed and thus only an examination of one scene from *The Caretaker* can be included below

(Part Three). His book offers a fresh and perceptive approach to Pinter.

The danger of a purely linguistic examination of dramatic texts is that it can neglect the theatrical forms of drama. John Russell Brown, Bernard Dukore and Ronald Knowles stress, that performance relates to dramatic structure, within which tensions are created moving the plays through comedy, tragedy, absurdity or menace. Such structures lend themselves to labels. It was Irving Wardle who coined the term 'comedies of menace' to describe these early plays. Bernard Dukore, meanwhile, in the subtitle to his first book on Pinter, *Where the Laughter Stops*, preferred the term 'tragicomedy'.[17] The search for such critical tags is fraught with danger, and Irving Wardle was soon to retract. Too late, the 'comedy of menace' has become part of Pinter's critical heritage even though it is an aspect from which Pinter in his later plays has tried to escape, without invalidating the earlier work:

> It was called 'comedy of menace' quite a long time ago. I never stuck categories on myself, or on any of us. But if what I understand the word menace to mean is certain elements that I have employed in the past in the shape of a particular play, then I don't think it's worthy of much more exploration. After *The Homecoming* I tried writing – odds and ends – and failed, for some time. . . . . No I'm not at all interested in 'threatening behaviour' any more, although I don't think this makes plays like *The Homecoming* and *The Birthday Party* invalid. But you're always stuck. You're stuck as a writer.[18]

At least Wardle's label in relation to these early plays did credit to the comic side of the drama. A problem with literary students, as C. S. Lewis commented in *Experiment in Criticism* in relation to Jane Austen, is that they can take their subject too sombrely. If, as Davison asserts, Pinter is in the tradition of the Music Hall and of such fifties comedians as Tony Hancock, then a critical response which fails to see the comic potentiality of the plays is fundamentally lacking. Like Shakespeare, Pinter is in the entertainment profession and is an accomplished practitioner of humour. As do great comedians, he creates a story by building audience expectations only to frustrate them or prove them to be incongruous with the characters presented. A good example comes in *The Caretaker* with Davies's story of the shoes (pages 13–15). It begins with: 'Them bastards at the monastery let me down again.' The incongruity of 'bastards' and 'monastery' establishes the comic context, but the story immediately moves away from this in order to present a variety of lesser jokes which seem irrelevant to the main narrative. It is a traditional comic device (employed currently, for example, by Ronnie Corbett in his story-spot during the popular *Two Ronnies* television series). Thus, we hear about the man looking after the 'best' convenience; of the 'very good soap' and of the tramp's need for soap but the thread of the original story is kept with Aston producing some shoes and Davies, after ignoring him for a while, emerging from a reverie to ask, 'You know what that bastard monk said to me?'

A further facet is introduced, exposing Davies's prejudices, as a link is made between the monks and the 'Blacks'. The tempo of the comic story increases with Aston offering the shoes and with the repetition of 'that bastard monk'. Pinter is directing the pace and leading audience expectations for a punch-line, but again he holds back thus intensifying the comedy. The size of the shoes is discussed as Aston tries to get Davies interested in them, but Pinter constantly stresses humorously the divide between the two men. Aston's phrases, such as 'Not bad trim', are juxtaposed with Davies's complaints, 'Can't wear shoes that don't fit. Nothing worse'. In this respect the Aston/Davies relationship for the audience reflects on the story the tramp is telling concerning himself and the monk. Monks usually signify charity, tramps are archetypically ungrateful: Aston seems to be trying to help, Davies doesn't want to know. It is within that structural development of comic tension that Pinter allows the humour to develop:

I said to this monk, here, I said, look here, mister, he opened the door, big door, he opened it, look here, mister, I said, I come all the way down here, look, I said, I showed him these, I said, you haven't got a pair of shoes have you, a pair of shoes, I said, enough to keep me on my way. Look at these, they've nearly out, I said, they're no good to me. I heard you got a stock of shoes here. Piss off, he said to me. (*The Caretaker*, p. 141)

The vocabulary is naturally incongruous with the figure of a monk, but the real humour of the passage comes from the teller rather than from the monk's supposed reply. The joke extends beyond 'Piss off' to the delivery, length and continuation of the story by Davies. This is Pinter at his comic best – entertaining through characterisation and story-telling. He is here in the best traditions of English comedy.

But the comedy is linked with threatening behaviour and with vulnerability. The dislocation of the language as found in the story of the monk or in the opening dialogue of *The Birthday Party* complements the dislocation of the characters themselves. What is the foundation of Stanley's existence? Where within himself, within his society, his individual history as presented by the play, can he find a defence against attack? The specific nature of the attack does not matter. It is rather the vulnerability of the victim that is the focus:

STANLEY: . . . I once gave a concert.

MEG: A concert?

STANLEY (*reflectively*): Yes. It was a good one, too. They were all there that night. Every single one of them. It was a great success. Yes. A concert. At Lower Edmonton.

MEG: What did you wear?

STANLEY (*to himself*): I had a unique touch. Absolutely unique. They came up to me. They came up to me and said they were grateful. Champagne we had that night, the lot. (*Pause.*) My father nearly came down to hear me. Well, I dropped him a card anyway. But I don't think he could make it. No, I – I lost the address, that was it. (*Pause.*) Yes. Lower Edmonton. Then after that, you know what they did? They carved me up. Carved me up. It was all arranged, it was all worked out. My next concert. Somewhere else it was. In winter. I went down there to play. Then, when I got there, the hall was closed, the place was shuttered up, not even a caretaker. They'd locked it up. . . .   [*The Birthday Party*, pp. 22–3]

The 'concert', 'they', 'Lower Edmonton', 'champagne', 'my father', are elements of stability. Each is positive. 'They', by being linked with 'champagne', are beneficent, friendly. His father 'nearly came'. He would have come, if he could have come; if he had known about it. His absence was not his fault but due rather to a lost address. As the story continues the credibility of the acceptance of him by others wanes. The language stutters: 'I – I lost the address'. The pause halts the flow. The use of the word 'Yes' and the return to the reference to the specific place 'Lower Edmonton' indicates a grasping for stability, for foundation, for some kind of roots. But they are not there. It's all fiction. The hall was locked up, and in the final resort all Stanley can do is show aggression to the one listening to him:

(*He replaces his glasses, then looks at* MEG.) Look at her. You're just an old piece of rock cake, aren't you? (*He rises and leans across the table to her.*) That's what you are, aren't you?
                                                                                                              [p. 23]

When there is no centre of stability, no foundation for one's existence, a victim can be an aggressor, an aggressor a victim, and words such as 'good' and 'evil' become meaningless – as Pinter has implied in answering a question about his not considering his characters to be villainous:

It's rather ridiculous to try to understand people in those kinds of terms. Evil people. What the hell does that mean? Or bad people. And who are you then if you say that, and what are you?[19]

The moral focus is unknown. What matters are the relationships, the interaction between individuals within 'a territorial struggle':

LENNY: Just give me the glass.

RUTH: No.

Pause
LENNY: I'll take it, then.
RUTH: If you take the glass . . . I'll take you.
        Pause
LENNY: How about me taking the glass without you taking me?
RUTH: Why don't I just take you?
        Pause
LENNY: You're joking.   [*The Homecoming*, p. 34]

Of all Pinter's early work, *The Homecoming* has produced the hottest
critical debate. Simon Trussler's evaluation of the play is the most
hostile piece in our selection (Part Four, below), although in his
perhaps under-rated book Trussler is usually the reverse in his
consideration of the other plays. To some extent Trussler overstates
his case in relation to *The Homecoming*, but his reservations are
important. What is critically questionable about the drama is its
emotional power. It taps areas of the human condition which, if done
in a gratuitous manner, comes close to pornography, but which if
expressed with artistic judgement must rank the play as one of
Pinter's major achievements. In contradiction to Trussler, Martin
Esslin sees the play as one of Pinter's 'finest', while Irving Wardle, in
an informative article, explains the bestial function in the work and
the struggle for territory – or, as Bernard Dukore sees it, for power.
From its opening in 1965, *The Homecoming* met critical disagreement.
Eric Shorter in the *Daily Telegraph* (4 June 1965) felt that 'this author
has never put his art to more absorbing, hilarious or stylish purpose',
and continued:

. . . the quality of its language, the variety of its mood, the tension of the dialogue (or
rather interlocking monologues), the feeling for cockney idiom and the cool confidence
with which the play unfurls its sordid theme are a constant source of pleasure.

Philip Hope Wallace, however, was sceptical, wishing the play to be
'about' something and consequently 'feeling cheated'. In our
selection in Part Four it is interesting to contrast this review with John
Elsom's review of Kevin Billington's revival of the play in 1978, where
he perceptively states:

The question arises as to whether we were simply incapable during the early 1960s of
taking Pinter's plays at their face value or whether a kind of 'art for art's sake'
intervened, changing the shocks just into effective moments, the power into mere
conjuring, the substance into decoration.

The substance of the play is within its structure, its enigmas, its
confrontations and its violence. Consequently there are moments

within *The Homecoming* which are comparable with some of the strongest scenes on the English stage. Ruth's first confrontation with Lenny succeeds in dramatising the transference of power from proposed aggressor to victim in as haunting a manner as Middleton provided four hundred years earlier in *The Changeling* (1623), while Lenny's characterisation and the setting of the East London 'coven' is as repulsively degenerate as anything presented by the Elizabethan revenge tradition. As with plays such as *The Revenger's Tragedy* (1606), Pinter's boundaries in *The Homecoming* are drawn by the animalistic needs of the community – the desire for food, violence, sex, aggression and power. It is a world of purulent physicality expressed even in a concern with one's own conception. Here is the Bastard ruminating on his beginnings in *The Revenger's Tragedy*:

> Faith, if the truth were known, I was begot
> After some gluttonous dinner, some stirring dish
> Was my first father, when deep healths went round,
> And ladies' cheeks were painted red with wine,
> Their tongues as short and nimble as their heels,
> Uttering words sweet and thick; and when they rose,
> Were merrily dispos'd to fall again, –
> In such a whisp'ring and withdrawing hour,
> When base male-bawds kept sentinel at stair-head,
> Was I stol'n softly . . .   [I ii 180–9]

Although the language and idiom are different, compare the individual aggression of that speech concerned with the character's very existence in relation to his parents' copulation, with Lenny's aggressive questioning of his father:

I'll tell you what, Dad, since you're in the mood for a bit of a . . . chat, I'll ask you a question. It's a question I've been meaning to ask you for some time. That night . . . you know . . . the night you got me . . . that night with Mum, what was it like? Eh? When I was just a glint in your eye. What was it like? What was the background to it? I mean, for instance, is it a fact that you had me in mind all the time, or is a fact that I was the last thing you had in mind?   [*The Homecoming*, p. 36]

In Lenny and Spurio, the Bastard, we find the same morbid, antagonistic, violent curiosity which depicts the panoramas of their respective plays. Whether or not in writing such passages dramatists are being self-indulgent or are attempting to portray, as clearly as their art allows, the picture of a particular society is a matter for critical debate but one which should be alert as much to the conditions and context which will determine the receptivity of the audience as any intentions or otherwise on the part of the dramatists.

During 'the London Controversy' Ionesco wrote:

A playwright simply writes plays, in which he can offer only a testimony, not a didactic message – a personal, affective testimony of his anguish and the anguish of others or, which is rare, of his happiness – or he can express his feelings, comic or tragic, about life.[20]

Similarly Pinter has argued that his art is neither didactic nor political. In this respect his plays are theatrical experiences provoking audience response, but in doing this they are naturally fulfilling a social and some would say a political role. Denial of a political role implies one. Silence is as powerful a political act as eloquence or as Pinter's own refusal as young man to be conscripted into the army. His art form does not have to be overtly didactic or moralistic since such elements are implicit within the dramatic experience the works provide. Through the complexity of his theatrical forms his plays express moments of existence, catching life as it passes. To talk of his theatricality as the focus of his achievement is not to deny his drama's social function but is rather to assert it. His plays express elements of human conduct and in that expression lie their strengths or their weakness as we accept or reject them.

NOTES

1. I had hoped to be able to include in this volume a section 'Pinter on Pinter' which would have provided a selection of Pinter interviews. Unfortunately fees proved prohibitive in this respect. Speech: Hamburg, 1970, an acceptance address on receiving the Hamburg Shakespeare Prize, was first published in *Theatre Quarterly* I, No. 3 (1971).
   2. Speech: Hamburg, 1970.
   3. Pinter, 'Between the Lines', *Sunday Times* (4/3/1962).
   5. Mel Gussow, 'A Conversation with Harold Pinter', *New York Times Magazine* (5/12/1971).
   5. Ibid.
   6. Kenneth Tynan, 'A Verbal Wizard in the Suburbs', *Observer* (5/6/1960).
   7. Harold Hobson, 'The Screw Turns Again', *Sunday Times* (25/5/1960). This review is reprinted in Martin Esslin, *Pinter The Playwright* (London, 1982), pp. 22–3.
   8. Francis A. Schaeffer, *Escape from Reason* (London, 1968), p. 67.
   9. *Observer* (22/6/1958); reprinted in Eugene Ionesco, *Notes and Counter Notes*, trans, D. Watson (London, 1964).
   10. Richard Schechner, 'Puzzling Pinter', *Tulane Drama Review*, 11 (Winter, 1966).
   11. See Lucina P. Gabbard, *The Dream Structure of Pinter's Plays: A Psychoanalytic Approach* (Rutherford, N.J., and London, 1976).
   12. Nigel Alexander, 'Past, Present and Pinter', *Essays and Studies*, 27 (1974) p. 10.
   13. *Sunday Times* (4/3/1962).
   14. Charles A. Carpenter, 'Victims of Duty: The Critics, Absurdity and *The Homecoming*', *Modern Drama*, xxv, No. 4 (Dec., 1982), p. 492.
   15. Austin E. Quigley, *The Pinter Problem* (Princeton, N.J., and London, 1975), p. 19.

16. Ibid., p. 31.
17. Bernard Dukore, *Where the Laughter Stops: Pinter's Tragicomedy* (Columbia, Mo., and London, 1976).
18. Gussow, op. cit.
19. Ibid.
20. Ionesco, op. cit. (note 9), p. 93.

PART ONE

General Studies

Ruby Cohn   The World of Harold Pinter
(1962)

Each of Harold Pinter's [first] four plays ends in the virtual annihilation of an individual. In Pinter's first play, *The Room*, after a blind Negro is kicked into inertness, the heroine, Rose, is suddenly stricken with blindness. In *The Dumb Waiter*, the curtain falls as Gus and his prospective murderer stare at each other. Stanley Webber, the hero of *The Birthday Party*, is taken from his refuge for 'special treatment'. In *The Caretaker*, the final curtain falls on an old man's fragmentary (and unheeded) pleas to remain in his refuge.

As Pinter focuses more sharply on the wriggle for existence, each of his successive hero-victims seems more vulnerable than the last. Villain assaults victim in a telling and murderous idiom. Although Pinter's first two plays are in one act, and the second two in three acts, each successive drama seems to begin closer to its own end, highlighting the final throes of the hero-victims.

But who are they – these nondescript villains and victims, acting out their dramas in dilapidated rooms? Victims emerge from a vague past to go to their ineluctable destruction. Villains are messengers from mysterious organisations – as in the works of Kafka or Beckett.

If Pinter has repeatedly been named as Beckett's heir on the English stage, it is because the characters of both lead lives of complex and unquiet desperation – a desperation expressed with extreme economy of theatrical resources. The clutter of our world is mocked by the stinginess of the stage-worlds of Beckett and Pinter. Sets, props, characters and language are stripped by both playwrights to what one is temped to call their essence.

However, Pinter is not only Beckett's spiritual son. He is at least a cousin of the Angry Young Englishmen of his generation, for Pinter's anger, like theirs, is directed vitriolically against the System. But his System cannot be reduced to a welfare state, red-brick universities and marriage above one's class. Of all the Angries, John Wain approaches closest to Pinter's intention when he states that the artist's function 'is always to *humanise* the society he is living in, to assert the importance of humanity in the teeth of whatever is currently trying to annihilate that importance' (*Declaration*). Pinter's assertion, however, takes a negative form; it is by his bitter dramas of *de*humanisation that he implies 'the importance of humanity'. The religion and society which have traditionally structured human morality, are, in Pinter's plays, the immoral agents that destroy the individual.

Like Osborne, Pinter looks back in anger; like Beckett, Pinter looks forward to nothing (not even Godot). Pinter has created his own distinctive and dramatic version of Man vs. the System. Situating him between Beckett and the Angries is only a first approximation of his achievement.

The house as human dwelling is a metaphor at least as old as the Bible, and on the stage that house is most easily reduced to a room (e.g. Graham Greene's *Living Room*, Beckett's *Endgame*). Pinter's rooms are stuffy, non-specific cubes, whose atmosphere grows steadily more stale and more tense. The titular Room of his first play is 'A room in a large house'; in *The Dumb Waiter*, we descend to 'a basement room'; in *The Birthday Party*, we have 'The living room of a house in a seaside town', and, in *The Caretaker*, it is simply 'A room'. Unlike the tree and road of *Godot*, which suggest vegetation and distance; or the shelter of *Endgame*, which looks out on earth and sea; unlike the realistic 'one-room flat . . . at the top of a large Victorian house' of *Look Back in Anger*, Pinter's rooms, parts of mysterious and infinite series, are like cells without a vista. At the opening curtain, these rooms look naturalistic, meaning no more than the eye can contain. But by the end of each play, they become sealed containers, virtual coffins.

Within each Pinter room, the props seem to be realistically functional, and only in retrospect do they acquire symbolic significance. Consider, for example, Pinter's treatment of such crucial details as food and clothing, in comparison with the casual realism of Osborne, or the frank symbolism of Beckett. The various preparations for tea in *Look Back in Anger* seem to be parallelled by the prosaic cocoa, tea, bread, sandwiches, crackers of Pinter's plays; in sharp contrast is the farcical and stylized carrot-turnip-radish 'business' of *Godot*. So too, three men grabbing for an old man's bag in *The Caretaker* has few of the symbolic overtones of the slapstick juggling of derbies in *Godot*.

It is, however, in their respective use of that innocuous prop, a pair of shoes, that the different symbolic techniques of Beckett and Pinter are in most graphic evidence. Earlier in *Godot*, Vladimir establishes shoes as a metaphysical symbol: 'There's man all over for you, blaming on his boots the faults of his feet.' At the end of *Godot*, it is by virtue of being barefoot that Estragon admits he has always compared himself to Christ. In Pinter's *Caretaker*, the old man keeps trying on different shoes that might enable him to get on the road to Sidcup, where he claims to have left his identity papers. Each pair of shoes is rejected for specific misfit – 'a bit small', 'too pointed', 'no laces' – before the curtain lines of the play: 'they're all right . . . if I was to . . . get my papers . . . would you . . . would you let . . . would you . . . if I got down . . . and got my. . . .' The finality of the fragments indicates that no shoes can ever fit, that the journey to Sidcup cannot be made. Thus, the symbolic significance of the shoes is instantaneous with Beckett, cumulative with Pinter.

Most crucial to an understanding of Pinter's theatre is the symbolism of his characters. For all their initially realistic appearance, their cumulative impact embraces the whole of humanity. In so generalising, Pinter extends the meaning of his characters beyond such particulars as Osborne treats; nevertheless, he does not achieve the metaphysical scope upon which Beckett insists, from his opening lines: 'Nothing to be done'.

Pinter's defenceless victims are a middle-aged wife, a man who asks too many questions, an ex-pianist, a broken old man. Ruthlessly robbed of any distinction, they come to portray the human condition. And Pinter's villains, initially as unprepossessing as the victims, gradually reveal their insidious significance through some of the most skilful dialogue on the English stage today. For it is language that betrays the villains – more pat, more cliché-ridden, with more brute power than that of their victims.

Even hostile critics have commented on the brilliance of Pinter's dialogue, and it is in the lines of his villains that he achieves precise dramatic timing and economical manipulation of commonplaces. Representatives of the System, Pinter's villains give direct expression to its dogma. In the plays of Osborne and Beckett, which also implicitly attack the System, the oppressive forces are presented through the words of their victims.

Jimmy Porter of Osborne's *Look Back in Anger* garbs the System in contemporary corporate metaphors:

JIMMY PORTER: . . . the Economics of the Supernatural. It's all a simple matter of payments and penalties . . . Reason and Progress, the old firm, is selling out. Everyone get out while the going's good. Those forgotten shares you had in the old traditions, the old beliefs are going up – up and up and up. There's going to be a changeover. A new Board of Directors, who are going to see that the dividends are always attractive, and that they go to the right people. Sell out everything you've got; all those stocks in the old, free inquiry. The Big Crash is coming, you can't escape it, so get in on the ground floor with Helena and her friends while there's still time. And there isn't much of it left. Tell me, what could be more gilt-edged than the next world! It's a capital gain, and its all yours.

Vladimir and Estragon, at the beginning of Beckett's *Godot*, describe the invisible deity figure in trivial human terms:

VLADIMIR: Let's wait and see what he says.
ESTRAGON: Who?
VLADIMIR: Godot.
ESTRAGON: Good idea.
VLADIMIR: Let's wait till we know exactly how we stand.
ESTRAGON: On the other hand it might be better to strike the iron before it freezes.
VLADIMIR: I'm curious to hear what he has to offer. Then we'll take it or leave it.
ESTRAGON: What exactly did we ask him for? . . . And what did he reply?
VLADIMIR: That he'd see.
ESTRAGON: That he couldn't promise anything.
VLADIMIR: That he'd have to think it over.
ESTRAGON: In the quiet of his home.
VLADIMIR: Consult his family.
ESTRAGON: His friends.
VLADIMIR: His agents.
ESTRAGON: His correspondents.
VLADIMIR: His books.
ESTRAGON: His bank account. . . . Where do we come in?
VLADIMIR: Come in?
ESTRAGON: Take your time.
VLADIMIR: Come in? On our hands and knees.

In Pinter's *Birthday Party*, Goldberg and McCann express the System by echoing modern commonplaces of social success. Pinter damns them with their own deadly clichés.

GOLDBERG: Between you and me, Stan, it's about time you had a new pair of glasses.
MCCANN: You can't see straight.
GOLDBERG: It's true. You've been cockeyed for years.
MCCANN: Now you're even more cockeyed.
GOLDBERG: He's right. You've gone from bad to worse.
MCCANN: Worse than worse.
GOLDBERG: You need a long convalescence.
MCCANN: A change of air.
GOLDBERG: Somewhere over the rainbow.
MCCANN: Where angels fear to tread. . . .
GOLDBERG: We'll make a man of you.
MCCANN: And a woman.
GOLDBERG: You'll be re-orientated.
MCCANN: You'll be rich.
GOLDBERG: You'll be adjusted.
MCCANN: You'll be our pride and joy.
GOLDBERG: You'll be a mensch.
MCCANN: You'll be a success.
GOLDBERG: You'll be integrated.
MCCANN: You'll give orders.

GOLDBERG: You'll make decisions.
MCCANN: You'll be a magnate.
GOLDBERG: A statesman.
MCCANN: You'll own yachts.
GOLDBERG: Animals.
MCCANN: Animals.   [p. 82, 83–4]

In comparing the three excerpts, we note that Osborne's sustained metaphors are almost lyrical with rebellion, but both Beckett and Pinter resort to pithy stichomythia. Although the passages are typical of the technique of each play the respective tonal differences depend upon the dramatic structure. Osborne's satiric hostility recurs throughout *Look Back in Anger*, but Beckett's attitude towards Godot is ambivalent. The quoted excerpt occurs early in the play, when the tramps, in spite of their pathetic plight, can still attempt to define the System in familiar human terms. But by the end of the drama, man and deity are poignantly reduced to their compulsive, impossible, problematical inter-relationship; 'in this immense confusion one thing alone is clear', says Vladimir. 'We are waiting for Godot to come.'

In the Pinter play, the messengers of the System glibly mouth its pat phrases – increasingly pointed as the dehumanisation of the victim progresses. In the quoted excerpt, which occurs towards the end of the drama, the seemingly irrelevant conclusion, 'Animals', corrosively climaxes the process. . . .

[Ruby Cohn's examination of these arguments in relation specifically to *The Birthday Party* is given below, in Part Three – Ed.]

SOURCE: extract from 'The World of Harold Pinter', *Tulane Drama Review*, 6 (March 1962), pp. 55–9.

*Katharine J. Worth   'Pinter and the *Realist Tradition'* (1972)   Tradition'

Pinter is the conjuror who comes into the realist tradition, takes over the well-worn material of the family play, the detective play and the cocktail comedy and works a dazzling transformation act with it. Of course, to the reviewers who were bewildered by *The Birthday Party* when it was first shown in London in 1958 – 'What all this means only Mr Pinter knows'[1] – the term 'realist' would have seemed a ludicrous one to use about him. It still would, if it were applied in a simple, unqualified way as it might reasonably be to playwrights like Alun Owen or Willis Hall. Pinter's brilliantly oblique and haunting drama is so unlike theirs that it might well seem to belong in a totally different mode.

There has been a critical tendency in the past to assume that it does, and to discuss him in terms of the absurdist, anti-realist drama: Martin Esslin's essay of 1963, 'Godot and his children: the theatre of Beckett and Pinter'[2] was followed by many in the same line. 'Isolated elements in his plays are intensely realistic', says one critic, 'the combination of elements is utterly absurd.'[3]

Certainly Pinter has always made plain his enormous admiration for Beckett. It may be that he was aiming at Beckettian effects in early plays like *The Room* and *The Dumb Waiter* – the symbolism does seem derivative – and there are still unmistakable echoes in plays. *Silence*, for instance, with its three characters in their separate 'areas' telling over their past, points pretty clearly to the three sad heads-in-urns of *Play* and to the pattern of movement among the three seated women in *Come and Go*; they break up into twos for intimate conversation rather as Bates and Ellen move out of their own areas, Bates to Ellen's, Ellen to Rumsey's, in Pinter's play.

But if the method – and the sad, backward-looking mood – is sometimes similar, the kind of interest Pinter raises is very different. His interest gathers round the revelation of character: he focuses attention on the subtext, the Freudian slips, compulsive repetitions and so on that give the characters away: we are drawn into 'reading' them and this usually involves looking back into their past as well as guessing about their future with the kind of curiosity that would be wildly inappropriate to Estragon or Clov or Winnie. Even *Silence* with its lyric-like structure and diaphanous texture offers solid character interest. A familiar real world can be sensed behind the shadowy recollections: one wants to piece the fragments together and reconstruct it: there's a feeling that it might turn out to be something like the Edwardian world of an L. P. Hartley novel with nice social distinctions (Bates lower class than Rumsey, Ellen somewhere in between) and wistful personal relationships. It was no surprise after *Silence*, at any rate, to learn that Pinter was actually working on the screen play of Hartley's *The Go-Between*.

This side of Pinter has begun to attract more attention lately. In his . . . full-length study of the plays, Martin Esslin stresses their Chekhovian aspects, referring to Chekhov, indeed, as Pinter's master.[4] It is a comparison Pinter would not be likely to quarrel with, to judge from the way he commonly speaks of his own work. 'I regard myself as an old-fashioned writer', he said in an interview in 1967,[5] 'I like to create character and follow a situation to its end. I write visually – I can say that. I watch the invisible faces quite closely. The characters take on a physical shape. I watch the faces as closely as I can.'

With remarks like this he places himself pretty firmly in the nineteenth-century Ibsen/Chekhov tradition.[6] One thinks of Ibsen's acute visual sense of his characters, the way he gropes after better knowledge of them in a detective-like manner (fascinatingly recorded in the various drafts of his plays) and then turns the groping into dramatic process. It's this analytical 'investigation' form that Pinter has inherited via Joyce and Eliot, as I suggested in speaking of them. He brings it right into our time, ruthlessly speeds it up and strips it down. When it emerges as the intense staccato form of *The Birthday Party* it's not surprising that its ancestry should go unrecognised. It is a long way from the stately investigations of *Rosmersholm* to this knockabout third degree sequence:

GOLDBERG: Webber, you're a fake. . . . When did you last wash up a cup?
STANLEY: The Christmas before last.
GOLDBERG: Where?
STANLEY: Lyons Corner House.
GOLDBERG: Which one?
STANLEY: Marble Arch.
GOLDBERG: Where was your wife?
STANLEY: In ——
GOLDBERG: Answer.
STANLEY (*turning, crouched*): What wife?
GOLDBERG: What have you done with your wife?
MCCANN: He's killed his wife.
GOLDBERG: Why did you kill your wife?
STANLEY (*sitting, his back to the audience*): What wife? [p. 39]

And yet there is a recognisable clear line running back from Pinter through Eliot to Joyce and the Ibsenian drama: the figure of the Rat Wife probing Rita's wish to be rid of the 'little gnawing things' in her house is a shadow in the background of Eliot's Reilly and Pinter's Goldberg and McCann. Other elements come in to make up Pinter's full inheritance, of course, from Chekhov and – very important, it seems to me – from Noel Coward. Pinter's most audacious strokes, those that make him look so dazzlingly new, are often developments from Coward or solutions to problems that Eliot wrestled with, solutions that allow him to remain inside the forms of realism.

His will to do this is most obviously demonstrated in his commitment to the proscenium stage. He told L. M. Bensky once: 'I *am* a very traditional playwright – for instance I insist on having a curtain in all my plays. I write curtain lines for that reason!'[7] When Bensky asked if he'd ever thought of trying freer techniques like those in the Weiss *Marat/Sade*, as a means of stimulating himself to write, he said categorically that he hadn't. Exceptionally, almost uniquely among the playwrights of the new wave, he seems to feel no pull towards an open stage, mixed forms, improvisation. All that 'jamboree', he says, is so noisy; what he likes is quietness.

'Quietness' is a key word for Pinter. His most characteristic effect is one of violence exploding with alarming unexpectedness into an almost equally alarming quietness. The entry of Ruth and Teddy in *The Homecoming* is quiet in this troubling way: they come into a sleeping house and stand there, making no move to disturb the silence. When Ruth suggests a normal action: 'Shouldn't you wake someone up? Tell them you're here?' Teddy refuses; instead he goes up the stairs 'stealthily' to look at the state of his room, coming back to tell her triumphantly: 'It's still there. My room. Empty. The bed's there.'

The weird touch of Peter Pan in this is a subtle preparation for the bizarre events that follow, when Teddy stands by, watching his wife taken over by his brothers and father, assimilated into the home as a kind of sensual Wendy-goddess. There's a very deep connection between the uncanny quietness of that first scene and the shock of the revelation – 'Old Lenny's got a tart in here!' Something repressed and unadmitted comes out in a form which is odd and perverse somehow because of the stillness that went before: the dam bursts and the waters flood out anarchically.

The scenes that tend to stay in one's mind from Pinter's drama, it seems to me, are those where the relation of quietness to violence is particularly sharp and meaningful. I think of Mick hurling the buddha to the ground in *The Caretaker*, a traumatic event in a play of such deep and melancholy quietness, or in a quite different, more feverish mood, the irruption of terrifying party games into the cosy, dull routines of *The Birthday Party*. Or in a [later] play, *Landscape*, Duff's desperate chat flowing under pressure from Beth's silence towards an outburst which is felt to be as much a relief as an attack:

You stood in the hall and banged the gong.
    (*Pause.*)
What the bloody hell are you doing banging that bloody gong?
    (*Pause.*)
It's bullshit. Standing in an empty hall banging a bloody gong. There's no one to listen. No one'll hear. There's not a soul in the house. Except me.

The force of this partly depends on the obscenity having the right effect. Pinter has made an interesting comment on this point. He objects to what he calls literal-minded persons' attempts to 'open up obscene language to general comment'. It should be, he says 'the dark secret language of the underworld'.[8]

This is very revealing. Secrecy is Pinter's great subject, his most compelling reason for always using the proscenium, the closed, framed stage where the characters can be shut up and spied on. It's the only way of getting at the sort of beings he is interested in, tightly closed characters who turn most of their energy to keeping themselves hidden from view, protecting the 'dark secret language' of their underworld. An open stage would be as wrong for them as it would for the characters in *Ghosts* or *Exiles* or *The Family Reunion*. The whole 'closed' situation has to be there, the frame the characters can't break out of, the eavesdropping audience. Pinter sometimes takes up the eavesdropping position himself in talking about his characters. Again like Ibsen, he tends to speak of them as though they are real people, having a life stretching before and after the action of the play: he professes to make guesses about what really happened to them. About *Landscape*, for instance, he says in a tentative, open-to-correction tone of voice that he 'believes' the man Beth is dreaming of is her husband: '. . . the man on the beach is Duff. I think there are memories of Mr Sykes in her memory of this Duff which she might be attributing to Duff, but the man remains Duff. I think that Duff detests and is jealous of Mr Sykes, although I do not believe that Mr Sykes and Beth were ever lovers.'[9]

If this happens to be one's own view, as it was mine, it's tempting to take Pinter's as the last word. He always does his best to prevent this kind of fixing, though, seldom being as explicit as this, and when he is, being careful to use words like 'believe' and 'think'. He hesitates nowadays to direct his own plays, he tells us, because he might be in danger of conveying to the actors – 'This is what's meant'. His great point is, after all, that motives can never be fully known. As he rather pedantically informed one of his first audiences: 'The desire for verification is understandable but cannot always be satisfied.'

It especially can't be satisfied in the area of strongest feeling. 'The more intense the feeling, the less articulate its expression.'[10] Pinter takes his exploration of this area as far as he can without undermining too drastically the sense of solid reality: he almost always seems to want that in. It's in his techniques for getting both – the inner and the outer reality – that he often comes remarkably close to Eliot, as I suggested earlier. They meet in the middle of the terrain from opposite ends, Eliot arguing that intense feelings tend to express themselves in verse and using a near-prose verse as a ground to take flight from; Pinter starting with the idea that intense feeling makes for incoherence and using a sharply stylised prose as his means of suggesting it. Pinter is often described as a poet: he has published verse, but he doesn't let his characters use it; the nearest they approach it is in the prose poem effects of a play like *Silence* or in imagery such as Ruth uses in *The Homecoming* to express her frustration. She is supposedly speaking of America:

It's all rock. And sand. It stretches . . . so far . . . everywhere you look. And there's lots of insects there. Pause. And there's lots of insects there.

This is moving quite a way towards 'open' verse: it even sets up a faint verbal echo from *The Cocktail Party* – Celia telling Edward that his voice seems like an insect's:

Dry, endless, meaningless, inhuman—
You might have made it by scraping your legs together.

It's in a Chekhovian type of subtext, though, that Pinter finds his real equivalent for Eliot's verse medium. . . . Thirties playwrights . . . sometimes seemed to be aiming at Chekhov without the subtext. Pinter's drama might be called all subtext: I suppose this is really what makes it so un-Chekhovian in mood and feeling despite the similarity of the technique. There's no sense of throw away, no casualness. Everything is pointed; even the humour, which is certainly relaxing in a way, as all good humour is, has its sharp edge uppermost pretty well all the time. The quarrel between Lenny and Ruth over the glass of water in *The Homecoming* is characteristic:

LENNY: And now perhaps I'll relieve you of your glass.
RUTH: I haven't quite finished.
LENNY: You've consumed quite enough, in my opinion.
RUTH: No, I haven't.
LENNY: Quite sufficient, in my own opinion.
RUTH: Not in mine, Leonard.
    (*Pause.*)
LENNY: Don't call me that, please.
RUTH: Why not?
LENNY: That's the name my mother gave me.
    (*Pause.*)
 Just give me the glass.
RUTH: No.
    (*Pause.*)
LENNY: I'll take it, then.
RUTH: If you take the glass . . . I'll take you.
    (*Pause.*)

LENNY: How about me taking the glass without you taking me?
RUTH: Why don't I just take you?   [p. 33–4]

The kind of social manoeuvring that is going on here is familiar
enough. To go outside the theatre for a moment, one thinks of
Trollope explaining why Mrs Proudie makes Mrs Quiverful sit down
while she herself stands and how Mrs Quiverful responds to the
manoeuvre without being able quite to 'translate' it.

The realism of the similar behaviour in Pinter's scene isn't
destroyed, I think, though it's certainly affected by the heavy
stressing he gives it. This and the many scenes like it in his drama
usually seem poised on the edge of realism: we can recognise what is
going on from our ordinary social experience – we all spend a good
deal of time reading subtext after all – but we're made to feel uneasy
and dubious by the bizarre, theatrical element in the style. The
careful pauses have something to do with this. Pinter himself worries
about these not seeming natural: he has found actors trying to time
them like musical notes, as if they were 'formal conventions or
stresses'. But this is not how they are intended. 'The pause is a pause',
he says, 'because of what has just happened in the minds and guts of
the characters. They spring out of the text.' If the character is being
properly played the actor should find the marked pause natural and
inevitable: a silence should simply mean that 'something has
happened to create the impossibility of anyone speaking for a certain
amount of time – until they can recover from whatever happened
before the silence'.[11]

The stylisation then, is a means of reading character. There are
many different degrees of it. Like Eliot, Pinter shades off from the
credible and the 'voiced' to the fantastic and 'unvoiced' but his
transitions are smoother: one of his greatest skills is his ability to keep
us doubtful about when we have moved from one plane to another.
His first level, corresponding to Eliot's verse dialogue, is 'straight'
subtext in the Chekhovian mode: tangential conversation, revealing
pauses and so on, all heightened and pointed to take on the faintly
unreal quality of the scene between Ruth and Lenny over the glass of
water, but still credible in ordinary social terms.

Then comes the level of sharper stylisation where distortion from
the characters' inner life creeps in – and yet still there is a way open to
taking the action as in some way actually happening in the outer
world. In this area one becomes very aware of Pinter's highly
developed filmic sense. Techniques adapted from film are important
in creating his peculiar illusion of things being real and yet not real,
happening in an observable way and happening only at a deep level of
the mind.

. . . In *The Homecoming*, in the very odd scene where Ruth lies on the floor being made love to by one brother-in-law while the other pokes her with his foot, her father-in-law peers at her face and her husband watches impassively. Can this really be happening? That it's only occuring inside the mind is artfully suggested by the curious lack of connection between what is seen and what is said. The physical acts flow on like a silent film sequence, no one seeming to be aware of anyone speaking, yet Max is speaking all the time and what he's saying is perfectly commonplace:

MAX: Listen, you think I don't know why you didn't tell me you were married? I know why. You were ashamed. You thought I'd be annoyed because you married a woman beneath you. You should have known me better. I'm broadminded. I'm a broadminded man.   [p. 59]

It's as if a pornographic silent film had been dubbed with a sound sequence from a suburban family comedy. Two elements in tension, a brilliant reflection of the state of feeling in which all the characters, except possibly Joey, seem to be trapped. . . .

At the point where he goes deepest into the mind's interior, especially when it's a mind possessed by guilt and dread, Pinter seems to look quite closely towards Eliot. Their use of ritual[12] is one link. The ritualistic procession round the birthday cake in *The Family Reunion*, for instance, seems to find a violent echo in *The Birthday Party* when Stanley marches round the table beating the child's drum, 'his face and the drum beat now savage and possessed'. The world 'possessed' points to the strongest and most persistent of these echoes, Pinter's variations on Eliot's 'guardian' motif. Whether accidentally or not, the word itself seems to be recalled in the title of *The Caretaker* (oddly, in its French translation, *Le Gardien*).

Aston, Davies and Mick are all caretakers or guardians of each other and of the house: the idea of being appointed a caretaker is central in the play. It's a role with an aggressive aspect – uppermost in Mick and Davies – and a benevolent one – prevailing in Aston, the double function that Eliot was aiming at in his presentation of Reilly, Julia and Alex in *The Cocktail Party*. Pinter makes the benevolence much more real and believable, though: this, to my mind, is what makes *The Caretaker* still his most touching play.

In *The Birthday Party* the emphasis falls, in Pinter's more usual way, on the aggressiveness of the 'guardian' figures. McCann and Goldberg arrive at the boarding house on Stanley's birthday, uninvited guests like Eliot's Reilly [in *The Cocktail Party*] or Lord Claverton's visitors in *The Elder Statesman*: they break him down by relentless inquisition, reducing him to an incoherent wreck. Yet they have come to do him good, or so they say when they cart him off to Monty's for further 'treatment': they have certainly released in full those nervous fears and the sense of nameless guilt that he seems to have been trying to suppress from the start of the play: 'I mean, you wouldn't think, to look at me, really . . . I mean, not really, that I was the sort of bloke to – to cause any trouble, would you?' Pinter brilliantly conveys the suggestion that the inquisitors are unreal beings, a projection of Stanley's obscure dread, without quite destroying the possibility of their being taken as real; this is what makes them so alarming. It's an effect that Eliot was trying for in *The Elder Statesman* by making Gomez and Mrs Carghill stagey, melodramatic figures who couldn't quite be believed in, who almost had to be ghost emanations from Lord Claverton's guilt-troubled mind.

The illusion wasn't bold enough, though, perhaps because Eliot hadn't a sharp enough ear for stage idiom. This is what Pinter has, of course, in the highest degree. It's no trouble to him to invent an idiom near enough to life to make for lifelike effect and sufficiently close to parody to raise doubts about it.

Goldberg's Jewish talk could *almost* be appropriate to a play of Wesker's:

When I was a youngster, of a Friday, I used to go for a walk down the canal with a girl who lived down my road. A beautiful girl. What a voice that bird had! A nightingale, my word of honour. Good? Pure? She wasn't a Sunday school teacher for nothing.

[p. 43]

Almost but not quite. Even in small units like this the sense of a careful selection of Jewish elements comes through, and the cumulative effect of his speech is overpoweringly one of caricature, a stage mask of Jewishness.

In coming to these deliberate effects of staginess we come to the heart of Pinter's drama, it seems to me. He uses false voices, phoney performances as a writer like O'Neill uses masks. And for a similar purpose, to convey the terrible sense of non-identity and disconnectedness that almost all his characters, like O'Neill's, suffer from. It's what Eliot's characters suffer from too. This is the ground where he and Pinter meet. But where Eliot mostly relies on imagery to communicate this nightmare, Pinter can act it out. His marvellous ear for idiom and his gift for mimicry allow him to suggest rather than state that all the world's a stage, all people characters endlessly strutting in parts they have created for themselves. One of his characters' most alarming tricks is their habit of mimicking the style they think their opponents aspire to, attacking their right to their part, like one actor upstaging another. This is what Lenny seems to be doing when he puts on an actor's grotesque version of a 'philosopher's' voice to tackle Teddy, the alleged philosopher. 'Do you detect a certain logical incoherence in the central affirmation of Christian theism?', he says, and poor Teddy backs away – 'That question doesn't fall within my province' – revealing himself in that one absurd reply to an absurd question as the man of straw he is, hardly there at all, least of all as a philosopher.

Some critics have taken him as one, though not, certainly, Nigel Dennis, whose account of Pinter's plays in the *New York Times Review of Books* was one that impressed Pinter enough for him to refer to it when he was asked by Mel Gussow[13] if any 'bad things' said by critics had interested him. From memory he quoted Dennis's view that the plays were 'simply acting exercises – for actors. . . . And that was it. There was absolutely nothing else. There was no content whatsoever, merely postures of actors being sad or happy or whatever.' Pinter went on to say that he was fascinated and troubled by this account. I think one can see why. It's so near the truth: there is so much posturing, acting, mimicry, one does begin to wonder, as very much in *Old Times* for instance, if there's anything real behind. I think, though, that this worry is Pinter's too, and that one of the reasons why he is generally found so absorbing and haunting, as well as funny, is that he is touching an uneasiness his audience knows from their experience of themselves. He has spoken of his own experience of looking in a mirror and wondering 'Who is that?' It's not a feeling confined to actors, though it's true that thoughts of Pinter having been a professional actor do often thrust into one's mind.

It's in this area of doubt about identity and the truth of feeling that he comes very close to the other English predecessor whom I named earlier on as an important figure in his background – Noel Coward. He doesn't part company with Eliot here, either. It sometimes seems that all roads in the modern English theatre lead back to the Master of *Hay Fever*! Pinter is more thoroughly at home with him than Eliot could be, of course. They have the same inside knowledge of the actor's world and a very similar line in jokes and repartee. Pinter once used the phrase 'the weasel under the cocktail cabinet' when asked what his plays were about. He's since repudiated it, saying – rather amusingly for someone so alert to Freudian slips – that it was a totally accidental remark. It seems no accident, really, though, that it points in the direction of Noel Coward and the Eliot of *The Cocktail Party*. Coward was quick to appreciate Pinter: the 'genuine original' among the new playwrights, he said. It was hardly surprising: there are so many similarities of style and interest. They have the same feeling for streamlined form, the same sharp ear for lifelike idiom and stage speech, the same love of mimicry and burlesque. . . .

SOURCE: extracts from ch. IV of *Revolutions in Modern English Drama* (London, 1972), pp. 86–93, 93–4, 94–7.

NOTES

[Reorganised and renumbered from the original]

1. *Manchester Guardian Review* (29/5/1958).
2. M. Esslin, in W. A. Armstrong (ed.), *Experimental Drama* (1963).
3. V. E. Amend, 'Pinter: Some Credits and Debits', *Modern Drama*, 10 (1967).
4. M. Esslin, *The Peopled Wound* (1970). A richly informative account of Pinter's career, this records interviews and dealings with the BBC as well as productions, etc.
5. Pinter, in 'Talk of the Town', *New Yorker* (25/2/1967).
6. Hugh Nelson points out that structurally Pinter's drama is closer to the well-made Ibsenite play than is generally realised – '*The Homecoming*: Kith and Kin', in J. Russell Brown (ed.), *Modern British Dramatists* (1968).
7. Pinter, in interview with L. M. Bensky, *Paris Review*, 39 (1966); reprinted in *Writers at Work* (New York, 1967).
8. Ibid.
9. Letter of Pinter to the German director of *Landscape* (performed in Hamburg, 10 Jan. 1970); quoted in Esslin, p. 192.
10. Pinter's note in programme for *The Room* and *The Dumb Waiter* at the Royal Court theatre (8 March 1960).
11. Pinter, in interview with Mel Gussow, *New York Times Magazine* (5/12/1971).
12. J. Russell Brown points out that when Pinter wants to show Stanley's 'deeper, inarticulate feelings', he gives him action rather than speech – 'Dialogue in Pinter and Others', *Modern British Dramatists* (1968).
13. Pinter interview with Gussow, op. cit.

Nigel Alexander   Past, Present and Pinter
(1974)

There is no future for the characters created by Harold Pinter. In play after play the curtain comes down on a terrible state of stasis in which the only possible development for the individuals concerned is, at best, continued stagnation, at worst, putrefaction. This is not a matter of accident. The characters frequently refer to the future – some of them may even be presumed to have an 'existence' to look forward to once the play is over. Yet the future which they imagine is quite clearly beyond their grasp. Their visions are perpetually betrayed by their actions – and their actions, as the audience come to realise, are conditioned by their history. This steady elimination of the future by the slow revelation of old times is the most distinctive mark of Pinter's dramatic technique. Its most interesting aspect is the way in which he subtly corrupts his audience into abandoning all hope for the characters. The menacing atmosphere of the plays is a product of the way in which the spectator is left prey to the pity and terror naturally associated with an unexpected visit to the inhabitants of inferno.

This mastery of technique is even more important than Pinter's grasp of language and it has not, perhaps, been sufficiently recognised. In an extremely interesting article in the *New York Review of Books* Nigel Dennis savaged those who sought for thought or philosophical coherence in Pinter's work but then found himself still with the task of explaining why. 'There is no doubt at all that his plays *work* – that the puzzles they represent in no way prevent them from being extremely theatrical.'[1] The solution favoured by Mr Dennis is that the plays work because they are, purely and simply, exercises for actors – an elaboration of standard drama school improvisations.

All playwrights must think themselves into their characters in order to put life into them, but Mr Pinter is perhaps the first playwright to think himself exclusively into the actor. It is this that he is 'obsessed with'. A dialogue such as the following:

ELLEN: It's very dark outside.
RUMSEY: It's high up.
ELLEN: Does it get darker the higher you get?
RUMSEY: No.
    (*Silence.*)

is virtually meaningless in thought or intellect, but put two good actors on the stage and see how it will hum – what deep significance, what frightening overtones, what enigmatic images it will produce. It is perfectly legitimate theatre, of a childish sort, and it is God's gift to the acting profession. An actor is not concerned with what something is about; he is only interested in how he can act. In Mr Pinter he has found a playwright who is equally uninterested in what the work is about: the work is simply the acting thereof.[2]

Mr Dennis is, I believe, right to attack those who seek to transmute the plays into the substance of the current higher metaphysics. There is nothing there, and it does a grave injustice to the more concrete problems of perception presented to us in dramatic form by Pinter. It is this dramatic form which Mr Dennis has ignored. If actors were really capable of making lines 'meaningless in thought and intellect' hum with significance the theatre would be a much busier place than it is. The lines are theatrically effective because they are in a context which is theatrically effective. They 'work' because Mr Pinter is one of those rare beings praised by Aristotle – the poet who is more the poet of his plots than of his verses. A Pinter plot is created not by intricate intrigue but by the manipulation of past and present.

One of the ways in which this is achieved may be demonstrated from *The Caretaker*. There all the characters believe in some miracle of rare device which will effectively transform their dreary present existence. Mick, the first character seen on stage although he does not enter the action until the end of the first act, is engaged (or rather says he is about to become engaged) in converting his old house into a penthouse containing

Curved chairs with cushioned seats, armchairs in oatmeal tweed, a beech frame settee with a woven sea-grass seat, white-topped heat-resistant coffee table, white tile surround.

Aston, his brother, appears to have a slightly more methodical approach to the same problem. He intends to clear the garden and build a shed so that he can do the carpentry necessary to get the house in order. Davies, the old man befriended by Aston, has an even more modest design. He hopes, if only the weather would break, to get down to Sidcup to collect the vital papers which prove his identity.

These are all predictions, made by the characters, of what they will do in the future. The reasons that will prevent them from ever being fulfilled emerge slowly from the past. It turns out that Davies left his papers with a man 'in the war . . . must be . . . about near on fifteen years ago'. The effort to reach Sidcup may, therefore, be continuous but it is unlikely to be successful – even supposing that the man or the papers still exist. Aston's shed will remain a pile of wood in the bedroom while he continually visits shops or men to find jigsaws or other items that are essential before he gets started – a state of compulsive and nervous inaction which has already involved him in treatment in a mental hospital. Mick's penthouse will never have the colours of its 'teal blue, copper and parchment linoleum squares' re-echoed in the walls because he depends upon people like Aston or Davies to act as interior decorators for him.

It is, of course, possible for the audience to think like the characters and imagine a future where the journey was completed, the shed built, and even the penthouse created – but in order to do so they would need to disbelieve everything that they see and hear about the characters in the course of the play. Their behaviour is both repetitive and compulsive and the audience is soon in a position to predict what these individuals will do next. Their view contradicts the projections of the characters' fancy. The audience thus 'know' the characters better than they know themselves and can, with greater accuracy, forecast their future. It is bleak because it is blank. The terrifying contrast between the expressed feelings of the characters and their actual behaviour is the subject revealed through the structure of Pinter's play.

The meaning of the play does not depend upon some display of thought or intellect voiced by the characters. It depends upon the conclusions which the audience draw from the process which they observe acted before them on the stage. The fact that a Pinter play does not contain 'great thoughts' which explain 'what it all means' does not deprive it of dramatic or philosophical significance. The demonstrable fact that Harold Pinter has a characteristic way of structuring his plays is important because it reveals some similarity in the kinds of conclusion towards which he directs his audience. In the control exercised over the feelings and thoughts of the audience is expressed the dramatist's 'view of life'.

It is important to try to be as clear as possible about the principles involved since they are vital to the art of the dramatist. Actors are required to appear upon the stage, or acting area, for any performance to take place. The routine with variations which they go through is the act or action of the play. This performance could be entirely static – as a pianist might give a concert performance by sitting without playing a note of music. It could be completely improvised – depending simply upon the reactions of the actors to each other – although even improvisation soon has a predictable element. These are extreme cases and, in general, more control is sought over the dramatic performance. Such control usually implies an author, and a script.

The script, or play, exercises control over the actors and the performance in two basic ways. It provides information about whom the actors represent – what sort of people they are, what they are doing in their present environment, what they have done in the past to get there. It also predicts what they are going to do next. This prediction, as we have seen, may be of two kinds. It may be a forecast provided by the characters themselves or a deduction and prognosis made by the audience. In either case the course of the drama may fulfil or frustrate such a prediction. That, in its turn, provides evidence upon which further speculation must be based. The kind and extent of the information may vary. The degree of prediction, and its accuracy, will fluctuate. There is, however, no play written or performed using words which does not contain some degree of prediction.

This provision of information and prediction by, and for, actors is taken to represent the passage of time – which may, or may not, correspond to the time taken for the performance. This is perhaps the most basic convention of all dramatic art. Although there are exceptions, the period of time represented is usually longer than that taken for its performance. All the essential elements of a performance or play may now be presented in the form of a diagram:

$$\text{TIME (dramatised)} = \frac{\text{ACTORS} \times \text{ACTION}}{\text{INFORMATION} \times \text{PREDICTION}}$$

This is the basic dramatic equation, if we may be permitted to abuse the language of mathematics, which every dramatist must solve in his own way. The fashion in which it is solved determines the kind, the style and the nature of the play.

Pinter's method is to allow the information which is supplied by or about his characters to contradict the predictions which they make about themselves until the audience is forced to make a much more pessimistic evaluation of their situation. This technique is hardly new, since it is the basis of the highly successful *Oedipus Tyrannus* by Sophocles, but it is not a technique that could be used easily by a man who was uninterested in what the work was about. . . .

[Nigel Alexander's examination of these arguments in relation specifically to *The Birthday Party* is given below, in Part Two – Ed.]

SOURCE: extract from article in *Essays and Studies*, 27 (1974), pp. 1–5.

NOTES

[Renumbered from the original]

1. Nigel Dennis, 'Pintermania', *New York Review of Books*, xv, No. 11 (1970), pp. 21–2.
2. Ibid.

Peter Hall   Directing Pinter   (1974)

INTERVIEW WITH CATHERINE ITZIN AND SIMON TRUSSLER

You're now the director one associates most closely with Pinter, but actually the association began relatively late in his career, didn't it?

In practice, yes. But Pinter had seen my production of *Godot* back in 1956 or 1957, and Michael Codron sent me *The Birthday Party* when it was first going to be done. I didn't know who Harold Pinter was, but I liked the play enormously. I couldn't do it though because I had commitments in New York that year: and then when *The Caretaker* was sent to me, I couldn't do that, either, because I was just setting up the new companies at Stratford and the Aldwych. But I did put £250 into the production of *The Caretaker* at the Arts, which I think was capitalised at £1000 or something very low, and it earned me a surprising amount of money – it's one of the few times I've made money out of investing in plays, a hobby I've long since given up! I then put most of the money back into the film of *The Caretaker*. So there were these very early possibilities for association with Pinter, which didn't come to anything.

Can you remember now how you reacted when you first read The Birthday Party *by this unknown dramatist?*

Well, I heard the voice of Beckett, without any question, and the voice of Kafka – the horror, the terror of the unknown. But I did think the play was rather too bound by its own naturalism: you know, the three-act structure, the French's acting edition set. That was why I was so thrilled when I read *The Caretaker*, which seemed to have reached a point where the form was uniquely the dramatist's own. I don't think *The Birthday Party* is quite free from being a 'rep' play.

You didn't see the short-lived first production, presumably?

No – I remember actually coming back from New York on the Sunday morning after the opening, and reading Hobson's review. He was the only one more or less to get *The Birthday Party* right, and there in the same paper was the news that it had closed the previous night.

You didn't consider The Caretaker *for the opening Aldwych season?*

Oh no, I couldn't. Michael Codron had an option on *The Caretaker*, having done *The Birthday Party* and lost his shirt on that.

How well did you like Donald McWhinnie's production?

I certainly liked it well enough to ask him to do I think three productions with the RSC. I didn't think it was quite hard enough, actually. It was a little explanatory – perhaps Pinter needed to be at that stage.

. . .

How did you respond to The Collection?

Well, working on Pinter's plays over the years, I'm conscious, retrospectively, of having developed a technique, an approach, a way of going about things. I certainly didn't have that when we began *The Collection*. I don't think I was fully at home with it as a technique until about half-way through the rehearsals of *The Homecoming*. But it was very much part of the same world as working on Beckett – making the actor trust what is given, making him accept the premise of the words. That goes as much for the architectural shape of the words as it does for any resonance that they may have for the actor emotionally. And since you cannot actually ignore or change the words, you may as well start from there. The parallel to me is with music – don't get me wrong, I don't think if you merely sing the right notes, you make any sense in human terms. You don't in opera, you don't in Pinter. But if you sing the *wrong* notes you are going to make nonsense. . . .

. . .

Can you describe the process of work on the play?

I can speak about how I work on a Pinter play. It doesn't mean to say this is *the way*. And I must make absolutely clear that although Harold and I have had a long association and I've directed a number of his stage plays, and we've worked together on films and so on, it is a totally pragmatic situation. I would hate anybody reading this to think *this is the way to direct Pinter*. This absolutely is not true: it's the way *I* direct Pinter. Having said that, my working arrangement with him has been, over twelve years, that in front of the actors – and I stress that – he can say anything he likes about what I'm doing, and the production, and the rights and wrongs of it. And in front of the actors I can say anything I like about the text, and the rights and wrongs of that. But I am the final arbiter of the production, and he, obviously, is the final arbiter of the text. I think this has, on occasion, been very tough on the actors, because we do develop a kind of Tweedledum and Tweedledee act, and we are, I think, very good for each other. But that doesn't necessarily mean we're very good for some of the actors surrounding us. It's all a bit high-powered, it's very wordy, and we split hairs with great glee. The scrutiny can get a bit much. But Harold will never say, 'You should do *that*.' He will say, 'That isn't right', which is something quite different.

Is there an example of that you could give?

Well, let's take *The Homecoming*. The problem there is that the biggest bastard in a house full of bastards is actually the man who at first sight appears to be the victim – that is, Teddy, the brother who brings his wife home. He is actually locked in a battle of wills with his father and with his brothers, and of course, with his wife, during which, in some sense, he destroys his wife, and his family, and his father, and himself, rather than give in. He is actually the protagonist. Now, it's very easy for an actor to fall into the 'martyred' role in that part, because Teddy says so little – just sits there while all the other characters are speculating about his wife's qualities in bed. But this is the point – its a tremendous act of will on his part to take it, and if he was actually feeling anything uncontrolled, he wouldn't be able to do it.

It wasn't until Michael Jayston did it in the film that I realised how hard Teddy actually had to be, and how much in control he was. I'd felt it, but I hadn't pushed it far enough. And Harold was always saying to me during the two stage productions, 'That's not quite right.'

Is that all he would say?

No, no, he would indicate that one should make it harder, but we never found the way. I don't want to denigrate Michael Bryant or Michael Craig who played the part on the stage. I think it was something to do with the personalities of the particular actors concerned, who are giving off vibrations which they may not know about, and which one has to allow for in certain ways. So my approach to a Pinter play is first of all to try and expose the underlying melodrama of the text. I try and find out who does hate who, and who loves who, and who's doing what to whom, and in the first stage of rehearsals play it very crudely.

Does this mean that you try to find what is actually happening, in fact, in so far as there might be a fact?

Yes. There is a fact. Certainly there is a fact. Why, in *The Homecoming*, is Lenny so obsessed from the word go with destroying his father? Talking about his cooking and his rotten meals and so on. Now that must not, in my view, be played with any kind of heaviness: but the underlying feeling is one of absolute naked hatred. Because I think at the base of a good deal of Harold's work is the cockney game of taking the piss: and part of that game is that you should not be quite sure whether the piss is being taken or not. In fact, if you know I'm not really doing it very well: and a good deal of Harold's tone has to do with that very veiled kind of mockery.

Now, actors can't play veiling until they know what they're veiling, so we play mockery, we play hatred, we play animosity, we play the extreme black-and-white terms of a character. That stage of rehearsal is very crude, but it's a very important stage, because unless the actor understands what game he is playing, what his actual underlying motivations are, the ambiguity of the text will mean nothing. People who think that all you've got to do in Pinter is to say it, hold the pause and then say the next line, are wrong. The mystery to me is that there is a communication in the theatre which is beyond words, and which is actually concerned with direct feeling. An actor who says to you, 'All right, I may be feeling that, but unless I show the audience that I'm feeling it, they won't understand', is actually wrong. If he feels it and masks it, the audience still gets it.

. . .

Do you find it's necessary to have any sort of scenario to present to the actors, if only for them to start off with?

No. I would never say to an actor, 'This is what it means', or 'This is what this scene's about'. I would start nudging as soon as they begin, by means of propositions. 'Because you've said that, might it not indicate that your feelings are this: could we explore that, could we play it at the extremity of that feeling?'

Do you find the actors have very definite feelings initially, even if they're wrong ones, rather than just feeling confused?

It very much depends on the actor. You see, because he has such a distinctive voice, very quickly there came to be a 'Pinter style', which is external. Actors know you speak Pinter in a dry, clipped way, and you hold the pause, and you don't inflect very much, and you don't show very much emotion. It's wrong, of course – a convention, nothing more. Like saying play Chekhov sad, or Shakespeare with a lot of lung power. But, very early on, one felt actors making Pinter patterns, and that's really dreadful – though I suppose it's better than actors trying to 'normalise' Pinter's speech rhythms, because the first thing I say to actors when we're beginning a Pinter play is 'Look, don't mislead yourselves into thinking that if there's a pause there, there shouldn't be a pause there, or, if there's a silence, there shouldn't be a silence, because there should. Our job is to find out why. And don't, in order to make it comfortable, turn a full-stop into a comma, or break it up in a colloquial way different to the way he's written it.'

I actually believe that Beckett and Pinter are poetic dramatists, in the proper sense of the word: they have a linear structure and a formal structure which you'd better just observe – don't learn it wrong, don't speak it wrong, you can't, you mustn't. But there are various things that you can exercise. One of the greatest influences on Pinter, obviously, is the early Eliot – particularly in the repeated phrase, the catching up of a phrase and repeating it over three sentences, keeping it up in the air, like a ball. Now, that is often written in three separate sentences: but it has to make a unit, and you don't find that unit till about the third week. So at the beginning it is better just to observe absolutely accurately what he's written.

I also know that the intensity of the feeling underlying Pinter's text is so very extreme, so very brutal, that you have to explore this melodramatic area that I was speaking about. And this of course raises the question of where the actors live in relation to each other, physically, because until you start letting loose the naked feeling, you don't know the answers to very basic questions, such as, are eyes necessary, or are they not? Are they part of the weaponry?

My vocabulary is all the time about hostility and battles and weaponry, but that is the way Pinter's characters operate, as if they were all stalking round a jungle, trying to kill each other, but trying to disguise from one another the fact that they are bent on murder. And whether you can see a character's face or whether you can't, whether you hold his eyes or not, is absolutely critical – and that to a very large extent comes out of the actor's psyche, once the feelings are being generated. So I wouldn't have anything to say about the physical life of a Pinter play until the emotions had been released, because I wouldn't know what they should be. Equally, Pinter deals in stillness, in confrontations which are unbroken, and I believe it mandatory to do as few moves in a Pinter play as possible. You don't want moves up to the drinks cabinet, or across to the table, in order to 'break it up', or to make it seem naturalistic. It isn't naturalistic.

I couldn't help feeling that John Bury's cavernous set for the Aldwych production of The Homecoming *almost cried out for the actors to make just those sorts of irrelevant moves. . .*

But they didn't.

No, but to some extent the set seemed to work against what you've just said.

No, I don't think that's true at all. Pinter wrote *The Homecoming* for the Aldwych, actually. His description of the set is that it is enormous, and actually the staircase was twice as tall as an actual staircase would have been. The area they were fighting over, which was the father's chair and the sofa where the seduction takes place, and the rug in front, was an island in the middle of antiseptic cleanliness – that scrubbed lino, acres of it. And the journey from that island where the family fought each other, across to the sideboard to get the apple, was very perilous, and this was all quite deliberate – a few objects in space, and a feeling of absolute chilliness and hostility.

Pinter has got a terrific selectivity about physical life on the stage. His stage directions, if he needs to give them, about where people move and what they do, are extremely precise, and if he doesn't give them, it's just as well to assume nothing is necessary. This also goes for design. If the set for *The Homecoming* is a naturalistic representation of a house in North London, then the glass of water makes almost no impression, because it's one glass among many knick-knacks. I think one of the troubles about *The Birthday Party* as a play was that Pinter hadn't yet achieved in formal terms, the absolute clarity of his vision. *The Birthday Party* exists in that rather cluttered room, it's all more unnecessarily naturalistic.

I'd agree about The Birthday Party, *but the clutter seems absolutely vital to* The Caretaker.

Oh, yes, it is. But that is a *decision* to be very cluttered, and that's a point in itself. Nobody would dream up that clutter in *The Caretaker* unless it was specified. Equally, *The Homecoming* is about space, and I think *Old Times* is about those two beds side by side. And sometimes they're sofas. Pinter has an immensely architectural sense, and John Bury's contribution to the plays has always been very great, because he thinks architecturally and spatially.

You've mentioned cockney piss-taking as a recurrent element in Pinter's plays. Are there other important features they share?

If anybody breaks down in a Pinter play, it is catatonic. . . total. A breakdown is a sign of great, great weakness – the end of the world. So most of the characters preserve their cool, however hot their cool is inside. Equally, physical violence can suddenly be unleashed, which is an expression of the tensions that have been developing beneath this often very urbane surface, and people crack each other over the head or beat each other up or kill each other. It's there in that sudden unleashing, that total breakdown of Deeley at the end of *Old Times*.

You don't think there's any difference in this respect between the two worlds in which Pinter's plays seem to be set — one of them the North London or the cockney world, the other the much more urbane, middle-class world from The Collection *onwards?*

I don't think there is very much difference. There are different kinds of sophistications, but his cockney characters are extremely clever, extremely sophisticated. But the other recurring characteristic concerns his treatment of women. It is very sensitive and well-observed – he creates wonderful women; but always one feels it's a *man* looking at women, the feminine enigma remains.

. . .

Do you find improvisation is of any value in trying to get at the nature of the underlying tensions?

You can't improvise easily as an aid to acting Pinter, because at the end of the day you still have to speak a very formal text. But you can improvise feeling patterns, or you can play the opposites – say, 'Let's play this scene with you hating instead of loving.' Or you can increase the obvious underlying tensions, you can swop roles – you can do all the things that make people aware of the underlying tensions. To that extent improvisation is helpful.

And you use it?

Yes, certainly. And at that point it doesn't matter, obviously, that what you're getting is something very crude. I like, by the end of the first ten days, to be able to have a melodramatic run-through, with books in hand – something which is very emotional and very, very crude. The next stage actually is to try to analyse exactly what games of hostility each character is playing with the others. Because they all play games, all the time. They all tease each other, they all try and get rises out of each other, they all try and disturb each other by saying the opposite of what the other one was hoping or expecting. This reaches its obvious climax in *Landscape*, where one character is apparently totally oblivious of the other, although she obviously hears every word he says.

One of the worrying things for actors in Pinter is that you can never trust what is said to be literally true. It is much safer, in fact, to assume that it is a ploy, rather than the truth, unless you can actually discover that it is the truth. So when the actors have found how to wear their hearts on their sleeves and actually show their emotions, you then have to start a process where they hide their emotions, because to show emotion in Pinter's world is, as I've said, a weakness, which is mercilessly punished by the other characters. You have to construct the mask of the character – because all Pinter's characters have masks – though it's no good having a mask unless you know what's underneath it. But the mask almost never slips. It's exactly like that Marceau mime, where he's laughing, and the mask gets stuck in the grin, and you know his heart is breaking underneath. Now, his breaking heart is what you feel, but he doesn't actually indicate that his heart is breaking at all. That's very like acting in Pinter.

So, the second stage is to find how to disguise the emotions which are quite evidently being felt. When Ruth returns with Teddy and comes downstairs in the morning and the father is so dreadful to her and to his son, 'having tarts in the house at night', the obvious realistic response would be to break down left and bury your head in the sofa, or whatever. But he beckons her over to him, the father does, and she crosses and looks him in the eye, and he says to her, 'How many kids have you got?' 'Three.' 'All yours, Ted?' Now, by any normal standards of improvisation, Ruth should be playing that scene hysterically, but she isn't. The alarm is underneath, but totally masked.

And the actress knows why she isn't hysterical?

Oh, of course. Because she's taking the old man on. If the old man is making that kind of challenge, she is accepting it. It doesn't mean to say she's not upset, underneath her mask, just as in the last section of the play, when Teddy is deliberately pushing the family, they retaliate with the proposition that his wife should be put on the game, as a dreadful joke at first, to see if he'll crack. And he is saying throughout the last twenty minutes of the play, 'You live your joke. Go on. You want to put her on the game? You needn't think I'll object. *Put* her on the game.' He's dying inside, because he doesn't, of course, want to lose his wife. But again, the mask is not allowed to slip.

There's one little crack at the end of the play, the most difficult moment of the play, when he's leaving the room, and Ruth says, 'Don't become a stranger.' It is very difficult to play. That's the first and only time she calls him Eddie, which is obviously the intimate and familiar name. It is all there, and it's all very . . . calculated is the wrong word, because I know Harold to be a deeply instinctive writer, who writes very quickly once it's there to be written, and it would not be true to say that he works it all out like an intellectual game.

It's almost as if you have to direct two plays each time you direct a Pinter play. . .?

Yes, you do, you certainly do. And I think the achievement of a Pinter production must be that the two plays meet. Because what stirs the audience is not the mask, not the control, but what is underneath it: that's what upsets them, that's what terrifies and moves them. In that sense Pinter's is a new form of theatre. It's very difficult to point to anybody else and say, 'That's the way he operates too'. Beckett, of course, sometimes.

Are you partly saying that there are really no weak characters in Pinter's plays – weak in the human sense? Ready to give in and to react naturally?

No, I don't think so. Uncle Sam is very weak, but he's also very sly and very cunning, because he knows the dangers of the game. That's why, when he makes the final revelation in *The Homecoming*, that 'McGregor had Jessie in the back of my cab as I drove them along', there's nothing for him to do but keel over, pass out, the pressure is so much.

I don't think that Harold has recognised from the beginning of his writing that if, say, I'm sitting in this room on my own, I'm in a totally relaxed state – I don't know how my face is behaving, I'm not concerned about it, I'm not presenting myself to anybody. A knock on the door, by you, is sufficient to make my face form a pattern, even before you've actually entered, and from that moment on, neither of us, either by word or by deed or in physical relation to each other, are expressing what we are actually feeling. We are modifying ourselves in relation to each other, and all the modifications, the signals of modern behaviour, are aimed at preserving the mask. We are playing a game – that is, social intercourse.

Pinter has worked from that premise, and taken very dreadful situations, usually, dreadful confrontations between people, which are about territorial battles, or battles over people. And where Pinter on the stage goes wrong is if the actors stop playing the game, if they actually show what they're feeling, because it becomes ludicrous – you know, those unfortunate laughs you can get in Pinter when it's played without underlying truth. Suddenly, something quite apparently serious is said, which pulls the rug away from everything. Now, Pinter *is* very funny, mainly because you can't believe people can maintain these signals, these masks, and it's so shocking, it makes you laugh. But if an actor indulges himself and actually drops the mask, and says, 'I want to show the audience that I'm breaking my heart', the whole scene collapses.

I think it's at this point, as you manufacture the masks, that you have to verify, in a very particular way, that you are saying what Pinter says, and hitting the rhythms that he wrote. It's no good doing it earlier because then you apply it like a funny hat to the actor. But once the play is beginning to live, you cannot be too meticulous. What Pinter wrote is always better than what a lazy actor will come up with. Now this may seem a very small and pedantic point, but most of our actors have a fairly easy-going, not to say contemptuous, attitude to what a dramatist has written, and for the average playwright, writing the average colloquial flim-flam, it doesn't much matter whether you say 'but' instead of 'and', or put in a few extra words. It does in Pinter, and it is excruciatingly difficult to get it completely accurate. But *when* you get it accurate, then the rhythm – and he has the most astonishing ability to write rhythms – begins to work. And you begin to feel the emotions underlying those rhythms. Let me put it like this. If you sing a Mozart aria correctly, certain responses begin to be necessary inside you. Now, you could say that's putting the cart before the horse, but that's the way it is – you're not improvising something of your own, you're singing some notes of Mozart. It's much the same with Pinter.

You can do that too early, and then you simply have the actor imitating surface rules. He must already be alive in himself, emotionally, otherwise it's an imposition. But there has to come a point – and this is the most unpleasant, agonising moment of rehearsal – when you actually get it right. It's not easy.

There is a difference in Pinter between a pause and a silence and three dots. A pause is really a bridge where the audience think that you're this side of the river, then when you speak again, you're the other side. That's a pause. And it's alarming, often. It's a gap, which retrospectively gets filled in. It's not a dead stop – that's a silence, where the confrontation has become so extreme, there is nothing to be said until either the temperature has gone down, or the temperature has gone up, and then something quite new happens. Three dots is a very tiny hesitation, but it's there, and it's different from a semi-colon, which Pinter almost never uses, and its different from a comma. A comma is something that you catch up on, you go through it. And a full stop's just a full stop. You stop.

Have you found that, because of the cliches that have developed about Pinter, actors try to leap over your first few weeks of rehearsal, and go straight into the significance bit?

Yes, and that's disastrous, that's disastrous. I'm now already about three-quarters of the way through rehearsals, and it's only at that stage where you know where people stand or sit.

What are the actors doing *before? How are you moving it?*

They're going anywhere. I never mind where actors go beforehand. Not in Pinter. Though on the whole I would advise them to stay still, providing they don't find that staying still is inhibiting or tying them up. If they need to move, they move. But the reality of where they need to stand will not be evident until the melodrama has been investigated, and then the mask has been investigated. *Then* they'll begin to know where they can stand and where they can't stand, and where they can move and where they can't move. And who they need to look at and when.

But it is very much a matter of 'can' and 'can't' by that stage, as opposed to 'want?'

Well, yes, because by that stage what they want begins to be something necessary for what they're having to do as characters. All actors like to move too much in the early stages – it frees them, it's a means of getting away from the actual problem. Anybody can light a cigarette in order to feel natural, or go and get a drink: but in the highly-charged Pinter play, you don't do *anything* without it having some significance to the other characters. So the physical life comes quite late, and with that, I like to allow a total absorption, once it begins to grow, in the inner life. The actors should indulge their private emotions. At this later stage the actors should be encouraged to over-pause, to over-silence, to think very, very deeply, and feel very deeply what it is that they're hiding. They should take all the time in the world, in fact, so that the emotion becomes very full inside them. And at that point the play is obviously meaningless to an outside observer.

At what point would Pinter himself normally have started to come along and tell you if things weren't right?

From the word go. He pops in every few days. The great thing about Pinter is that he knows what work processes are, he's not one of those dramatists who judges today's work as if it was the first night. He's a practical man of the theatre.

So. . . what happens next, after getting the moves right?

The next stage actually is to encourage the actors, if they see a chink in another character's armour, to challenge it. This gets things very right and tense. If you really are feeling very heavy, it's almost axiomatic in Pinter that you play very light. But if you're revealing the heaviness, the other actor should say, 'I can see what you're feeling: you're vulnerable'. And this creates a terrific frisson.

You're setting up your own game to get at his game?

Exactly. Your own game. And this again is a very difficult stage of rehearsal, because often actors feel that those feelings, which they have so carefully nurtured, if they're going to be that evident, and that criticised, they're going to throw them away altogether, and start feeling like hollow shells with a mask on top. So it's all a matter of balance, of going from one extreme, then back to the other again. After that stage I have a very technical, shaping period of rehearsal which is equally horrible, because I shape what's been found – that is, I make certain quick bits quicker, slow up some slow bits, find motives to make this pause longer or that pause shorter. I do a whole rehearsal of the play in which the main thing is to see how quickly you can take the cues, if there isn't a pause or a silence. I orchestrate it, actually. But only from what has been reached. Shape what has been found.

By what time are you working on the actual stage, with the set?

Well, I would already like to be there, from about the third week. I'm usually not, but I would like to be there.

The third week out of how many weeks?

I think a Pinter play usually needs about five or six weeks. One of the reasons why it needs a long time is that a concentrated Pinter rehearsal is so exhausting for actors they can't take more than about four hours a day without actually cheating for the fifth or sixth, or just getting so taut that it doesn't work. Four to five hours a day is about the maximum they can take.

It sounds from the way you've understated it as though the moves almost happen by themselves. . .

Well, they do. And if a scene is not operating, it is sometimes because the physical life is not right, and you try other things. I once said that staging a Pinter play is not difficult: of course it *is*, but it isn't difficult if the actors are actually creating in the right way.

Likewise with the set?

Likewise with the set. The ideal way to work on a Pinter play would be to rehearse it for three weeks, and then design the set. Of course, we're never in that situation. I've only been able to do that once in my life, and that was for an Albee production. When it comes to sets, costumes, props, I think everything burns itself so strongly on the audience's mind in a Pinter play that the coffee cup really has to be very carefully considered. It sounds very fanciful, but the apples in *The Homecoming* had to be green – they could not be yellow or red, because they simply didn't disturb visually. The moment when Sam picks up the apple and eats it and says, 'Feeling a bit peckish' to the old man, is a kick in the crutch to him, and a soft yellow apple would not have had the effect, I sound obsessive, I am. The furniture, the costumes, are very, very carefully scrutinised and a lot of things change, until one builds up something where one can feel that each second is charged with something, and is right.

   The artist that I have thought about visually for Pinter, ever since I read *The Birthday Party*, is Magritte – that hard-edged, very elegant, very precise style. Again, you see, you can't overstate. . . .

   . . .

How much more or less vital is the whole preliminary casting process in a Pinter play?

Well, I think the one thing you've got to do in casting a Pinter play is cast rich personalities, because his characters are like three-dimensional masks – we look at them from different sides and we see different aspects of them, and they've got to be fascinating people, in the first instance. So I wouldn't cast good, dull actors. They have got to have enormous verbal dexterity, and enormously good breath control, because Pinter doesn't allow you to take ordinary breaths, you know. You can't colloquialise it. Experience in Shakespeare is a help.

Yet one of the seeming things about a Pinter text is its apparent linguistic simplicity. . . .

That really is only apparent. You take a piece of Pinter and read it aloud as if you were in a Wednesday Play, and you'll find that the emphases come at the wrong moments, because you've run out of breath, and you can't quite get your tongue round it, it doesn't quite work. Pinter requires great verbal dexterity. My experience has been that the actor with a fair amount of classical training and experience can handle it, but the actor who is used to colloquial behaviourism can't do it at all.

But it depends on the actor. Michael Hordern didn't find it difficult. Yet Paul Rogers – a marvellous classical actor – found the discipline in the early stages of rehearsal intolerable – the pauses were like dreadful corsets round him. But he licked it brilliantly.

Getting back to the progress of rehearsals – have we got to the stage when it's 'fixed', but very difficult to hold?

We're at the nit-picking stage. I've shaped it and orchestrated it, and it goes absolutely dead, and at this point you have to do some exercises about what's actually being felt all over again. You may even take the mask off in a couple of scenes, in order to revitalise the emotional levels. I've done that before now.

Does anybody panic?

Well, yes, people panic. I remember one very eminent actress panicking very badly at that stage, because she was being confronted with an intensity of emotional life which she didn't actually want to admit, certainly not on the stage, and certainly not in life. But she played it, she played a whole scene with tears running down her face, in actual agony, and the other actors wanted to stop it but didn't dare, because there was such a release going on. That is a measure of the intensity of feeling required. Once she'd got that, once we'd gone through that, it was all right. I don't believe in engineering rows in order to upset people, I think they're totally unproductive, but I think that complete immersion in the play can sometimes produce staggering emotional reactions, and they're of course very important.

So, at this stage, I would say one is nit-picking about precise timings, precise inflections, precise patterns, precise orchestrations, which is all formalised and deadening. And at the other extreme, one is stoking up the fires of feeling all the time, so it's a crisis-ridden time. The other important point is that an actor's responsibility to his fellows in Pinter is absolutely critical. If an actor gives too much away or too little on a feed-line, it makes it absolutely impossible to play the answering line. So the actors must have developed – by now we're in the fifth week – a trust and an understanding of each other. At this point one is running the play probably once a day or certainly once every two days, and doing exercises to make it more emotional on the one hand, and shaping it technically on the other.

And then the most difficult thing of all comes when you meet the audience, because a Pinter actor has to control the audience in a quite deliberate way. It requires a degree of control in the actor, a degree of arrogance in the actor, towards the audience. For instance, you need to let an audience laugh in Pinter, so that at the precise moment when they have laughed themselves out, you can hit them hard with the actuality. The plays are constructed like that, and it has to do with that tenth part of the actors' mind, which has got nothing to do with truth, but with control and technique – the tenth of you standing outside and watching the whole thing. You have to be absolutely adroit.

You've described the creation of a very precisely-honed instrument, which is the finished production . . . how do you reconcile the precision of the thing on the other hand, and the erraticism of the audience on the other?

Audiences are not that erratic for Pinter, actually. I think the precision is the instrument of control, and you can slightly increase the pause, or slightly increase the length of a laugh in order to grip a particular audience. Pinter audiences get off the hook and laugh at people as objects if you don't control them. You really have to make them listen, you really do have to hear that pin drop, and that takes a degree of expertise in the actor which is, I think, pretty considerable. But all the time, the paradox remains, about this intensity of feeling. That has to be utterly true. Because I have seen my own productions of Pinter, without the actors being aware of it, dry out in a fortnight or three weeks, so that the level of intensity underlying the masks has dropped, and actually what is being seen is a very chic series of patterns.

I was going to ask about this difficulty of having tuned a production to this pitch of intensity, and then having to keep it playing in the repertoire for months or even years.

You've got to keep attending to the emotional life underlying the play. That's the main thing.

Do you re-rehearse?

Yes, I do.

. . .

Though Pinter himself now has a lot of experience as a director, he seems to have stopped directing his own plays. . . .

Well, we tried this. I persuaded him to do the Aldwych revival of *The Birthday Party* himself. I think he is a very fine director and I'm very pleased when I can work with him in a producer-director relationship. But the curious thing about *The Birthday Party* when he directed it was that the actors were not working in a free and open way with the director, they were working with the *author*. So when Harold said, and I heard him say it, 'I don't know, what does it say?' or 'Why don't you try. . .?' they took it as god's writ. Therefore they acted results and simplifications. They didn't go on a quest. They didn't make something complex, which changed from second to second. This is the pain and the fascination of playing Pinter. You have this storm of emotion inside you, and you change tack, as we do in life, from second to second, behind the mask. This didn't happen in *The Birthday Party* production, because however Harold reacted, whether he said nothing or whether he said something, they took it to be *the answer*, and he said to me after he'd done that, 'I'm not going to direct any of my plays again. Not my plays. That's it'. Because it really didn't work.

. . .

In *The Homecoming*, Harold envisaged that vast room. 'We knocked the wall down several years ago to make an open living area. My mother was dead'. Because of the big Aldwych stage John Bury's first solution had a big iron beam across where they'd knocked the wall down. The iron was very evident, and I remember Harold saying, 'Now I think they would have put that big steel beam up, to keep the house up, that's right, and I like the whole proportion of it, but I don't want to see all that iron, that makes too much of a statement.' So we covered it with plaster. So you thought, well, maybe it's a big iron beam they've got there, but you weren't absolutely sure. That's an image, actually, of the whole process – the iron beam is there, but covered over.

. . .

How important do you think the Jewishness is in Pinter?

Very, in some areas – the extremity of family affection – the family unit being something which holds and encloses and makes everything possible, and yet also destroys everything. I don't say that is something which is special to the Jewish race, but it's something which they seem to have an extreme instinct for. But we all do it. Again, though, they are not 'Jewish' plays; to say that *The Homecoming* is about a Jewish family is already wrong. It isn't. And we went out of our way to make sure that they were not 'Jewish' actors.

We've talked about Beckett, and one can see the Beckettian associations, of course. But, whereas one feels that Beckett's characters are always hovering on the edge of some extremity of existence, in however comic a fashion, Pinter's world is much more part of one's own experience . . . almost, more normal.

I think that Pinter is concerned with the family unit, the husband-wife relationship, the child – the hope of making the bourgeois unit: whereas Sam's work is entirely concerned with 'me alone in a dark tunnel' – or you alone in a dark tunnel.

. . .

Is there such a thing as a Pinter world-view?

Oh, Christ. Speaking personally, I get a very bleak, very uncompromising, very hostile view of life out of him. Counterbalanced by a longing for contact and relation and . . . not getting into a situation of deep regrets, which is very painful. Because all his characters do have regrets, do crucify themselves, and everybody else. But I think what is for me wonderful about Pinter is that in an unblinkingly hostile situation where everybody does go wrong in some way or another, there are little moments of light and tenderness which are cherished. He is a very pessimistic dramatist: but I don't really understand how anybody could honestly be writing in the 1960s or 1970s and be particularly sunny. People are always saying to me, 'Why don't you do happy plays, that are life-enhancing?' to which the answer is 'Well, why don't people write them?' But I find the great thing about him is that his tenderness and his compassion are not sentimental, but absolutely, unblinkingly accurate.

Not cynical. . . .

Not at all, he's not cynical, he's unblinking. He scrutinises life unyieldingly, and I think my job as a director is to scrutinise it, if I can, as carefully as he has.

SOURCE: extracts from Peter Hall's interview-article, *Theatre Quarterly*, IV, No. 16 (1974/75), pp. 4–17.

Andrew Kennedy (1975)   'In Search of a Language'

'I am pretty well obsessed with words when they get going', Pinter once said when an interviewer asked whether his creative imagination was not more visual that verbal. Pinter went on to stress the doubleness of drama: 'It is a matter of tying the words to the image of the character standing on the stage. The two things go very closely together.'[1] This dual stress is important, for Pinter has explored the whole scale of verbal-visual power in the different dramatic media: film scripts as well as plays for radio and television flank his major plays for the theatre. Yet one is entitled to single out that obsession with words. It is impossible to think of a Pinter play in terms of mime, for the groping attempt of two or more characters to mark out contested territory with indefinite words – as animals, we learn from Lorenz and Tinbergen, mark out territory with definite posture, movement, colour and sound – is central.[2] The new patterns of dialogue can be regarded as the principal interest in each play. All other interests – including structure and insight into character – are inseparable from the 'transactions' in the dialogue. Pinter has worked out his plays, and the plays work on us, through words.

On the level of artistic creation this means that Pinter has a particular acute sense of the 'blank page' as 'both an exciting and frightening thing. It's what you start from.'[3] The words on the page *are* the shaping medium of the play, occasionally showing a strain of inbreeding, words multiplying words in scenes that seem autonomous.[4] On the level of 'audience impact' the words compel patient listening, attention to *how* things are being said, sometimes against *what* is being said. For certain patterns in a Pinter play may gain an almost hypnotic hold on ear or mind, even though they do not inform, have no emotional charge, and offer only neutral clues to the speaker.

On the linguistic level proper Pinter's dialogue is precise enough to provide samples for a work on the Varieties of Contemporary English; and the conversational rhythms alone could be used to train 'aural perception' in foreign students of spoken English. (It would be a much less mechanical primer than the one that inspired Ionesco's *The Bald Primadonna*.[5]) The precision is matched by the social–cultural range of the dialogue across Pinter's entire work (only once, in *The Homecoming*, within the texture of *one* play): from the 'non-standard' and inarticulate speech that keeps recurring in *The Room*, *The Dumb Waiter*, *The Birthday Party* and *The Caretaker*, to the euphemistic props of 'U-speech' in *A Slight Ache*, and to the sophisticated urban word-consciousness in plays like *The Collection*, *The Lover* and *Old Times*. Pinter has a facility for starting with a particular speech-style at a level of mimesis which Beckett found uncongenial and which Eliot could only achieve with strain. Yet a particular speech-style is not left 'to speak for itself', each is gradually made to exhibit its 'absurd' potential; the tramp's inarticulateness is intensified; the genteel phrases of Edward and Flora in *A Slight Ache* turn into a disturbed, mock-euphemistic litany by the end of the play; the mannered verbal games enacted by the married couple as adulterous lovers are underlined: 'To hear your command of contemporary phraseology, your delicate use of the very latest idiomatic expression, so subtly employed' (Richard in *The Lover*, p. 75). Not only is the dialogue 'idiomatic', it is saturated with idioms 'played' to show up their idiocy.[6] Similarly, jargon is used to draw attention to the misuse of language as a comic-aggressive smokescreen (Goldberg's cliché-patter, Mick's finance and interior-decorator terms; the academic jargon of Teddy, the cellarmanship of Duff).[7] The low slang in *The*

Homecoming is arranged to sound as if the cloaca of language had been dredged to exhibit the 'underground' of ceremonious family talk. The words 'get going' with obsessive patterns.

One characteristic of Pinter's dramatic language has become so familiar that terms like 'Pinterish' and 'Pinteresque' have come to denote – as Ronald Hayman reminds us – the irrationality of everyday conversation, its 'bad syntax, tautologies, pleonasms, repetitions, *non sequiturs* and self-contradictions'. Hayman goes so far as to claim that 'Pinter has capitalised in a way that no playwright had ever done before . . . on the fact that real-life conversations don't proceed smoothly and logically from point to point.'[8] Pinter certainly is an innovator, yet it needs to be stressed that what is original in his dialogue is the fusion of the minimal language in naturalism (Chekhov) and the aesthetic expressiveness found in implicit speech from the Symbolists to Beckett.

Most important of all: we experience – and can only experience – the plays through listening to the way everyday language gets deflected by – and the way it alienates – the speakers from one another. In James Boulton's words:

Evocative or disturbing speech, language which is an accurate reflection of colloquial English and yet reflects the mystery that Pinter sees as an inevitable feature of human relationships: this is a starting point for a consideration of his vision. It leads directly to what is perhaps the chief irony in his plays: the discrepancy between the implicit claim in any *patois* that it is the currency accepted and understood by all its users, and the dramatic fact that all such language in actual usage reveals not complete communication between man and man but their essential apartness.[9]

Pinter has, then, invented a drama of 'human relations at the level of language itself'. The phrase just quoted is taken from Jean Vannier's definition of what is really new in the theatre of Beckett and Ionesco: while the traditional theatre, says Vannier, presents 'psychological relationships which language only *translates*', in the new drama the characters' language is 'literally *exposed* upon the stage' so that there appears '*a theatre of language* where man's words are held up to us as a spectacle'.[10]

Yet Pinter stands in sharp contrast to Beckett and Ionesco.[11] Beckett – who seems to have been present at some latter-day Fall or Babel of literary language – has created his dialogue out of the stylised breakdown of hyper-literary styles. Pinter, to develop the image, has taken the linguistic Babel for granted (perhaps too glibly at times) at the level of everyday exchanges, talk, chat, verbal games – with an ear for local usage, or rather abusage and verbiage. He seems to carry no literary 'burden of the past'. He has created his dialogue out of the failures of language that might occur *as* English is spoken, by frightened or evasive or sadistically playful characters. The words come much less from 'eavesdropping'[12] – that naive picture of the dramatist in the bus queue – than is sometimes supposed. The patterning in the dialogue frequently goes with violent or mannered distortion. Yet a Pinter character's speech can, eventually, be 'pinned down' to an identifiable person even when it is used to conceal identity. In sum, Pinter's dialogue tends to 'correspond' to what we hear outside the world of the play, even though it is made to 'cohere' with the overall rhythm of the play.

Consider a simple contrast, something like a paradigm. *The Caretaker* opens with a micro-naturalistically presented conversation between the host and the invited tramp (Aston and Davies) and after some Uuh-ing and Huh-ing the tramp bursts into this 'life-like' narrative: 'Ten minutes off for tea-break in the middle of the night in that place and I couldn't find a seat, not one. All them Greeks had it . . .' While *Waiting for Godot* begins with the stylised duologue of two literary tramps (or traditional clowns or questers) whose lines could be swapped around. 'Nothing to be done' – Estragon's classical opening line – at once creates a 'gesture to the universe', with that literate non-personal passive voice. (No wonder that one down-to-earth producer insisted that the correct English must be 'Nothing doing'.[13]) Or take the exchange between Stella and James, the married couple in *The Collection* (1961), at one of the points where they are teasing out the verbal tangle created around Bill as a potential or hypothetical adulterous partner. . . .

In the present context what matters is to see that the texture of Pinter's dramatic language is quite different from Beckett's. Yet clearly this is related to other important differences which can only be listed here. The structure of many Pinter plays – notably *The Caretaker* and *The Homecoming* – can be plotted as a half-submerged but otherwise forward-moving action (*implicit* exposition, denouement, and so on), while Beckett's plays turn in a static-perennial cycle. A Pinter character can nearly always be extrapolated (the dots can be connected to draw a familiar figure, as in the child's puzzle), and hours can be spent discussing quite traditional questions of motive and psychological interaction. The time-scale for a Pinter play can be measured by the clock; there are no 'timeless moments', and no openings to time lost beyond redemption. Pinter's silences are perfectly timed to fit characterisation and to create a rhythm, but we do not feel – as we do in Beckett – that language is created out of a silence that is, in the end, all-consuming. (Though *Landscape* and even more *Silence* are Pinter's attempt at reaching this dimension.)

In sum, Pinter has little of Beckett's intense 'metaphysical' anguish; and, again, little of the sheer intensity of feeling – that to speak is to suffer and that all language is exhausted. But Pinter has learnt to exploit his own sense of language-nausea:

Such a weight of words confronts us day in, day out, words spoken in contexts such as this, words written by me and by others, the bulk of it stale and dead terminology; ideas endlessly repeated and permutated, become platitudinous, trite, meaningless. Given this nausea, it's very easy to be overcome by it and step back into paralysis. I imagine most writers know something of this paralysis. But if it is possible to confront this nausea, to follow it to its hilt, then it is possible to say something has occurred, that something has been achieved.[14]

In his most authentic work Pinter succeeds in just that: in 'making something occur' out of the felt paralysis of words. He can re-create the rhythms of difficult or failing utterance with a detached, almost ego-empty method of writing, in a dialogue 'not subjected to false articulation'. This is a specialised, reduced version of one of the aims of classical naturalism:

Given characters who possess a momentum of their own, my job is not to impose upon them, not to subject them to false articulation, by which I mean forcing a character to speak where he could not speak, of making him speak of what he could never speak.[15]

Paradoxically, the pursuit of this aim can also lead Pinter to indulgent pattern-making, and mannerism. . . .

In the early plays (as in *The Room*) it is the patterns of 'non-communication' that sometimes become decorative or facile. In the later plays, particularly in the 'sophisticated' television plays, the verbal games with their 'intriguing' sexual ambiguity are too dependent on the linguistic equivalent of 'suspense' – once the code is deciphered, we are left with a cliché.

Yet the progression of Pinter's work as a whole shows a determination to avoid cliché and self-repetition. Each of the four major stage plays has attempted to do something different – and the urge to innovate, to re-create the language in and for each new play is something Pinter shares with Eliot and Beckett. Pinter keeps renewing his dramatic form and language, at the cost of what looks like increasing critical self-consciousness. He himself has complained of the relative difficulty of writing *The Homecoming* and when that play was written he felt once more: 'I want to write a play, it buzzes all the time in me, and I can't put pen to paper'.[16] He connects this with the difficulty of avoiding 'the searchlights' in contrast with his direct concern with *writing* – 'completely unselfconsciously' – when he wrote his first three plays. We may assume that writing against 'the searchlights' means, among other things, the dramatist writing with intensified stylistic consciousness: aware of his own achieved work – and the public's attitude to it – as something inhibiting (the taboo on repetition colliding with the expectation of something 'Pinteresque'). But in the narrower sense of scrupulous attention to the words on the page Pinter has been a highly self-conscious writer from the outset. The price is recurrent mannerism. The achievement: the shaping of an essentially mimetic dialogue towards a new kind of expressiveness in a 'theatre of language'.

Pinter's 'double thing': shapes for listening

Ideas concerning his own dramatic language take up a good third of Pinter's tentative yet firmly thought-out article 'Writing for the Theatre'.[17] There are comments here on the ambiguity of dialogue, on the growth of language out of human indeterminacy, out of what is 'inexpressive, elusive, evasive, obstructive, unwilling' in the characters. This goes with a conscious exploration of a 'language where under what is said another thing is being said'. These points define genuine discoveries, and they remain essential keys to Pinter's dialogue. But so much has been heard of these ideas in our over-communicative time that they have become critical commonplaces (Pinter's 'failure of communication', 'subtext').[18] There is need for new questions, and a fresh inquiry, and it might as well start with a neglected point from Pinter's statement on playwriting:

The function of selection and arrangement is mine. I do all the donkey-work, in fact, and I think I can say I pay meticulous attention to the shape of things, from the shape of a sentence to the overall structure of the play. This shaping, to put it mildly, is of the first importance. But I think a double thing happens. You arrange *and* you listen, following the clues you leave for yourself, through the characters.[19]

Just how does this 'double thing' happen – in particular dialogue sequences and across a whole play? How does Pinter solve the tension between 'spontaneity' and 'design' in language? . . . This is to test . . . a persistent tension in post-naturalist drama: between the diffuseness and fragmented banality of most 'conversation', and the need for dialogue to concentrate and express, to quicken the beat in the action – so that in under two hours a pattern of experience may be felt upon our pulses. There is here an affinity between Pinter's 'double thing' and Eliot's early hope for 'a new form . . . out of colloquial speech' (first attempted in *Sweeny Agonistes*). But Pinter has no interest in formal 'verse drama', and he seems to be free from the pains of Eliot's linguistic dualism: that partial taboo on 'language of the tribe', the hollowness of words against the Word.[20]

We may first define the two poles of Pinter's dramatic language: moving from the seeming record of eavesdropping towards rhythmic abstraction. One can point to two distinct, as it were nuclear, styles, to be seen at their simplest in Pinter's revue sketches (each sketch being homogeneous enough to make us perceive the 'shape' of the dialogue instantly). Contrast, for example, the rambling, inane, yet humanly authentic conversation of two old women in an all-night café:

SECOND: Yes, there's not too much noise.
FIRST: There's always a bit of noise.
SECOND: Yes, there's always a bit of life.

(where the pattern is woven 'along with' and 'from within' the conversation) with the comic-parodic build-up of the cross-examination of the Applicant by a secretary, equipped with nerve-testing electrodes and earphones:

After a day's work do you feel tired? Edgy? Fretty? Irritable? At a loose end? Morose? Frustrated? Morbid? Unable to concentrate? Unable to sleep? Unable to eat? Unable to remain seated? Unable to remain upright? Lustful? Indolent? On heat? Randy? Full of desire? Full of energy? Full of dread? Drained? of energy, of dread? of desire?[21]

The applicant is caught up in a crescendo of bewilderment, he 'can't get a word in edgeways', and finally collapses – after trying to cover up his earphones – to the sound of drum-beat, cymbal, trombone and a piercing buzz. Such a simple situational convention (aptly called, in relation to Pinter's early plays, 'comedy of menace') is enough to enable Pinter to exploit the energies of rhythmic formalisation, in this instance a question-catalogue.

In *The Dumb Waiter* (a one-act play, much more complex than any revue sketch, but more immediately 'transparent' than any of the major plays) the guided inconsequentiality of the dialogue between Ben and Gus is transformed into a sharper pattern when – following the comic food orders received through the dumb waiter – the speaking tube is introduced. That ill-functioning instrument of communication 'dictates' a parodic ritual, with its own rhythm of pauses, as Ben listens, holds the tube to his ear and to his mouth, alternately:

BEN: The Eccles cake was stale.

> The chocolate was melted.
> The milk was sour.

GUS: What about the crisps?

BEN: The biscuits were mouldy.
Well, we're very sorry about that.
What? What? Yes. Yes. Yes certainly. Certainly. Right away.[22]

Such 'shapes for listening' are several removes from casual conversation, from some putative 'tape-recording ear'. (One could make a rough analogy: Pinter's speaking tube is nearer to Eliot's telephone in *Sweeny Agonistes* in its function than to the concealed tape-recorder of the descriptive linguistic.) And it can hardly be an accident that it is immediately after the little food-litany induced by the unseen and unheard presence in the speaking tube that the play reaches a rhythmic crescendo: the ritualistic reiteration of orders:

> Shut the door behind him.
> Shut the door behind him.
> Without divulging your presence.
> Without divulging my presence (. . .)

and the anguished litany of the victim's unanswered questions (ending with 'What's he playing these games for?').

Through his entire work Pinter has been working out different kinds of dialogue 'shaping'. In the early plays, particularly in *The Birthday Party*, *The Dumb Waiter* and *A Slight Ache*, quasi-ritualistic patterns are used repeatedly to give a rhythmic intensity to climactic scenes. Yet the rhythms of ritual – responses, catechismic cross-examination, litanies – are used parodistically or playfully to dehumanise speech. . . . Then, in *The Caretaker* . . . a language of lived encounter is created out of the fragmented speech of two inarticulate persons: Aston and Davies set against the sadistically elaborate jargon-speeches of Mick. To that extent *The Caretaker* is Pinter's most valuable achievement in unified 'listening' and 'shaping', in fusing the human abstract attributes of dramatic language.

'Design' is more palpably or ingeniously imposed in all the later plays, in which we may distinguish three dominant interests, pressing to shape the dialogue. There is the ritualised interplay between decorum and scatological violence in *The Homecoming* (the language of the tribe in para-animal display within one family). Then there are the highly patterned, though colloquially based, verbal games people play,[23] taken from and presented to a psycho-sexually 'sophisticated', knowing society: in *The Collection* and *The Lover* (1961, 1963), later in *The Tea Party* and *The Basement* (1965, 1967), all originally written for television, and so exploiting visual clues (devices of close-up, mixing, fading and quick scene-shift) to intensify the omission of verbal clues. In all these plays the conventional comedy of manners is 're-packaged' as a modish language of hints and guesses, nourished by the energies of imagined or potential adultery. Such patterns of verbal fantasy and near-farcical titillation make up much of the texture of *Old Times* (1971), where the mannerist dialogue – the many-coloured bubbles of talk from three corners of the triangle – is shaped to re-enact a still unpurged trauma, with gathering intensity. The third way of shaping dialogue can be seen in the 'word-painting' and 'sound-painting' patterns of *Landscape* and *Silence* (1968, 1969): a semi-abstract scoring of speech fragments in a small-scale 'musical' design, as precise as Webern or Boulez. . . .

[Andrew Kennedy's examination of these arguments in relation specifically to *The Birthday Party* and *The Homecoming* is given below, in Part Three and Part Four, respectively – Ed.]

Source: extracts from ch. 4 in *Six Dramatists in Search of a Language* (London, 1975), pp. 165–70, 171–2, 173–8.

notes

[Reorganised and renumbered from the original]

1. 'Harold Pinter Replies', *New Theatre Magazine* (Jan. 1961), p. 9.

2. A similar analogy is offered by Ronald Hayman in *Harold Pinter* (London, 1969), p. 91. (It occurred to me independently.)

3. 'Between the Lines', *Sunday Times* (4/3/1962), p. 25, subsequently published in a revised form as 'Writing for the Theatre', *Evergreen Review* (Aug.–Sept. 1964), pp. 80–3. All further references will be to the second version.

4. Pinter himself says: 'Too many words irritate me sometimes, but I can't help them, they just seem to come out – out of the fellow's mouth. I don't really examine my words too much, but I am aware that quite often in what I write some fellow at some point says an awful lot.' Interview with Lawrence Bensky, *Paris Review*, no. 39 (Fall 1966), p. 26. . . . See also Richard Schechner's unqualified gloss on Pinter as the 'disinterested artist . . . He is meticulous in scenic structure and dialogue for their own sake.' 'Puzzling Pinter', *Tulane Drama Review* (Winter 1966), p. 184.

5. The contrast can be tested by setting the banal conversational opening of, say, *The Dumb Waiter* or *The Collection* against the opening scene of *La Cantatrice chauve*. Pinter's patterns, though 'empty', are at once casual-seeming and humanly authentic. Ionesco *starts* with the denatured logic of language, the talking machine. Cf. also 'La Tragédie du langage', *Notes et contre-notes* (Paris, 1962) pp. 155–60. The essay confirms Ionesco's primary interests: 'la démarche tout à fait cartésienne de l'auteur de mon manuel d'anglais' and 'les automatismes de langage', for example. By contrast Pinter *starts* with a seemingly 'raw' language, as if untouched by schooling. See also n. 12.

6. Some examples: the idiom-catalogue of Edward on his wife in *A Slight Ache* (p. 24); Ben and Gus in sustained dispute over the phrase 'light the kettle' in *The Dumb Waiter* (pp. 47–8); Bill fencing with James over the extent to which he is a 'wow' at parties in *The Collection* (p. 22); or the variations rung on 'going the whole hog' in *The Homecoming*

(p. 68) until Joey concludes that 'Now and again . . . you can be happy . . . without going any hog at all.' See also Martin Esslin's amusing account of 'Pinter Translated', *Encounter* (March 1968), and *Brief Chronicles*, pp. 190–5. The translators' howlers are all due to Pinter's dialogue being steeped in English idioms.

7. *The Birthday Party*, Act III (2nd ed.), pp. 77–8; and below: pp. 180–1; n. 42; p. 187; p. 189. *The Caretaker*, Act II, pp. 37–8; Act III, pp. 63–4, used again, with dramatic irony, p. 76; *The Homecoming*, Act II, pp. 51–2 and 61–2; '*Landscape*' *and* '*Silence*', pp. 25–7.

8. *Harold Pinter*, London (2nd ed.), 1969, pp. 1–2 (a play-by-play discussion which *starts* with language). Attentive listening and systematic linguistic description both confirm that spoken English, at most levels of usage, is *inexplicit* – broken or jumbled-up syntax, word searching, unrelated repetitions and overlaps are frequent. See David Crystal and Derek Davy, *Investigating English Style* (London, 1969), Part II, Ch. 4. The linguistic features are there, but not the dramatic shaping.

9. James T. Boulton, 'Harold Pinter: *The Caretaker* and Other Plays', *Modern Drama* (Sept. 1963), pp. 131–40. But Boulton does not develop this point on dialogue.

10. Jean Vannier, 'Theatre of Language', *Tulane Drama Review* (Spring 1963), p. 182. (Paraphrase with extracts.)

11. Pinter has explicitly stated: 'I'd never heard of Ionesco until after I'd written the first few plays.' *The Paris Review*, no. 39, p. 19. . . . By contrast, the debt to Beckett is repeatedly acknowledged: in *Paris Review* (p. 20); in 'Harold Pinter Replies' (*loc. cit.* p. 8); and in a cheerful private letter, in *Beckett at 60, A Festschrift* (London, 1967), p. 86.

12. Pinter on 'eavesdropping': 'I spend no time listening in that sense. Occasionally I hear something, as we all do, walking about. But the words come as I'm writing the characters, not before.' *Paris Review*, no. 39, p. 26. That stress on *writing the characters* (here and elsewhere) accords with what we find in the dialogue.

13. See Colin Duckworth (ed.), *En Attendant Godot* (London, 1966), p. 91.

14. 'Writing for the Theatre', *Evergreen Review*, no. 33 (Aug. – Sept. 1964), p. 81.

15. Ibid.

16. *Paris Review*, no. 39, pp. 35–6. Contrast Pinter on his early plays: 'It was a kind of 'no-holds barred feeling, like diving into a world of words' – 'In an Empty Bandstand', *Listener* (6/11/1969), p. 651.

17. *Evergreen Review*, no. 33.

18. The most sustained study on 'subtext' is John Russell Brown's 'Dialogue in Pinter and Others', *Critical Quarterly* (Autumn 1965), pp. 225–43, later used in the same author's *Theatre Language* (London 1972), ch. I. See also Introduction, pp. 21–2. In 'Writing for the Theatre', Pinter himself has objected to the 'grimy, tired phrase, failure of communication' as applied to his work. Victor Amend points to the inherent dramatic limitations of 'demonstrating failure of communication through man's chief means of communication' in 'Harold Pinter – Some Credits and Debits', *Modern Drama* (Sept. 1967), p. 173. In sum, the devices of non-communication tend to get obvious, contrived and self-exhausting.

19. 'Writing for the Theatre', loc. cit., p. 82.

20. Raymond Williams draws an evolutionary line from Eliot's early comic-strip characters, and the first scene of *The Cocktail Party*, to *The Birthday Party* – Pinter taking further the stylisation of 'the dead phrases, the gaps of an accepted articulacy', etc., in the context of ordinary English speech, *Drama from Ibsen to Brecht* (London, 1968), p. 325.

21. Quoted respectively, from *The Black and White* and *The Applicant*, in '*A Slight Ache*' *and Other Plays* (1961), (London, 1966), pp. 126 and 135. Among the other revue sketches *Request Stop* and *Last to Go* resemble the first, *Trouble in the Works* the second pattern.

22. '*The Room*' *and* '*The Dumb Waiter*' (1960), (London, 1966), p. 62.

23. I am alluding to Eric Berne's book *Games People Play* (1964), (London, 1966), because these plays by Pinter seem to be working exactly on that level of serio-sophistication. Also, Pinter's 'games' can be seen – as in Berne's work – as open-ended forms of ritual. If ritual provides fixed rhythmic patterns, 'games' are a source of half-ritualised ambiguity – in situation and language. I think that *Old Times* (1971) – first performed after the completion of this chapter – is comparable in approach and method, in a sustained and complex way.

Guido Almansi   Pinter's Idiom of Lies
(1981)

Were I to trace with the firm hand of a surveyor or an accountant the graph of Harold Pinter's progress, or regress, or dramatic itinerary, from the early works to his latest plays, a few trends would emerge: a progressive baring of the symbolic superstructure; new disguises of a violence which becomes purely verbal or goes underground; monologues spreading, following some Beckettian suggestions, while stichomythia, which reached its apex with the interrogation of Stanley in *The Birthday Party*, recedes; intensification of pauses and silences, becoming the natural repositories of meaning (for instance in *The Basement*, *Landscape* and *Silence*, respectively of 1967, 1968 and 1969). But the fundamental element, language, has hardly changed. From *The Room* (written in 1957) to *Betrayal* (performed in 1978), Pinter has systematically forced his characters to use a perverse, deviant language to conceal or ignore the truth. In twenty years of playwriting he has never stooped to use the degraded language of honesty, sincerity, or innocence which has contaminated the theatre for so long. Nor did Pinter have to wait for his own maturity as a dramatist before he acquired the language of deceit and meretriciousness (as often happens with writers who only reach a strategic idiom after a first juvenile production of free-wheeling expressionism). His language was never chaste, but corrupt from birth. In his plays, even the virginal page protected by its candour is polluted, for the blank space conveys evil intentions and vile meanings. Pinter's idiom is essentially human because it is an idiom of lies.

Irving Wardle in a celebrated article[1] suggested that Pinter's characters ought to be analysed from an ethological perspective, as humanised animals fighting for territory (the room in *The Room*, *The Caretaker*, *The Basement*; the boarding house in *The Birthday Party*; the old house of *The Homecoming*; the flat of *No Man's Land*) rather than for sex, or power, or pleasure, or glory, or immortality.[2] But although the Pinterian hero is often as inarticulate as a pig, stumbling pathetically on every word, covering a pitifully narrow area of meaning with his utterances, blathering through his life, he does not, like any honest animal, seem to whine or grunt or giggle or grumble to give an outlet to his instincts, desires, passions or fears. He grunts in order to hide something else. Even when he grunts ('Oh, I see. Well, that's handy. Well, that's . . . I tell you what, I might do that . . . just till I get myself sorted out'.[3]), his grunt is a lie. Pinter's characters are often abject, stupid, vile, aggressive: but they are always intelligent enough in their capacity as conscientious and persistent liars, whether lying to others or to themselves, to hide the truth if they know truth's truthful abode. They are too cunning in their cowardice to be compared to noble animals. They are perverted in their actions and speech: hence human.

On the traditional stage, characters use dialogue for their underhand strategy, but reveal their true selves in monologues. This is not true of Pinter's plays, where both dialogue and monologue follow a fool-proof technique of deviance. You can trust his characters neither when they are talking to others nor when they are talking to themselves: this is what makes *Landscape*, *Old Times*, *No Man's Land* such difficult plays. Characters shift position crab-like, move forward like knights on a chess-board,[4] an oblique tentative step rather than a bold progress. In Pinter's games players do not advance towards their goal (except for the kill, as in Spooner's final speech in *No Man's Land*): they dribble. This requires a picklock-language, used askew, whose crooked insinuation – penetrating between the reality of the *thing* and the reality of the *word*[5] – mocks the straight approach of the honest key.

With Pinter, expression is no longer the specular reflection of an emotion nor the *word* of a *thing*: the mirror is slanted, and the expression therefore does not reflect the opposite and apposite emotion but the adjacent one, so that each sound and image is systematically distorted (Robert to Emma: 'I've always liked Jerry. To be honest, I've always liked him rather more than I've liked you. Maybe I should have had an affair with him myself. (*Silence*) Tell me, are you looking forward to our trip to Torcello?' (p. 87)) The stage – and the post-Shavian English stage in particular – was used to a perpendicular language, reflecting the inner world of mind and heart with geometric inevitability. Pinter replaced the right angle by an obtuse angle, so that repartees do not rebound directly: this is his special effect which gives the odd ring to his conversations. Not the language of thinking robots, like Shaw's; not the language of men aping apes, like Artaud's; not the language of hysterical clowns, like Ionesco's; not the language of existential preoccupations, like Beckett's: his is a language of hide-and seek, human/inhuman ('*inhuman*: the characteristic quality of the human race', Ambrose Bierce[6]). Pinter's world is plausible and understandable in so far as everyone attempts not to be understood.

Yet, in a sense, Pinter's characters do behave like beasts. Their language articulates the three basic survival techniques of animals: fight, flight and mimetism. Stanley, Davies, Teddy, Spooner, Jerry use language either to attack, or to retreat, or to disguise what they are (and what they are is neither here nor there, to crack the wind of a poor pun). In some often quoted statements from early speeches and interviews, Pinter attempted to distinguish himself from the Absurdist tradition by shifting the issue from the difficulty of communication to the danger of communication:

I think we communicate only too well, in our silence, in what is unsaid, and that what takes place is continual evasion, desperate rearguard attempts to keep ourselves to ourselves. Communication is too alarming. To enter into someone else's life is too frightening, to disclose to others the poverty within us is too fearsome a possibility.[7]

Sincerity, honesty, linguistic generosity, openness, are diabolical inventions that must be shunned because they create chaos. Survival is based on a policy of reciprocal misunderstanding and mis-information. If we were to choose a straightforward approach, we would be at the mercy of others, or of language itself; or even worse: of ourselves, that part of ourselves we do everything to ignore – and this drive towards self-ignorance is the one intellectual enterprise in which we excel. Nothing is more frightening than making Yakov Petrovitch Golyadkin's ordeal of meeting his doppelgänger on the Fontanka Quay close to the Ismailovsky Bridge[8] into a daily routine. Mirrors are 'deceptive' says Bill in *The Collection* [III, 146], and this is our salvation.

In *Uno, Nessuno e Centomila* (*One, No One and One Hundred Thousand*) by Luigi Pirandello,[9] Vitangelo Moscarda, shaving in the morning, realises for the first time in his life that his nose is crooked. This means that mirrors are 'deceptive': they have either deceived him in the past, when he was thinking of himself as a straight-nosed individual, or they are deceiving him now, as he discovers the crooked nature of his trump. Vitangelo creates a breathing space for himself in the antagonism between his two alter-egos (the straight-nosed Cleopatra of history facing the crooked-nosed Cleopatra of hypothesis), and eventually finds solace and comfort in the serene harbour of madness where all opposites are reconciled. Rimbaud's frightening 'Je est un autre' ('I *is* another one')[10], or Lacan's ironical 'L'inconscient, c'est le discours de l'autre' ('The unconscious is the discourse of the Other')[11] require intellectual heroes. Like us, Pinter's characters lack this boldness and continue to pretend to be themselves with thorough and impudent bad faith (think of the supreme bad faith of Deeley in *Old Times*) because they are aware that their secrets are so well hidden that they themselves have forgotten where they are. No one is likely to dig them out: not Goldberg or McCann, who must resort to real violence to *get* at Stanley; not Mick with Davies; or Lenny with Ruth, or Anna with Deeley; not Foster and Biggs either, who are defeated by Spooner's proteanism. 'Now-a-days to be intelligible is to be found out', says Lord Darlington in *Lady Windermere's Fan*.[12] But, as usual, Wilde is at his best when he does not really know what he is saying. Pinter, whose style abhors the paradoxical truisms *à la Wilde* (the reference to mirrors in *The Collection* is almost a slip), seems to know what he is doing; he wants characters who are *born* liars, and an audience who mistrust them.

In spite of this, critics seem to refuse their new roles as unbelievers. No matter how improbable the statement, implausible the situation, extravagant the motivation, tall the story, honourable critics ponderously assess and discuss the declarations of the Pinterian character as if they were reliable. Spooner 'is acquainted with the impeccably aristocratic Lord Lancer. He is able to organise a poetry reading for Hirst that will include . . . a dinner party at a fine Indian restaurant. . . .'[13] Mick dreams 'of seeing the derelict house as a luxurious penthouse'.[14] 'It is made quite clear by Ruth that when Teddy met and married her she was a nude photographic model – and this is widely known as a euphemism for a prostitute'.[15] When Davies is invited by Aston to stay, 'Mick's jealousy is instantly aroused'.[16] 'In his anger Micks picks up and smashes the figure of the Buddha which is one of Aston's favourite pieces in the room'.[17] 'Now there is a serious question as to whether Lenny really did this (belting the old lady in the nose, and kicking her to finish the job) . . . at all, much less with such terrifying indifference'.[18] 'Mick had believed Davies to be an interior decorator . . .' (!?!)[19] In all these instances, critics give the Pinterian hero a credit that he does not deserve and does not require. I don't think we are supposed to believe that Spooner is acquainted with Lord Lancer; that Mick is jealous and angry; that Ruth was a prostitute; that Lenny met a woman who made him 'a certain proposal' and beat her, or that he had kicked the old lady who wanted the mangle removed. Least of all are we expected to believe that Mick believed that Davies was an interior decorator. All we know is that there are characters who are making these statements: not that these statements are valid. The Pinterian hero lies as he breathes: consistently and uncompromisingly. Not to lie is as inconceivable to him as to 'eat a crocodile'[20] or make love to a spider. Goldberg, Mick, Edward, Ben, Lenny, Spooner, are not just occasionally unreliable: they are untrustworthy by definition, since their words only bear witness to their capacity for speech, not to their past or present experience. Pinter's opus, like Pirandello's, is a long disquisition on the masks[21] of the liar: the liar as the man who panics (Davies, Edward, Stanley, Hirst); the liar as the man who conceals his panic (Mick, Ben, Lenny, Spooner, Robert); the liar as the man who chats ('I talked too much. That was my mistake.' says Aston in *The Caretaker* (p. 54); but these words would fit Gus, Duff, Foster). In Pinter mendacity is avoidance of identity: the existential equivalent of our daily avoidance of responsibility. . . .

SOURCE: extract from article in *Stratford-upon-Avon Studies*, No. 19: *Contemporary English Drama*, General Editors, Malcolm Bradbury and David Palmer (London, 1981), pp. 79–83.

NOTES

1. Irving Wardle, 'The Territorial Struggle', in John and Anthea Lahr (eds), *A Casebook on Harold Pinter's 'The Homecoming'* (New York, 1971); reprinted (1974) in an edition which is used in this article, pp. 37–44.

2. The same idea reappears in self-conscious form with other critics. See, for instance, Ronald Hayman, *Harold Pinter* (1975) – especially the Conclusion, where the animal comparison is taken so literally as to become ludicrous.

3. All quotations from the early plays are from the three-volume (Methuen) edition, and will be incorporated in the text. This quotation is from II, 25.

4. 'Knight-move' is the title of a celebrated article by V. Sklovsky about literary strategies.

5. I use the terms of Michel Foucalt in his classical study, *Les Mots et les choses* (Paris, 1966); English edition, *The Order of Things: An Archeology of the Human Sciences* (London, 1970).

6. Ambrose Bierce, *The Enlarged Devil's Dictionary* (Harmondsworth, 1971).

7. Harold Pinter, *Sunday Times* (4/3/1962).

8. I am referring to the scene in Dostoevsky's *The Double* when the protagonist crosses his double in the street.

9. The first edition was 1962; I use the recent Oscar Mondadori edition (Milan, 1979).

10. Letter to Georges Izambard, 13 May 1871.

11. J. Lacan, 'Le seminaire sur *La Lettre Volée*', in *Ecrits* I (Paris, 1966), p. 24.

12. Act I. Wilde's witticism is quoted by Arthur Ganz in his interesting introduction to a collection of essays on Pinter (Englewood Cliffs, N.J., 1972).

13. Lucina Paquet Gabbard, *The Dream Structure of Pinter's Plays* (N.J., and London, 1976), p. 260.

14. M. Esslin, *The Peopled Wound* (London, 1970), p. 99.

15. Ibid, p. 151.

16. John Russell Taylor, *Anger and After. A Guide to the New British Drama* (London, 1962), p. 247.

17. Esslin, p. 100.

18. Bert O. States, 'Pinter's *Homecoming*: The Shock of Nonrecognition', in *The Hudson Review* XII, 3 (Autumn 1968), pp. 474–86. The quotation is from p. 482.

19. Nigel Alexander, 'Past, Present and Pinter', in *Essays and Studies 1974*, edited by Kenneth Muir for the English Association (1974). The quotation is on p. 10.

20. *Hamlet* [v i 264]

21. Pirandello's theatrical works are in fact, collected under the general title of *Maschere Nude* (Naked Masks).

PART TWO

The Birthday Party

Harold Pinter   A Letter to Peter Wood
(1958)

This letter was written to Peter Wood, the director of *The Birthday Party*, just before rehearsals started for the first production of the play in April 1958. I had forgotten all about it, until I came across a copy in an old file a few months ago. It had been sitting there for some twenty-two years. It is not the kind of letter I could possible write now and therefore I found it of interest.

The debate between Peter Wood and me proved to be academic as the play closed in London after a run of one week.

30 March 1958

Dear Peter,

The first image of this play, the first thing that about a year ago was put on paper was a kitchen, Meg, Stanley, corn flakes and sour milk. There they were, they sat, they stood, they bent, they turned, they were incontravertable, or perhaps I should say incontrovertible. Not long before Goldberg and McCann turned up. They had come with a purpose, a job in hand – to take Stanley away. This they did, Meg unknowing, Peter helpless, Stanley sucked in. Play over. That was the pure line and I couldn't get away from it. I had no idea at the time what or why. The thing germinated and bred itself. It proceeded according to its own logic. What did I do? I followed the indications, I kept a sharp eye on the clues I found myself dropping. The writing arranged itself with no trouble into dramatic terms. The characters sounded in my ears – it was apparent to me what one would say and what would be the other's response, at any given point. It was apparent to me what they would not, could not, ever, say, whatever one might wish. I interfered with them only on the technical level. My task was not to damage their consistency at any time – through any external notion of my own.

When the thing was well cooked I began to form certain conclusions. The point is, however, that by that time the play was now its own world. It was determined by its own original engendering image. My conclusions were only useful in that they were informed by the growth of the work itself. When I began to think *analytically* about it (as far as I can manage to do that, which isn't very far) I did so by keeping in step with what was being suggested, by judging the whole caper through an accurate assessment of the happenings described, or what I concluded was an accurate assessment. I never held up the work in hand to another mirror – I related it to nothing outside itself. Certainly to no other work of literature or to any consideration of public approbation should it reach a stage.

The play is itself. It is no other. It has its own life (whatever its merit in dramatic terms or accomplishment may be and despite the dissatisfaction others may experience with regard to it). I take it you would like me to insert a clarification or moral judgement or author's angle on it, straight from the horse's mouth. I appreciate your desire for this but I can't do it.

I confused the issue by talking of what 'I thought' of the characters. Who I would invite to tea, etc. That's irrelevant. The play exists now apart from me, you or anybody. I believe that what happens on this stage will possess a potent dramatic image and a great deal of this will be visual – I mean one will *see* the people, which will be a great aid to the expression of the thing, the getting across. The curtain goes up and down. Something has happened. Right? Cockeyed, brutish, absurd, with no comment. Where is the comment, the slant, the explanatory note? In the play. Everything to do with the play is in the play.

All right. You know what I think about Stanley. I think he has the right whatever he does and is to do and be just that and fuck the expense. That's what I think. But that is not the point of the play. It is a conclusion I draw from it. Is that *a* point expressed in the play? Only by implication, agreed. I conclude what I conclude upon that implication. Stanley fights for his life, he doesn't want to be drowned. Who does? But he is not *articulate*. The play in fact merely states that two men come down to take away another man and do so. Will the audience absorb the implications or will they not? Ask the barber.

Audience reaction, it seems to me, might be one of three – (a) They should have left him alone. (b) The silly bugger deserved it. (c) It's all a load of crap. There is also, of course, (d) How fascinating, but what does it mean? To which I reply – Meaning begins in the words, in action, continues in your head and ends nowhere. There is no end to meaning. Meaning which is resolved, parcelled, labelled and ready for export is dead, impertinent – and meaningless. I examine my own play and ask, what's going on here? I note – this seems to lead from that, I would conclude this, but the characters themselves do nothing but move through an occurrence, a morning, a night, a morning. This occurrence has, admittedly, any number of implications. Anyone is entitled to see the show. The dramatic progression and the implications implicit in it will either find a home in some part of their nut or not.

To put such words as we discussed into Stanley's mouth would be an inexcusable imposition and falsity on my part. Stanley *cannot* perceive his only valid justification – which is he is what he is – therefore he certainly can never be articulate about it. He knows only to attempt to justify himself by dream, by pretence and by bluff, through fright. If he had cottoned on to the fact that he need only admit to himself what he actually is and is not – then Goldberg and McCann would not have paid their visit, or if they had, the same course of events would have been by no means assured. Stanley would have been another man. The play would have been another play. A play with a 'sensitive intellectual' articulate hero in its centre, able to examine himself in any way clearly, would also have been another play.

Stanley is the king of his castle and loses his kingdom because he assessed it and himself inaccurately. We all have to be very careful. The boot is itching to squash and very efficient.

Goldberg and McCann? Dying, rotting, scabrous, the decayed spiders, the flower of our society. They know their way around. Our mentors. Our ancestry. Them. Fuck 'em.

What would you, as they say? In the third act Stanley can do nothing but make a noise. What else? What else has he discovered? He has been reduced to the fact that he is nothing but a gerk in the throat. But does this sound signify anything? It might very well. I think it does. He is trying to go further. He is on the edge of utterance. But it's a long, impossible edge and utterance, were he to succeed in falling into it, might very well prove to be only one cataclysmic, profound fart. You think I'm joking? Test me. In the rattle in his throat Stanley approximates nearer to the true nature of himself than ever before and certainly ever after. But it is late. Late in the day. He can go no further.

At that juncture, you will appreciate, he cannot be expected to suddenly recover the old gift of the gab and speak a set piece of self analysis or self realisation, to point a tiny little moral. Nor could he earlier in the play for it would never occur to him to justify himself in that manner. Nor, for instance, could Petey in his last chat with Goldberg and McCann deliver the thought for today or the what we learn from these nasty experiences homily since, apart from anything else, we are not dealing with an articulate household and there is no Chorus in his play. In other words, I am afraid I do not find myself disposed to add a programme note to this piece.

None of what I have said means that I disclaim responsibility for my characters. On the contrary. I am responsible both for them and to them. The play dictated itself but I confess that I wrote it – with intent, maliciously, purposefully, in command of growth. Does this appear to contradict all I said earlier? Splendid. You may suggest that this 'command' was not strict enough and not lucid enough but who supposes I'm striving for lucidity? I think the house is in pretty good order. We've agreed; the hierarchy, the Establishment, the arbiters, the socio-religious monsters arrive to effect alteration and censure upon a member of the club who has discarded responsibility (that word again) towards himself and others. (What is your opinion by the way, of the act of suicide?) He does possess, however, for my money, a certain fibre – he fights for his life. It doesn't last long, this fight. His core being a quagmire of delusion, his mind a tenuous fusebox, he collapses under the weight of their accusation – an accusation compounded of the shitstained strictures of centuries of 'tradition'. Though nonconformist he is neither hero nor exemplar of revolt. Nothing salutary for the audience to identify itself with. And yet, at the same time, I believe that a greater degree of identification will take place than might seem likely. A great deal, it seems to me, will depend on the actor. If he copes with Stanley's loss of himself successfully I believe a certain amount of poignancy will emanate. Couldn't we all find ourselves in Stanley's position at any given moment?

As for the practical question of the end of Act Two where's the difficulty? Stanley behaves strangely. Why? Because his alteration-diminution has set in, he is rendered offcock (not off cock), he has lost any adult comprehension and reverts to a childhood malice and mischief, as his first shelter. This is the beginning of his change, his fall. In the third act we see the next phase.

The play is a comedy because the whole state of affairs is absurd and inglorious. It is, however, as you know, a very serious piece of work.

A simple matter, don't you think?

Yours,

Harold Pinter

SOURCE: Letter of 30 March 1958, printed for the first time in *Drama* (Winter, 1981), pp. 4–5.

Harold Pinter   A View of the Party   (1958)

i

The thought that Goldberg was
A man she might have known
Never crossed Meg's words
That morning in the room.

The thought that Goldberg was
A man another knew
Never crossed her eyes
When, glad, she welcomed him.

The thought that Goldberg was
A man to dread and know
Jarred Stanley in the blood
When, still, he heard his name.

While Petey knew, not then,
But later, when the light
Full up upon their scene,
He looked into the room.

And by morning Petey saw
The light begin to dim
(That daylight full of sun)
Though nothing could be done.

ii

Nat Goldberg, who arrived
With a smile on every face,
Accompanied by McCann,
Set a change upon the place.

The thought that Goldberg was
Sat in the centre of the room,
A man of weight and time,
To supervise the game.

The thought that was McCann
Walked in upon this feast,
A man of skin and bone,
With a green stain on his chest.

Allied in their theme,
They imposed upon the room
A dislocation and doom,
Though Meg saw nothing done.

The party they began,
To hail the birthday in,
Was generous and affable,
Though Stanley sat alone.

The toasts were said and sung,
All spoke of other years,
Lulu, on Goldberg's breast,
Looked up into his eyes.

And Stanley sat – alone,
A man he might have known,
Triumphant on his hearth,
Which never was his own.

For Stanley had no home.
Only where Goldberg was,
And his bloodhound McCann,
Did Stanley remember his name.

They played at blind man's buff,
Blindfold the game was run,
McCann tracked Stanley down,
The darkness down and gone.

Found the game lost and won,
Meg, all memory gone,
Lulu's lovenight spent,
Petey impotent;

A man they never knew
In the centre of the room,
And Stanley's final eyes
Broken by McCann.

Source: poem of 1958 included in Harold Pinter's *Poems and Prose, 1949–1977*
(London, 1978), pp. 32–4.

Ruby Cohn   'Pinter's Thread'   (1962)

. . . Until his first three-act play, *The Birthday Party*, the threats in Pinter's drama emanate mysteriously from a vague apparatus of master-messenger-organisation. But with his third play, Pinter not only defines the enemy more explicitly, but casts a retrospective light upon the villains of the earlier plays. Goldberg and McCann, who represent the System in *The Birthday Party*, do not appear on scene until the end of the first act, and until they do, the living room of the Boles's boardinghouse is Pinter's most photographically real set. Although Stanley Webber's reaction against the two prospective boarders seems disproportionate, and his review of his earlier concert career ambiguous, we do not definitively leave the realistic surface until Goldberg and McCann actually enter by the back door. Partners like Ben and Gus [in *The Dumb Waiter*], they carry no revolvers, but pose as casual vacationers in the seaside boarding-house where Stanley has taken refuge. Their first monosyllabic exchange establishes their relationship:

MCCANN: Is this it?
GOLDBERG: This is it.
MCCANN: Are you sure?
GOLDBERG: Sure I'm sure.   [p. 27]

Their Jewish-Irish names and dialects suggests a vaudeville skit, and it is not long before we realise that that skit is the Judaeo-Christian tradition as it appears in our present civilisation. Goldberg is the senior partner; he utters the sacred clichés of family, class, prudence, proportion. McCann is the brawny yes-man whose strength re-enforces Goldberg's doctrine.

Although Meg and Petey Boles have sheltered Stanley in their home, they are unable to recognise that the sinister new guests threaten the welfare of their guest. Meg acquiesces joyously in Goldberg's suggestion of a birthday party for Stanley 'to bring him out of himself'. Villains and victim, Goldberg-McCann and Stanley are not brought face to face in Act I, but Stanley already begins to feel trapped.

Before the party that fills Act II, Stanley tries to convince McCann that he is not 'the sort of bloke to – to cause any trouble', that it is all a mistake, that Goldberg and McCann have to leave because their room is rented. Having forced Stanley to sit down, Goldberg and, secondarily, McCann engage in a verbal fencing-match with Stanley, in which Pinter parodies the contemporary emptiness of the Judaeo-Christian heritage.

Interrupting Stanley's efforts at self-defense, Meg comes down ready for the party. In the maudlin mixture of drinking, pawing and reminiscing that follows, a game of Blindman's Buff is played. An increasingly desperate Stanley tries to strangle Meg, a mother-surrogate, and rape Lulu, the sexy neighbor, but Goldberg and McCann advance upon him each time. As Act II closes, '[Stanley's] giggle rises and grows as he flattens himself against the wall. Their [Goldberg and McCann] figures converge upon him'.

Act III is a virtual *post mortem*. Goldberg, McCann and Petey talk about Stanley's 'nervous breakdown'. McCann complains to Goldberg about this job, and Goldberg encourages him by an interweaving of clichés, in which the Biblical tradition is the warp, and modern success formulas the woof: 'Play up, play up, and play the game. Honour thy father and thy mother. All along the line. Follow the line, the line, McCann, and you can't go wrong.'

When McCann finally ushers Stanley down, 'dressed in striped trousers, black jacket, and white collar', the victim has lost the power of speech, and his glasses are broken. Again, Goldberg and McCann attack him verbally, in even pithier phrases, but this time they promise him worldly success if he complies. Stanley only gurgles unintelligibly.

'Still the same old Stan', Goldberg pronounces, and he and McCann start to lead Stanley to an unexplained Monty. When Petey Boles objects that Stanley can stay on at the boarding-house, the macabre pair scornfully invite Petey to join them, 'Come with us to Monty. There's plenty of room in the car'. An automaton propped between the partners, Stanley is helped out while Petey, broken-hearted, calls, 'Stan, don't let them tell you what to do!' But Goldberg's car is heard starting up, then fading into the distance. When Meg Boles comes down with a morning hangover, Petey does not even tell her Stan is gone, but encourages her to dream of the birthday party, at which she was the 'belle of the ball'.

The thread running through all Pinter's plays now appears more clearly. If we recall *The Room* in the light of *The Birthday Party*, we see resemblances between Goldberg and Mr Kidd, who had a Jewish mother. Both emphasise the value of property, of progress, of family, of tradition. Similarly, the Irish names of Riley and McCann seem to indicate a Christian continuance of the Judaic legacy; in both plays they are the weaker members, although never as weak as Gus of *The Dumb Waiter*, who is metamorphosed into a victim.

In *The Birthday Party* and *The Dumb Waiter*, there is a higher, invisible power behind the messengers, but Monty remains even more mysterious than Wilson, and more authority is invested in Goldberg than in Ben. In all the plays, the motor van becomes a clear symbol of modern power. In the first play, *The Room*, the van belongs to Bert Hudd, but is the object of Mr. Kidd's admiration. In *The Birthday Party*, as in *The Dumb Waiter*, the van is the property of one of the messengers – in each case, of the dominant and senior partner. It seems to be the older, crueller tradition which best embraces modern mechanisation. Only the recalcitrant individual must be quashed.

As the victim-villain conflict in *The Room* is somewhat diffused by the socially satirised Sands couple, so the Boles couple in *The Birthday Party* provides a comic relief from the mounting tension. And yet the latter couple functions more directly in the symbolic context, for the Boles are not, like Mr Kidd, mere landlords; they provide a temporary if tawdry refuge for Stanley. Distasteful as are the attentions of Meg-mother-mistress, impersonal as is Petey's presence, the Boles express affection and concern for Stanley. But human emotions are tricked or brushed aside by the ruthless team of a dogmatic system. . . .

Source: extract from 'The World of Harold Pinter', *Tulane Drama review*, 6 (March 1962), pp. 63–5.

John Russell Brown (1972)   Words and Silence

. . . The opening of his first full-length play, *The Birthday Party* (1958), illustrates some of his simpler strategies. . . .

The play starts with silence; if this is held for a moment, the audience will wait for Petey to speak. But Pinter breaks the silence with words from an unseen source, so gathering a further curiosity. After 'Is that you, Petey?', a pause repeats the exploitation of theatrical vacuum and still further develops the audience's desire for it to be filled. Pinter does not let go of this tension until line 6, with Petey's 'Yes, it's me', and then Meg appears on stage.

He is not merely withholding information, for the repetitions of words have been carefully judged. This is, indeed, a basic device in all the plays. Meg's first three questions seem at first to repeat the same inquiry, but the slight changes in the use of words reveal progressively that the questions she asks are not truly questions at all, but a challenge. 'Petey' is placed first at the end of the sentence, then more commandingly at the beginning, and then becomes the single questioning word. Moreover, when Petey's voice gives sufficient answer, three more questions follow at once, repeating the ostensible inquiry. Meg is not satisfied until she *sees* Petey, and then she herself responds with an assertion that she has done a job for him. At this point she breaks contact to bring the cornflakes to the kitchen hatch, and this action will make him rise from the table, go to her, and take them from her. Her questions, statements and action all establish that she is calling the tune; she wishes to make him acknowledge her presence and his dependence.

Other repetitions in this passage still further suggest the drama underneath the seemingly inconsequential exchanges. Petey starts by evading any statement – 'What?' – but his second speech begins with 'Yes', as if he were intent on cutting off the exchange. He continues, however, with 'it's me', a repetition of the information given in 'Yes' that is unnecessary and therefore seems insistent or, more likely, irritated or mocking. Petey's third speech defines more closely his desire to disengage by repeating for the third time the essential message with a second 'Yes', which now, in contrast with his previous speech, sounds brief, uninviting and yet, possibly, submissive.

Meg's first entrance on to the stage itself and the preceding pause will gain the audience's attention for her 'Are they nice?'. If the audience has begun to question the validity of speech, it may consider that cornflakes are not likely to vary in themselves and therefore her question may sound like a challenge, asking for attention or praise, rather than a genuine inquiry. The repetition of 'nice' in her next response – 'I thought they'd be nice' – shows that this interpretation is correct, and because this speech adds nothing substantial to the exposition the audience is more likely to become at least partly aware of her pursuit of gratification.

During these speeches Petey is hidden behind the '*propped up*' newspaper, but now Meg challenges this protection with a further question which is now – and the contrast with earlier exchanges will make this point more clearly – overtly a challenge: 'You got your paper?' Then the attack implicit in 'Are they nice?' is repeated in her 'Is it good?'; and the similarity again helps to define the point. A '*Pause*' is now repeated, followed by a new question, this time more apparently concerned for Petey, as if she were recognising – without ever saying so – that he has not been satisfying the needs which have launched her upon the whole conversation and make her, instinctively, prolong it: 'Have you been working hard this morning?'

But as soon as he answers with rather more detail than he has given in earlier exchanges, she accepts the small victory, and now the repetition of 'nice' signals a reversion to her basic, selfish concerns. After the next *'Pause'*, these particular repetitions momentarily cease; this in itself suggests a shift of engagement and throws the new questions about Stanley into relief. But then there follows another *'pause'* in which Meg looks and moves around the room and gets some darning to do; settled again, she tries another inquiry – 'What time did you go out this morning, Petey?' This reverts to the more personal challenge of Petey and leads to another question which in form is like 'Is it nice?' or 'Is it good?'; but this time, there is an unexpected 'Was it dark?' This could be a far-reaching modification, expressing fear and apprehension; and it stands out as the first directly affecting word in the play. Now, for the first time, she seems to question his response, and she then repeats *his* words – 'Oh, in winter' – and then she repeats merely her own ejaculation of acceptance or reassurance: 'Oh.' Satisfaction is restored in the pause, for she returns to the earlier, challenging question in a less avoidable form, not 'What does it say?' but 'What are you reading?'

Petey's speeches are as full of repetitions as Meg's. 'Yes' is common, and it is noticeable that when it comes for the last time, in 'Yes, it gets light later in winter', it comes without prompting from a question. At this point it is an attack rather than an evasion. Three times he simply repeats Meg's words or phrasing:

> Is that you? . . . Yes, it's me.
> Are they nice? . . . Very nice.
> Is it nice out? . . . Very nice.

And with as little disturbance of the phrasing, he parries or contradicts her:

> Is it good? . . . Not bad.
> Was it dark? . . . No, it was light.

Petey is disclosing as little as possible, protecting himself, holding himself still; yet he is rather furtively ready to take small advantages.

The passage about Stanley is different from the other exchanges. To Meg's first question, 'Is Stanley up yet?', Petey answers briefly – 'I don't know' – but he adds a question: 'Is he?' Other than his first defensive 'What?', this is his only question in the episode, and it provokes Meg to a repetition of his words, and then a statement of her own knowledge which sounds like an excuse: 'I don't know. I haven't seen him down yet.' Now Petey takes advantage and almost attacks – 'Well then, he can't be up.' Now Meg asks an obvious question and gets the obvious answer; and then she concludes with a further obvious statement or excuse. Here the repetitions show questions unnecessarily asked and statements unnecessarily made: Meg goes on, it must seem, because of the subject and because she is apologetic, not because she cannot work matters out for herself.

The repetitions, the disproportions, the easy use of 'nice', 'good' and 'bad', are all occasions for comedy. So are the movements underneath the dialogue as shown by these devices. But, more than this, the two characters are at work with sly, mocking, perhaps anguished, smokescreens. There is 'continual evasion'; even in attack, as little as possible is given away.

The device of repetition, so prevalent here, is not, of course, Pinter's own discovery. It is the stock-in-trade of oratory, comedy and drama, and of all speech. But Pinter uses it with astonishing persistence, repeating the simplest phrases until they yield the secret of their character's hidden activity. . . .

Talking of his characters and their speech, Pinter uses words like 'true', 'necessary', 'firmly based'; he asks 'Would this be said? Is this possible?':

You create characters, which is a bit of a liberty anyway, then you give them words to speak and you give them a situation to play. And I find you've got to be very careful.[1]

If the subtextual reality of each character has been imagined with fullness and accuracy, and if the actors have given a precise, solid and detailed actuality to it in their performance, then reader and audience may fitfully, progressively and perhaps, at last, with a kind of certainty, come to recognise it, each for themselves and in their own measure and time. The repetitions in the first episode of *The Birthday Party* can all be explained on slow analysis, but in performance the conflict between Petey and Meg is not put into irrevocable words at this stage of the play and therefore it is there only to be 'sensed' by the audience. Pinter's plays are realistic in one important and unusual way: audience and readers do not know everything, and what certainty there is comes very late in the play. The plays offer an opportunity for understanding very like those fleeting and uncertain opportunities that are offered by life.

In effect, Pinter seems to play a game with his audience, giving only a few signposts on the way, a few landmarks or buoys to distinguish the hidden rock and sand. Like his characters, he seems to evade, to obscure intentionally, to blaze false trails. But his concentration on the truth of the dramatic fiction is such that we come to realise that he plays these games of necessity, without setting out to do so. His view of his own characters and the situations in which they are placed makes his task a wary one. He plays hide-and-seek with his audience because he is deeply involved in this very game himself. This is how he sees and hears the world around him and within him.

When Pinter is fully engaged as dramatist, he is fully caught. He knows more than his audience and he knows the direction in which the play will go; but his involvement is to watch, wait and explore, and then to stretch out carefully in order to touch something which is not wholly expected, not wholly prepared for. The plays, written in this way, offer a sequence of partial discoveries, which the audience seem to make for themselves and out of which a sense of overall coherence and meaning seems to be born in each attentive consciousness. Pinter offers his own experience of discovery, and in the same mode of perception.

No detail of Pinter's writing can be adequately considered outside the context of the complete drama in which it must play its part. But by examining some short passages, his continuous control may be seen at work, and his awareness of the part words play in dramatic confrontations of considerable complexity but little explicit verbal statement. The more recurrent devices of language illustrate the nature of his perception and the means whereby he ensures that that perception is communicated in his writing.

The most difficult to describe is Pinter's manipulation of rhythms. Speeches run in one kind of phrasing, until some subtextual pressure lengthens, shortens or quickens the utterance and so, by sound alone, betrays the change of engagement. The last episode of *The Birthday Party* illustrates this:

> (MEG *comes past the window and enters by the back door.* PETEY *studies the front page of the paper.*)
> MEG (*coming downstage*): The car's gone.
> PETEY: Yes.
> MEG: Have they gone?
> PETEY: Yes.
> MEG: Won't they be in for lunch?
> PETEY: No.
> MEG: Oh, what a shame. (*She puts her bag on the table,*) It's hot out. (*She hangs her coat on a hook.*) What are you doing?
> PETEY: Reading.
> MEG: Is it good?
> PETEY: All right.
> (*She sits by the table.*)
> MEG: Where's Stan?
> (*Pause.*)

Is Stan down yet, Petey?
PETEY: No . . . he's . . .
MEG: Is he still in bed?
PETEY: Yes, he's . . . still asleep.
MEG: Still? He'll be late for his breakfast.
PETEY: Let him . . . sleep.
    (*Pause.*)
MEG: Wasn't it a lovely party last night?
PETEY: I wasn't there.
MEG: Weren't you?
PETEY: I came in afterwards.
MEG: Oh.
    (*Pause.*)
It was a lovely party. I haven't laughed so much for years. We had dancing and singing. And games. You should have been there.
PETEY: It was good, eh?
    (*Pause*)
MEG: I was the belle of the ball.
PETEY: Were you?
MEG: Oh yes. They all said I was.
PETEY: I bet you were, too.
MEG: Oh, it's true. I was.
    (*Pause.*)
I know I was.

CURTAIN   [p. 86–7]

Meg's first three speeches have two main stresses each, the third containing a greater number of unstressed syllables; then, as she registers Petey's 'No', the rhythm changes, starting with a single syllable 'Oh', and then after a comma three more, the middle one being unstressed: 'Oh, what a shame.' She then moves about the room and begins speech again in much the same rhythms as at first. But when Petey replies this time the phrasing grows shorter: 'Is it good?' and then, having sat down, a simple two-stressed, two-syllabled 'Where's Stan?'. At this point there is a '*Pause*' during which her energy changes rhythm, for there now comes a slightly longer question, less emphatic, and 'Petey' at the end following a comma's pause: 'Is Stan down yet, Petey?' When Petey answers with broken phrasing and hesitation 'No . . . he's . . .', she first gains speed – 'Is he still in bed?' – with light front vowels and no more than two stresses. But she then seems to halt with a monosyllabic question (that repeats 'still' for the second time), but soon runs on with her observation, 'He'll be late for his breakfast'. This assumption of knowledge seems to allow her to change the whole mood of her thoughts, for a pause is now of her making; and when she speaks again, the rhythm is almost lilting, as if she were happily lost in idle thoughts: 'Wasn't it a lovely party last night?' Petey's disclaimer breaks the mood momentarily, but after another pause, again of her own making, she picks up with a longer speech that has varied rhythms within it. The rhythmical jingle of '. . . dancing and singing' is followed by the shorter and slightly disturbing rhythm of a short, verbless sentence 'And games'; this alludes to the frightening part of the evening. But then, as she remembers Petey was not there, the tension is again relaxed. Meg's final speeches begin again with a dreamy ease: 'I was the belle of the ball'; but Petey's question and then his support tighten the rhythms. Her reply to the question starts with a two-syllable assertion 'Oh yes', and then a rather longer agreement, 'They all said I was'. Her reply to his token of support is short but with two pauses, the first slight and the second more emphatic: 'Oh, it's true. I was.' A *'Pause'* follows and then her last speech with two very short elements and a repeated 'I', in its single phrase: 'I know I was.' The rhythm of this last utterance is short, contained and simple; and, since 'know' carries more stress than 'was', it has a slight falling-off. This tightening of the rhythms of speech is all the more effective for contrast with the lighter rhythms and longer reach of her preceding speeches.

Petey's rhythms start with stark monosyllables: 'Yes . . . Yes . . . No.' When Meg returns to the attack, they are less firm with two-syllables: 'Reading . . . All right', the second giving an abrupt sound in comparison with the light ending of the first. When he is questioned about Stanley, his rhythms are broken, finding their firmest point on the concluding monosyllable, 'sleep'. Petey's next replies seem light, unstressed and smooth in comparison, as if yielding even as he contradicts Meg. When she enters her reverie, he seems to give light compliance with 'It was good, eh?' and 'I bet you were, too', each with a single syllable after a brief pause at the end of the line. The strongest contrast here is in the two-syllabled 'Were you?' that could be delivered slowly or a little weighted.

The two characters have their own rhythms that are shown off by varied contrasts throughout the episode. But there is one point where they seem to speak almost in the same 'breath', with similar shortness of phrase, though with varying emphasis. This is when Petey's answers grow to 'Reading' and 'All right', and Meg shortens her questions to 'Is it good?' and then 'Where's Stan?' This rhythmic 'meeting' may represent an unspoken acknowledgement of the one urgent matter they must both learn to face and live with. It lasts for only a moment that continues into the pause; then Meg's uncertainty forces the pace again.

If only the sounds of the words were heard, or if the dialogue was followed by someone not knowing a word of English, much of the pressures, tactics and moments of decision in this episode would be communicated. Such response might be more valid and exciting than if a reader registered the words without recreating their sound in his mind as well as registering their implications. Sound and the interplay of rhythms are constant factors in the effectiveness of Pinter's dialogue.

The same passage illustrates further devices of more occasional value. Most notable is barefaced, inescapable falsehood: the apparently simple statement of facts that the audience knows to be wrong. Here Petey fumbles towards his lie, but when it comes it is sharp enough to alert the audience: 'Yes' – Stanley is still in bed. (The audience has just seen Petey watch Stanley march out of the room between Goldberg and McCann, despite his own protest.) The effect is not complete when Petey has given the simple lie, for so briefly is it effected that the elaboration which follows after another hesitation will also be listened to sharply for verification: 'Yes, he's . . . still asleep.' The audience now hears Petey as a man managing his wife and also his own unspoken thoughts. Meg's obvious lie – that 'We had dancing' when, in fact, she had been unable to find a partner – is less crucially managed. It follows the more general deception of 'It was a lovely party' and 'They all said' she was 'the belle of the ball'. Here the comparatively small factual error is sufficient to alert attention and so give a momentary awareness of how far Meg is indulging her fantasy of rosy success.

Falsehoods are important for Pinter's dialogue, not least when they can be detected only by careful reference from one scene to another. . . .

Some of the more blatant lies are so casually delivered that the audience is encouraged to look for more than is going to be disclosed. This is a part of Pinter's two-pronged tactic of awakening the audience's desire for verification and repeatedly disappointing this desire. In *The Birthday Party* and *The Caretaker*, he may be said to create mystification by contrary statements and by the absence of verification for what can only be assumed. Where do the characters come from? (Answers are sometimes suggested, but never substantiated.) Is Goldberg's name Nat or Simey, or Benny? (Each name is used.) Was his son called Manney (Emanuel) or Timmy? (Again, each name is used.) Was Stanley married or not? (He is said to have a wife and also not to be married.) Why does Mick, in *The Caretaker*, invent such unlikely and impossible exploits for his uncle's brother who 'married a Chinaman and went to Jamaica'? Why does Aston say Davies snores when on all but one, late, occasion he does not? The effect of such falsehoods, half-truths and contradictions is to raise suspicion about statements that could possibly be true, and which if true, might be significant. So the audience doubts and questions the characters' progress through the play, the clues they seem to drop, the assurance they seem to possess. Their words are undermined, their credit short.

A notable example is Aston's speech at the end of Act Two of *The Caretaker* which follows his strange stories about victimisation. Here he tells of a mental hospital more in terms of primitive nightmare than medical practice. Yet there are details that could be true, like needing a guardian's permission for treatment and, more potentially reassuring for an audience, the credibility of its tone as a crazed man's account of actuality.

A fact which the audience has no cause to doubt is sometimes presented so that it awakens the possibility of relevance to some other statement of fact. For instance, is it significant that Stanley, in *The Birthday Party*, speaks of living in Basingstoke (p. 45), when Goldberg has said his Uncle Barney had had a home just outside this town (p. 29)? Uncle Barney, the audience is told later, is the one whom Goldberg's father had said on his death-bed would always 'see him in the clear' (p. 81). Coincidences like these tend to draw attention to each other. Why does Stanley say he connects McCann with a Fuller's teashop, a Boots Library and the High Street at Maidenhead (p. 42), when, later in the same Act, Goldberg, who did not hear this conversation, imagines his own life with some precisely similar detail: 'Not size but quality. A little Austin, tea in Fullers, a library book from Boots, and I'm satisfied' (p. 59)? Has McCann reported back, or are Goldberg and Stanley connected in some previous activity? How does Goldberg know, or why does he say he knows, the date of Stanley's birthday? Or is that invention? Is there a connection between Goldberg talking of his surviving son (the other two sons were 'lost – in an accident') and his pursuit of Stanley? (He says he 'often' wonders what that son is doing now.) Or are McCann's two references to 'the organisation', while joining Goldberg in interrogating Stanley, a more reliable clue to the unknown past? Many of the accusations hurled at Stanley are absurd or impossible, so is any one of them 'true'? Goldberg says, at length, that Stanley is being taken to Monty; but why does he merely hint that Monty is a doctor?

In a programme note for *The Caretaker*, Pinter claimed uncertainty as a key dramatic device:

Given a man in a room, he will sooner or later receive a visitor . . .
There is no guarantee, however, that he will possess a visiting card, with detailed

information as to his last place of residence, last job, next job, number of dependents, etc. Nor, for the comfort of all, an identity card, nor a label on his chest. The desire for verification is understandable but cannot always be satisfied. There are no hard distinctions between what is real and what is unreal, nor between what is true and what is false. The thing is not necessarily either true or false; it can be both true and false. The assumption that to verify what has happened and what is happening presents few problems I take to be inaccurate. A character on the stage who can present no convincing argument or information as to his past experience, his present behaviour or his aspirations, nor give a comprehensive analysis of his motives is as legitimate and as worthy of attention as one who, alarmingly, can do all these things. The more acute the experience the less articulate its expression.[2]

So presented, Pinter sounds as if he is making paradoxical play with words; and this is suitable. A more direct statement came in a letter to the *New York Times* in 1967, when *The Birthday Party* was presented on Broadway. A theatre-goer had written to say that Mr Pinter was shirking his job and should tell her who the two visitors were, where Stanley came from and whether they were 'all supposed to be normal'. Pinter replied that he couldn't understand her letter, and therefore couldn't reply until she had answered *his* questions: who was she, where did she come from, and was she 'supposed to be normal'? Pinter, in fact, is exploring Whitehead's dilemma,[3] the inability of anyone to describe the fact that he exists and that he is attempting to communicate with others. The philosopher's questions have yielded the dramatic device of blatant falsehood and continuous mystification and suspicion. Used with exaggeration and meticulous control, the device sharpens the audience's awareness of an uneasiness latent in all human encounters.

Of course, the lies Pinter introduces are not any lies. Often the clearest falsehoods introduce, or are accompanied by, the most potent words, words which are found to reveal several levels of meaning or suggest a large wake of association. Petey's

> Yes, he's . . . still asleep.
> Let him . . . sleep.

says more than that Stanley, according to him, is in bed (which was the wording offered by Meg). As Petey had watched Stanley being escorted to the waiting black car, dressed in black, almost blind without his spectacles and quite silent, he could have seen him as if he were going to his own funeral. Moreover, the audience has witnessed Stanley reduced to child-like cries, and then drawing '*a long breath which shudders down his body*'. Just before Petey's entry he had crouched on a chair, shuddered, relaxed, dropped his head and become '*still again, stooped*'. After his 'Birthday', Stanley has regressed as if into the womb, in a foetal position, but quiet and still as if dead. Is Stanley indeed being 'put to sleep'? Or is Petey expressing his own fearful response in trying to let the sleeping lie? After this falsehood, Petey is, certainly, silent, as Stanley was and, probably, still is: is Petey 'sleeping' too, intentionally?

Equally, Meg's 'We had dancing and singing. And games. You should have been there', may be both, 'true and false'. Blind-man's-buff was not the only 'game' played; Lulu had had hers, Goldberg and McCann theirs; Stanley had been about to '*strangle*' her (p. 66). Petey's absence at his 'game' of chess had affected the course of the Birthday Party.

Pinter has an acute ear for those words which carry suggestions or traces of secondary implications. He places them carefully, often with a lie, as a stepping-off point for a long speech, or as a suddenly satisfactory conclusion to one, or as a conversation-stopper. They are often placed in unremarkable verbal surroundings, or seem to be uttered without reflection and then seized upon, as if a secret source of appropriateness has been unwittingly discovered. . . .

A single word is sufficient for a conversation to turn upon its hidden axis. So Stanley, in *The Birthday Party*, counters Meg's question with ironic impatience, and Meg greedily devours the attack for the satisfaction of her own fantasy:

> Was it nice?
> STANLEY: What?
> MEG: The fried bread.
> STANLEY: Succulent.
> MEG: You shouldn't say that word.
> STANLEY: What word?
> MEG: That word you said.
> STANLEY: What, succulent –?
> MEG: Don't say it!
> STANLEY: What's the matter with it?
> MEG: You shouldn't say that word to a married woman.   [p. 18]

Later she returns to the word in a different way, gently and inviting:

> MEG: Stan?
> STANLEY: What?
> MEG (*shyly*): Am I really succulent?
> STANLEY: Oh, you are. I'd rather have you than a cold in the nose any day.
> MEG: You're just saying that.   [p. 19]

Meg hears what she wants to hear. Double meanings, allusions, tones of voice, gratification and fear are continuously changing, even with the speaking of a single word. By making this verbal encounter turn on 'succulent', Pinter reveals the inner drama, making the normally hidden intention almost explicit for the moment. . . .

Perhaps the most basic strategy in Pinter's use of words is a movement towards a verbal statement that 'is irrevocable, and can never be taken back'.[4] The course of a conversation or soliloquy can be deflected by another more powerful need, triggered off by a seemingly chance choice of word, or by a lack of response, or a physical action. So the verbal expression is, at least momentarily, 'truer', more instinctive, more necessary, less calculated or less able to deceive. Stanley's fantasy about playing in a concert reveals his desire to be accepted, his concern for his father, fear of persecution, desire to be tough and, then, his aggression towards Meg and his desire to fix her in his mind and in his world. Here are many words, written with relish and precision. The rhythms of speech alternate between those of fear and confidence. Underneath there is loneliness and panic, and the dead weight of custom and lethargy. The phrase, 'old piece of rock cake', comes unexpectedly, blatantly and with revealing coarseness and weariness. Perhaps the most 'irrevocable' statement, where words carry most solid and exact meaning, is the final demanding question, 'That's what you are, aren't you?':

STANLEY: Played the piano? I've played the piano all over the world. All over the country. (*Pause*) I once gave a concert.
MEG: A concert?
STANLEY (*reflectively*): Yes. It was a good one, too. They were all there that night. Every single one of them. It was a great success. Yes. A concert. At Lower Edmonton.
MEG: What did you wear?
STANLEY (*to himself*): I had a unique touch. Absolutely unique. They came up to me. They came up to me and said they were grateful. Champagne we had that night, the lot. (*Pause*) My father nearly came down to hear me. Well, I dropped him a card anyway. But I don't think he could make it. No, I – I lost the address, that was it. (*Pause*.) Yes. Lower Edmonton. Then after that, you know what they did? They carved me up. Carved me up. It was all arranged, it was all worked out. My next concert. Somewhere else it was. In winter. I went down there to play. Then, when I got there, the hall was closed, the place was shuttered up, not even a caretaker. They'd locked it up. (*Takes off his glasses and wipes them on his pyjama jacket.*) A fast one. They pulled a fast one. I'd like to know who was responsible for that. (*Bitterly.*) All right, Jack, I can take a tip. They want me to crawl down on my bended knees. Well I can take a tip . . . any day of the week. (*He replaces his glasses, then looks at* MEG.) Look at her. You're just an old piece of rock cake, aren't you? (*He rises and leans across the table to her.*) That's what you are, aren't you?   [p. 22–3]

Pinter not only uses words meticulously and with constant awareness of the 'other language' that can be locked underneath the spoken words, but he is an essentially dramatic writer in that he knows how to acknowledge the effects of time. His writing has tension and climax, and is continually dynamic. Words run ahead or lag behind the thoughts of his characters; they surprise, digress, tantalise and, occasionally, seem to clinch the dramatic conflict.

Pinter has spoken of the nausea which he sometimes feels for words, and describes his encounters with words as if he had had to penetrate and master them. This, too, as well as the perplexity and delight of words, he communicates to his audience. At a performance one can be lost – like an actor in early rehearsals – bewildered, amazed, infuriated, bored, and then find that some precarious statement seems to clarify, to be held for attention, understanding and wonder. Even when the discovery is of a simple or dogged reaction, the experience of so recognising it gives an essential dramatic excitement to the statement.

In his plays Pinter has faced his distrust of words and explored the means whereby the theatre can express in lively form his perceptions and discoveries. Not only has he increased the language of the theatre – its ability to speak – but he has done so in a manner that makes it difficult for his audiences and readers to forget what they have found; he has given them an experience in which they have discovered for themselves. . . .

SOURCE: extracts from chapter, 'Words and Silence' in *Theatre Language: A Study of Arden, Osborne, Pinter and Wesker* (London, 1972), pp. 20, 22–5, 32–8, 39–43, 48, 49–51.

NOTES

[Reorganised and renumbered from the original]

1. 'In an Empty Bandstand: Harold Pinter in conversation with Joan Bakewell', *Listener* (6/11/1969), p. 31.
2. Pinter's note in programme for *The Caretaker*, Arts Theatre, 1960.
3. [Ed.] See A. N. Whitehead, *Adventures in Ideas* (London, 1933).
4. 'Between the Lines', *Sunday Times* (4/3/1962).

Nigel Alexander   'A Defence Against "Mere Theatricality"'   (1974)

The Birthday Party, Pinter's first major work presented in 1958 . . . contains elements which are open to the charge of being 'merely theatrical'. At the seaside boarding house run by Meg and Petey, the deck chair attendant, there is only one guest, Stanley Webber. One day two strangers turn up whose names are Goldberg and McCann. It becomes clear that they have not only been associated with Stanley in the past – they have some kind of hold over him. In the course of the birthday party given by Meg for Stanley they succeed in subjecting him to a form of brain-washing, break his mental stability, and then carry him off to 'Monty' to be 'cured'.

Any audience is bound to speculate about the connection between Stanley and the mystery men. The lady who wrote to Pinter asking where they came from was, after all, making a reasonable request for information which had been provoked by the dramatist himself. An author who cannot, or will not, satisfy such a demand must expect to arouse the irritation of unfulfilled expectation. If the past is about to overtake and destroy Stanley Webber then it ought to be dramatised. It is not sufficient to say that the play requires their presence and the exact details of the intrigue that brings them there are unimportant. Spectators are not entertained by the dramatist's need to keep them in the theatre but by the logic and coherence of the pattern that he stages within it. If part of that pattern is simply missed out then the author is liable to be accused of using a 'theatrical' rather than a 'dramatic' device – one that is justified not by any necessary or probable connection with the plot but only by the fact that it is a play performed in a theatre.

In actual fact, although formal details of the intrigue or the 'organisation' to which they belong are never supplied, the past is effectively dramatised. The opening sequence opens a gap between the aspirations of the characters and their behaviour that is maintained in increasingly painful fashion until the end of the play.

MEG: Here's your cornflakes.
  Are they nice?
PETEY: Very nice.
MEG: I thought they'd be nice. (*She sits at the table.*) You got your paper?
PETEY: Yes.
MEG: Is it good?
PETEY: Not bad.
MEG: What does it say?
PETEY: Nothing much.   [pp. 9–10]

What is established is a domestic routine of almost killing boredom. Yet Meg's enquiries about the cornflakes, and her interest in the girl baby that the newspaper announces has been born to Lady Mary Splatt, indicate great expectations that have somehow withstood the withering of age and the staling of custom. One of the reasons that she sounds like a silly old woman is that her vocabulary is still that of a bride enjoying providing breakfast for her husband and looking forward to the baby that she hopes will be a boy. Her unquenchable folly, and Petey's resigned acceptance of her good intentions, have a quality of heroism which survives even the laughter of the audience.

The placing of these laughs for maximum effect '– some girl (*laugh*), I don't think you'd know her (*laugh*), no (*laugh*) –' indicate an inspired touch for comedy. What is unusual is the use of this comedy to provide information which allows an audience to predict the relationship between Meg and Stanley before he ever appears on the stage. The compound of maternal sexuality in which her frustrations find expression is clearly dangerously unstable and liable to cause an explosion. Stanley's frenzied outburst has been predicted although its form will be unexpected. His own relationship with his parents has been uneasy. As he says of his 'great success' – the concert at Lower Edmonton

> My father nearly came down to hear me. Well, I dropped him a card anyway. But I don't think he could make it. No, I – I lost the address, that was it. [p. 23]

He certainly does not wish to recognise himself as the son and lover of Meg's desire. The furies which seize him do not need localisation. They have always been part of his history.

The ritual of the birthday party encourages self-expression – and the trouble is that what usually gets expressed is the hatred and self-loathing that lurks in every individual. At the party all speak in glowing terms of the past – especially Goldberg. Neither he nor the others can make it match the present or open a way to the future. Comparing Goldberg to her first lover Lulu becomes the architect of her own seduction. He visits her bedroom where she opens his briefcase and performs the part that she finds in it:

> LULU: I wouldn't do those things again, not even for a Sultan!
> GOLDBERG: One night doesn't make a harem.
> LULU: You taught me things a girl shouldn't know until she's been married at least three times!*

Her position is both ludicrous and pathetic since she finds herself outraged and shamed by her own wish. Although she has been engaged in the same action as Goldberg they have been playing different games by different rules. The compatible qualities of Goldberg and McCann, sentimental seduction and mindless violence, are the source of their power. They gain control by turning

---

* This passage occurs in the 1st edition (1960), p. 84, of the play. It was changed in the 2nd edition (1965) – Ed.

all play into perversion. They need no further identification since they are an inevitable part of the circle in which each individual plays blind man's buff with his own desires.

In this context it is significant that Petey, the only character without fantasies of the past or future, is absent from the party because he is playing chess. His presence would have checked the wilder forms of the Goldberg controlled games but he can now do nothing to avert their consequences. Faced with the barely concealed threat of accompanying Stanley to 'Monty', Petey's weary acceptance and resignation can now accomplish nothing except to protect Meg, however temporarily, from the knowledge of her loss. The mysterious agents from the past who have deprived them of Stanley have not extinguished the ashes of their love – but there is no Phoenix to rise from them. . . .

SOURCE: extract from 'Past, Present and Pinter' in *Essays and Studies*, 27 (1974). pp. 5–8.

Andrew Kennedy   'The two Styles of *The* *Birthday Party*'   (1975)

. . . When *The Birthday Party* was first performed,[1] critical response included the feeling that there was a violent yet imperfectly controlled style-switch in the play. This seemed to amount to an abrupt change from microscopic naturalism (typified by the opening exchanges of Meg and Pete on cornflakes and 'nice bits' from the newspaper), to highly stylised 'absurdist' patterns reaching a climax in the Goldberg–McCann brainwashing patter of Act II, and the final incantation with its orchestrated clichés in Act III. The two styles then actually seemed to work negatively against one another, instead of creating a theatrical counterpoint: for Stanley's situation as a persecuted and guilty figure was never worked out on the human level 'promised' by the seeming naturalism, while the Goldberg–McCann variations stood out too blatantly as an already familiar theatre style. Now, with repeated hearing and reading, one can see that Pinter does in fact control his 'two styles' with skill, but the controls are precariously dependent on performers (and auditors) having learned the 'codes' of early Pinter. And, in later plays, Pinter developed a subtler and more unified 'shaping' for the dialogue.

One way in which Pinter controls the two styles can only be

appreciated when seeing the play whole – in practice, seeing it twice or reading it backwards. One then sees, with sudden clarity, that the 'ordinary' conversational opening and ending are a frame for, a connivance at the 'extraordinary' events in the house. The empty, natural-seeming but denatured talk – which goes with stupor, with Meg's sentimental naiveté and Pete's good-natured impotence – makes the atrocious inquisition possible.

Another kind of control turns on emphasis. Take, for example, the phrase 'This house is on the list', repeated like a *leitmotif* four times, in increasingly alarming contexts, and amounting to gradual intensification. First we have the casual-seeming exchange between Meg and Pete:

MEG: This house is on the list.
PETE: It is.
MEG: I know it is.

The pattern is next used in a teasing exchange between Meg and Stanley, when the latter is trying to cast doubt on Meg's talk of 'visitors':

STANLEY: (. . .) I'm your visitor.
MEG: You're a liar. The house is on the list.
STANLEY: I bet it is.
MEG: I know it is.

And it re-emerges in Stanley's first anxious questioning about the visitors ('Why?' 'This house is on the list.' 'But who are they?') and in his panicky questions after the arrival of Goldberg and McCann:

STANLEY (*turning*): But why here? Why not somewhere else?
MEG: This house is on the list.
STANLEY (*coming down*): What are they called? What are their names?[2]

On the simplest level these are just signals (don't miss 'the list' – it is sinister like a 'black list'). But something else is also happening: the gradual stylisation – in the last two examples an insistent, 'catechismic' questioning – prepares the way for the fully stylised ritual inquisition later in the play.

Then there is the rather simple yet often effective heightening: the chain of idiomatic – and idiosyncratic – phrases, where the 'chain' amounts to a stylised verbal smokescreen, what Pinter himself calls that other silence, a 'torrent of language'.[3] Here is Goldberg, on arrival in the house:

(*sitting at table*) The secret is breathing. Take my tip. It's a well known fact. Breathe in, breathe out, take a chance, let yourself go, what can you lose? Look at me. When I was an apprentice yet, McCann, every second Friday of the month my Uncle Barney used to take me to the seaside, regular as clockwork, Brighton, Canvey Island, Rottingdean – Uncle Barney wasn't particular. After lunch on Shabbus we'd go and sit in a couple of deck chairs – you know the ones with canopies we'd have a little paddle, we'd catch the tide coming in, going out, the sun coming down – golden days, believe me McCann . . .

[p. 27]

We recognise here, on the naturalistic level, the complacent clichés and rhythms of a semi-educated Jewish dealer with a flair for 'flannelling'. ('What can you lose?', and the raconteur's use of *would*: 'on Shabbus we'd go . . .') Yet it is highly patterned, and the cumulative effect of Goldberg's speeches (and they tend to dominate the play) is to parody a type of culture-patter: the sinister complacencies of the successful Head of Family and Business. So a highly individual language is used to expose the way elements in our language compel conformity. In Act II the function of Goldberg's speeches is quite clear: the farcical paean about the joys of boyhood ('I'd tip my hat to the toddlers. . .') and the fit man's cheerful waking to sunshine ('all the little birds, the smell of grass, church bells, tomato juice. . .') amount to a verbal limbering up for the verbal torture of Stanley; and the birthday celebration speeches, after the inquisition inflicted on the victim, are experienced as a black ritual.[4] But by Act III Goldberg's patterned loquacity becomes more arbitrary. In particular, Goldberg's speeches when left alone with McCann seem to have little function apart from 'creating a scene' and reinforcing the cultural bankruptcy of Goldberg through making him mouth a medley of slogans – Judaic, British and miscellaneous culture-props – with the dramatic breakdown over 'Because I believe': logorrhoea into vacancy. There is a strong local interest here but the connection with the context of the whole play is tenuous. It is, more than anything else, a verbal and rhythmic bravura act.[5]

In the cross-examination of Stanley, and, even more clearly, in the Goldberg–McCann incantation in the penultimate scene of the play, we see the extent of Pinter's attraction to the patterns and rhythms of ritual – apparently without wishing to evoke (as Eliot wished to do) a primitive or sacred rhythm of sacrifice. Nor do these scenes have the human pressure – the political-religious terror – which we find in such a work as *Darkness at Noon*, and in authentic documents of persecution. The pressure is induced through rhythmic intensification, through the paralysing spell of a disconnected language, for example the jump from random cliché-questions to random fantasy-questions ('What about the Albigensenist heresy?/Who watered the wicket at

Melbourne?'). But the cross-examination scene at least externalises that sense of 'meaningless proceedings' which Kafka's K.[6] – never interrogated – so resents. The final incantation is, however, more gratuitous:

GOLDBERG: We'll watch over you.
MCCANN: Advise you.
GOLDBERG: Give you proper care and treatment.
MCCANN: Let you use the club bar.
GOLDBERG: Keep a table reserved.
MCCANN: Help you acknowledge the fast days.
GOLDBERG: Bake you cakes.   [pp. 82–3]

followed by those spell-unbinding parodic responses: 'We'll provide the skipping rope./The vest and pants./The ointment./The hot poultice./The fingerstall./The abdomen belt./The ear plugs./The baby powder . . .'
We do respond here to the violent parody of institutionalised caring. But the detail of the mumbo-jumbo is so far-fetched (or farcical) that it is only in performance – through the image of the helpless victim and his reduction to gurgling speechlessness – that we connect this ritual with any pattern of felt persecution. The 'shaping' is preponderant, the texture of the language mannerist. . . .

SOURCE: extract from *Six Dramatists in Search of a Language* (London, 1975), pp. 178–82.

NOTES

[Reorganised and renumbered from the original]

1. Arts Theatre, Cambridge, April 1958. The response here recorded is based on a note I wrote after the first performance.
2. *The Birthday Party*, 2nd revised edn (London, 1965), pp. 12, 17, 20 and 34 respectively. (I note that the build-up of the 'catechism' is slightly more marked in the first edition – 'I mean, why . . .?' following 'But who are they?' in the third 'list' exchange. (Cf. 1963, p. 21 and 1965, p. 20.) More significantly: the third exchange is followed (in both editions) by Stanley's onslaught of Where/What/What/Who/Who questions over his tea. The whole sequence is rhythmically heightened and in effect establishes Stanley himself as the first inquisitor.
3. 'Writing for the Theatre', *Evergreen Review*, 33 (Aug.–Sept., 1964), p. 82.
4. *The Birthday Party*, pp. 43, 44–5, 56.
5. Ibid. pp. 77–8. As far as I am aware no published criticism has seen this dialogue-sequence in context. A critic friend, Christopher Gillie, has suggested to me one possible function of this scene: Goldberg and McCann are demoralised in and by the absence of Stanley, the victim they need.
6. Franz Kafka, *The Trial*, ch. II (Harmondsworth, 1970), esp. pp. 54–5.

106

Bernard F. Dukore   'From the Comic to the Non-Comic'   (1982)

. . . True to its title *The Birthday Party* contains a birthday party – for Stanley who insists it is not his birthday. Birthday not only means the anniversary of one's birth, it also means the day of one's birth, and in *The Birthday Party* the celebration of the former helps to create the latter. The intruders turn Stanley into what McCann calls a new man. At their hands he is reborn, made into a different kind of person on a birthday that becomes a birth-day.

What happens on stage is what the audience perceives, not the symbolic nature of actions or speeches. For instance McCann calmly tears a newspaper into five equal strips while Stanley nervously paces. To be sure one can interpret McCann's action as the destruction of a medium of communication, which it is, yet this interpretation reveals nothing essential about the play for communication is not a major theme. More important is that the action simultaneously calms McCann and unnerves Stanley.

When Stanley hears of two visitors he apprehensively questions Meg about them, paces the room, and insists they will not come. Pinter does not explain why he is nervous. What matters is that he is nervous. When Goldberg and McCann arrive Stanley peeks at them through the kitchen serving-hatch and sneaks out through the rear door. Mystery and menace increase when McCann asks Goldberg if they are in the right house, for he saw no number on the gate. 'I wasn't looking for a number', says Goldberg [p. 28]. They intensify when Goldberg questions Meg about her lodger and, upon learning it is the lodger's birthday, decides – not impulsively but *'thoughtfully'* – that a party should celebrate the event. *'We're* going to give him a party' (author's italics) [p. 33]. No reason is offered. What matters is that Goldberg's decision is deliberative and that he immediately assumes command of the household. After he and McCann go to their rooms Stanley questions Meg about the newcomers. Upon hearing that one is named Goldberg he responds by slowly sitting at the table. When she asks if he knows them he does not reply – then or later. What the play shows is that their presence and Goldberg's name unsettle him.

Meg's first actions in relationship to Stanley are very funny. She calls to him, as she would to a child, to come down to breakfast; she races to his room, rousing him, while he shouts and she laughs wildly; finally he enters – not a boy, but a bespectacled, groggy man in his thirties, unshaven, and wearing his pyjama jacket. Underlying these activities, what is often called the subtext, is that someone makes Stanley do what he does not want to do – a comic foreshadowing of a non-comic resolution. Furthermore Stanley's comic dissatisfaction with his reward, breakfast, hints at a more disturbing dissatisfaction to come. This attempt to make someone go where he does not wish to go becomes a leitmotif. Meg suggests that Stanley go shopping with her; he refuses. Lulu urges him to go outside for a walk; he refuses. At the end he is forced to leave the house, not merely his room – a non-comic departure this time. Goldberg and McCann say they will take him to Monty but do not explain who Monty is or what he represents. That Pinter does not have them do so indicates that the specific reason for his removal is unimportant. The dramatic point is that they take him, in contrast to his going of his own volition. His removal, the theatrical climax of this leitmotif, resembles a symphonic finale of a musical theme, not a discursive explanation of a literary theme.

Present speech and action are more important than exposition. Stanley's references to his career as a pianist dwindle, both comically and pathetically, from giving concerts through the world to giving them all over the country to once giving a concert. Dramatically what matters is not which if any of these statements is true but that Stanley makes them in this sequence, for by doing so he verbally non-entitises himself. Later Meg further undercuts his status as a pianist when, after twice saying she enjoyed watching him play the piano, she repeats his story about the concert and (comically) gets the details wrong. She undercuts that status still further (again comically) when she gives him a toy drum as a birthday present – because he does not have a piano.

What happens on stage contributes to the audience's sense, feeling or understanding. The passages that describe Stanley as a pianist convey the impression that he is an artist, an artist-manqué, or a parody of an artist. By contrast, partly because an artist is often regarded as one who does not conform to customary social roles and partly because Goldberg's conventional appearance contrasts with that of the unkempt Stanley, Goldberg suggests social conformity (he even carries a briefcase). His speeches sometimes seem to parody jargon, at other times overflow with the clichés of middle-class conformity. In large measure he and McCann convey an ambience of conformity (family, state and church) and appear as representatives of society who press Stanley into a mould. As if in summary they promise Stanley he will be adjusted. Appropriately they represent the two traditionalist religions of European civilisation, Judaism and

Catholicism. For *Protestants* to make Stanley conform would be inappropriate.

Pinter creates atmosphere by the theatrical nature of words: rhythms and quantity. When the visitors interrogate the lodger what they say is contradictory or illogical, but how they say it, and Stanley's inarticulateness or silence, have theatrical meaning. They accuse him of killing his wife and of not marrying, of not paying the rent and of contaminating womankind, of picking his nose and of being a traitor to the cloth. Stanley hardly has an opportunity to get a word in edgeways. Clearly the scene's effectiveness is unrelated to causal logic. As Glynne Wickham explains, 'Three characters are speaking in this interrogation episode, but the rhythmic structure is a single sequence. The horror of this remarkable scene, and its impact on the audience, is achieved by the deliberate antithesis of verbal *non sequitur* against the remorselessly mounting insistence of the verbal rhythm.[1] In addition, according to one critic, impact and ambience derive not from the accuracy or relevance of any particular accusation but from 'the sheer weight, variety, and quantity of usage'.[2] Here language is used theatrically, not referentially, as it is in the duo's final scene with Stanley where a stage direction says, '*They begin to woo him, gently and with relish*' [p. 82]. In these speeches two voices speak with one rhythm.

Implicit in some of the previous analysis is the play's comedy which links to later sequences that are not comic. *The Birthday Party* begins with humour derived from incongruity and verbal repetition. After Meg thrice asks her husband whether it is he who has entered, he responds: 'What?' 'Is that you?' 'Yes, it's me.' 'What?' [p. 9]. The opening exchange of Act III balances that of Act I, but the later scene is not funny. Furthermore Meg is mistaken about the visitor: as in Act I Petey enters, but in Act III Meg asks if it is Stanley. Identity, the subject of both exchanges, is thematically relevant. In Act I Stanley asks Meg whether, when she addresses him, she knows exactly whom she talks to. In Act II he tells McCann he is the same as he has always been. In Act III, however, the intruders promise to change his identity.

In Act I comedy derives from food Meg offers Petey and Stanley: fried bread that Stanley mockingly calls succulent, milk he calls sour, and tea he compares to gravy. By contrast there is no food left for either in Act III, since the intruders have eaten everything. Food suggests sustenance, and there is none for Petey who is too feeble to resist the well-nourished Goldberg and McCann, or for Stanley who is incapable of resisting them. Apropos, when Stanley calls the bread succulent, Meg does not understand the meaning of the word which sounds sexual. As the comic misunderstanding demonstrates, a word's meaning is not necessarily referential; in the interrogation scene the rhythms not the meanings of words have a devastatingly non-comic effect on Stanley.

Anticipating later conflicts, the first act has Meg and Stanley engage in a minor, comic struggle for domination. When he requests tea she demands: 'Say please.' 'Please.' 'Say sorry first.' 'Sorry first' [p. 7]. His mockery suggests his victory. In the next act a battle for domination revolves around whether Stanley will sit as directed. The battle is comic, suggestive of a child's game, with I'll-sit-if-you-sit and Stanley rising immediately after Goldberg and McCann sit. When Goldberg then rises, McCann reprimands Stanley and shouts at him to sit. Stanley tries to appear casual by whistling and strolling, but he obeys. Next the two menacingly interrogate him. Though the request to sit is apparently as trivial as the request to say please, and though it is initially as comic, what underlies both demands – what happens – is that a person or persons make another do what he does not want to do. The manoeuvre that is comic foreshadows menace.

In *The Birthday Party* Pinter links the visual wth the verbal. In Act I, for example, when Goldberg and McCann meet Meg they say: 'How often do you meet someone it's a pleasure to meet?' 'Never.' 'But today it's different. How are you keeping, Mrs Boles?' [p. 30]. How might Meg respond to Goldberg's first question? Is she pleased or does the flattery pass her by? In either case how does she respond to McCann's thoughtless answer? Does she understand its implications? Does Goldberg respond to it? The answer to this determines how and to whom he says that today is different. He might reassure Meg or he might reprimand his colleague, and the different possibilities determine his rendering of the next question. Whether one interprets the brief exchange as two visitors hurrying the mistress of the house through a perfunctory introduction or as a comic scene in which Goldberg finesses McCann's social blunder, it is important to consider not only the dialogue but also the relationship between the speakers and the silent character. Visual links with verbal.

Directorial embellishments can visually fortify the verbal. Alan Schneider's Broadway production did so. Perhaps taking a cue from Goldberg's assertion that McCann is a defrocked priest, Edward Winter (McCann), during the scene in which he exhorts Lulu to confess, placed two strips of torn newspaper over each of his shoulders as if they were a priest's vestment.

At the close of Act I the visual combines with non-verbal sound to create meaning: a climax of terror as Stanley, drum hanging from his neck, marches around the table beating the drum regularly, then erratically and uncontrolled, and when he arrives at Meg's chair his face and drumbeat are savage. At the climax of Act II the lights suddenly go out. From the darkness spectators hear groping for a torch, grunts from Goldberg and McCann, the sustained beating of a drumstick on a drum, whimpers from Lulu, people stumbling against each other, and dialogue – for a page and a half, a long time in the theatre. McCann finds the torch and shines it over the room until he picks out Stanley, bent over a spreadeagled Lulu. The light draws closer to him, he backs up against the serving-hatch, and he giggles as Goldberg and McCann converge upon him. Through theatrical elements, not discursive language, Pinter conveys Stanley's increasing breakdown.

When Stanley appears in the last act the very sight of him indicates the intruders' triumph and his conformity. No longer unkempt, as in Act I, he is as immaculate as a corpse and walks like a zombie. Clean-shaven, he wears a dark, well-tailored suit and white collar, and he holds his broken glasses. A stage direction has Goldberg easily seat him in a chair – in contrast to Act II when Stanley resists sitting. Although stage directions tell what Stanley wears, they do not indicate what Goldberg and McCann wear. In Pinter's 1964 production all three were dressed identically. The early editions of the play, and early productions, suggested conformity differently: Stanley wore striped trousers, a black jacket, and a bowler hat. . . .

SOURCE: extract from *Harold Pinter*, Modern Dramatists series (London and Basingstoke, 1982), pp. 29–35.

NOTES

[Reorganised and renumbered from the original]

1. Glynne Wickham, *Drama in a World of Science* (London, 1962), pp. 28–9.
2. Austin E. Quigley, *The Pinter Problem* (Princeton, N.J., 1975), pp. 64–5.

Irving Wardle   'A Rare Pleasure'   (1958)

REVIEW OF FIRST LONDON PRODUCTION, LYRIC, HAMMERSMITH

Reviewing a production after everybody else has had a crack at it is like entering a magnetic field; protesting, qualifying, rephrasing, you are swept off to belittling embrace with whatever positive or negative pole has exerted the strongest pull. Only occasionally can you saunter out on the field and find it still littered with iron filings.

Mr Harold Pinter's *The Birthday Party* offers this rare pleasure. When the play flared up briefly at the Lyric Opera House in May it provoked such anarchy of opinions, all very dogmatically held, that you have to look towards French government before finding a fit comparison. Nowadays there are two ways of saying you don't understand a play: the first is to bowl it out with that word 'obscurity', once so popular in poetry reviews; the second way is to say that the seminal influence of Ionesco can be detected.

Mr Pinter received the full treatment. As well as standing for *x* in the formulae outlined above, he was described as inferior N. F. Simpson, a lagging surrealist, and as the equal of Henry James. Remembering James's melancholy affair with the theatre this last one carries a nasty sting; and, within a couple of days of receiving it, *The Birthday Party* was over.

The comparison with James is quite baffling. Far from being a cautious verbal artist struggling to 'throw away cargo to save the ship', Mr Pinter has no difficulty in putting theatrical requirements first. No matter what you may think of the contents, the ship is afloat. And it is his very instinct for what will work in the theatre that has prompted hostility. One character in *The Birthday Party*, for instance, is given to tearing up newspapers: we are not told why. But the spectacle of John Stratton, as the inflammable McCann, holding his breath while rapt in the task of tearing each strip of paper to the same width, took on a malevolent power perfectly in key with the play and requiring no explanation. This device is an extreme example of the playwright's habit of introducing an intrinsically theatrical idea and letting it find its own road back towards common sense. Mr Pinter's way is the opposite of setting out deliberately to embody a theme in action.

All the same a theme does emerge, closely resembling that of *The Iceman Cometh*: the play demonstrates that a man who has withdrawn to protect his illusions is not going to be helped by being propelled into the outer world. Stanley, the man in question, is an obese, shambling, unpresentable creature who has moved into a dilapidated seaside boarding house where, as the only guest, he is able to lord it over his adoring landlady and gain recognition as a concert pianist of superhuman accomplishment. But even in this protected atmosphere there are menacing intrusions: he cannot banish the memory of arriving to give a recital and finding the hall locked up; there are enemies. And when they arrive – in the persons of a suspiciously fluent Jew and his Irish henchman – they seem as much furies emerging from Stanley's night thoughts as physical characters. His downfall is swift. Scrubbed, shaved, hoisted out of his shapeless trousers and stuffed into a morning suit he is led away at the end in a catatonic trance.

Theatrically the play loses its grip only when the two intruders appear alone. They have no need to keep up the mystery, but they do keep it up arbitrarily and begin to reveal distressingly human weaknesses which undermine their power to shock. John Slater, as the leader, almost redeemed these scenes by handling them with operatic licence – treating the lines as cadenced gibberish and alternating blandly honeyed rhetoric with a savage stamp of the foot or a chilling facial contortion. In company, however, the intruders had no need to adopt extraordinary practices: the wink, the muffled threat, the ogrish leer carried them effortlessly through scenes of introduction, accusation, and through the nightmarish birthday party in which Stanley sat bowed and speechless, as his guests, ludicrous in paper hats, worked themselves from giggling gentility into a frenzied *totentanz*.

Peter Wood's production, which seized tigerishly on the play and left it picked clean, contained two major performances – Beatrix Lehmann's Meg (the landlady), and Richard Pearson's Stanley. How these came to be cold-shouldered in the Press is a puzzle more unfathomable than any set by Mr Pinter.

SOURCE: review in *Encore* (July 1958); reproduced in *The Encore Reader* (London, 1965), pp. 76–8.

Irving Wardle   'A Reassessment'   (1975)

REVIEW OF KEVIN BILLINGTON'S PRODUCTION, SHAW THEATRE

Seventeen years after its famous flop at the Lyric, Hammersmith, and trailing lists of international productions and doctoral theses in its wake, Harold Pinter's first full-length play is at last getting a solid run in a London theatre.

I suppose that is an invitation to some kind of reassessment but the time has gone by for clocking in at the Pinter factory. More to the point, Kevin Billington's revival succeeds better than Pinter's own 1964 production in revealing *The Birthday Party* as a fine play whose innovations all serve character and situation.

It is full of dream images: the spectre of the fatal wheel-barrow, the great black car abruptly materialising outside the house; the basic dread of being tracked down to a supposedly impregnable hideout. Pinter anchors those nebulous dreads in a solid domestic environment, and explores his characters with a patience and respect in some ways similar to their own inquisitorial scenes.

The tactics of the Shaw production is to keep things normal for as long as possible. John Hallé's set simply represents a large room in a run-down seaside boarding house; there is nothing to suggest that it is right off the map.

The opening breakfast conversation follows a line of resolute banality between two people buried in unalterable routine. There is nothing grotesque about Basil Lord's Petey or Anna Wing's Meg; their minds have clearly packed in years ago but the comedy is kindly: it comes from the contrast between the dreadful food they eat and the solicitude with which it is served.

Likewise John Alderton's Stanley, the solitary lodger, prised out of bed at noon for a sulky *téte-à-tète* with his doting landlady. Even when paranoia starts twisting the dialogue in odd directions and ugly shadows begin stealing across the faded wallpaper, the relationship remains credible in simple human terms.

The two invaders again conform to the same unemphatic style. I have seen them played like Furies out of *The Family Reunion*; but here it is simply the arrival of two gentlemen out of season. Sydney Tafler's Goldberg is a pink, scrubbed advertisement for natty suiting; a bit florid in manner but he might well have a solid business in Hatton Garden. Tony Doyle's McCann is similarly subdued, a tense immobile figure, taking everything in with gimlet eyes, and occasionally springing a swift economical gesture.

Some of the sheer theatrical effects, like McCann's paper-tearing routine, are minimised and Paula Wilcox's Lulu shows a sophistication that undermines her credibility (it is, admittedly, the weakest part). Otherwise the comedy, the marvellous speech rhythms, and the surviving sense of entering fresh dramatic territory come through as strongly as ever; and this is the first production I have seen that clarifies what happens during the party.

Source: review in *The Times* (9/1/1975).

PART THREE

The Caretaker

John Arden   'Pinter's "Realism"' (1960)

There was a great deal of self-conscious bewilderment among the critics after the first production of *The Birthday Party* and it is not yet entirely dispersed – 'What,' they said, 'Does Pinter symbolise? Why are his characters so dreary? And why why why, can't he tell a story properly, with all the points underlined so that nobody has to listen with more than one ear?' But the 'stories' of Harold Pinter's plays are surely perfectly clear. It is not whether we listen with one ear or two, but what we expect to hear, that is important. Hitherto, plays we can call Realist have tended to follow the Ibsen model: in other words, a series of events was developed, connected by a strictly logical progression of fact, and we could be sure that anything done or said on the stage had its place in the *concrete* structure of the plot. If a character is seen to be fiddling with an electric plug in the first act, then later in the play there is going to be a power-cut or an electric shock, or some other necessary incident to provide a twist in the plot. Or, if the play is Symbolic as well as Realist, the point will be made (pretty heavily) that the electric light represents, say, the Bonds of Civilisation; in which case, the declaration of war in Act Three will coincide with a blown fuse, and the symbolism will be unmistakable to the most inattentive.

But Mr Pinter does not work like this. Instead, he gives a perfectly straightforward story that might almost have been overheard in a public bar – a tramp is picked up and offered lodging by a man engaged in decorating a flat. The man turns out to have been in a mental hospital, and the tramp tries to side against him with the younger brother (a go-ahead character, who owns the house) and establish him firmly as the cuckoo-in-the-nest. But he finds that the brothers both combine against him despite their apparent differences: and the play ends with his expulsion from the premises. The conventional treatment of this sort of story is not difficult to imagine – it might make a Willis Hall or Ted Willis TV piece – and the interesting thing is the closeness with which Mr Pinter's writing in fact does approach such a treatment. But he leaves his corners never quite joined up. There is a deliberate haze about the past, and indeed the present, of all of his characters, which never quite becomes so opaque that we are entirely bewildered. Their inconsistencies are never quite contradictory. We never quite catch a complete view of them. They are seen in vivid glimpses for moments, and then seem to disappear. Thus, the elder brother's account of his brain-operation is highly detailed and circumstantial. But is it true? If it is true, why isn't Mr Pinter writing that serious social play to denounce the cruelty prevalent in mental hospitals? And if it *isn't* true, why does it take the crucial place in the text – the climax of Act Two?

Of course, these questions are impertinent. Because they are based on the old idea of Realism – that the dramatist has no room in his plays for the inconsequence of life; except, perhaps, for the odd 'fey' character or the carefully-placed piece of apparent irrelevance. But after all, it is a very long time since Desdemona first said 'Faith, half asleep' when asked how she felt after her husband had called her whore, and we are surely ready for that degree of 'Realist' writing that will show us all the time, not merely what they would have said if the author had thought it up for them, but what they actually *did* say. Clearly this too is only a convention: and it is a convention that can easily become sterile. But in Mr Pinter's works it is fresh and exciting – and with the production of his second full-length play it seems that it is at last being understood.

There is more to Pinter than Realism, however. Exactly what, can be best discovered, perhaps, by examining his expert use of 'casual' language and broken trains of thought. The number of 'Pauses' marked in the stage-direction is remarkable and paralleled to my knowledge only in Beckett. This orchestration of the play implies an orchestration of observed life on the part of the writer – there is in fact a care in the selection of the 'not quiteness' of it all that is at least as calculated as the construction of the average 'well-made' play. I do not think we should feel bound to look for any allegorical interpretations – they may be there: but there are no clues as to how to find them, and the play stands up perfectly without them. Therefore any such search is surely more of a parlour game than serious literary appreciation. Taken purely at its face value this play is a study of the unexpected strength of family ties against an intruder. That in itself is a subject deep enough to carry many layers of meaning without our having to superimpose any extra scheme of Symbols. It also, by its verbal patterns alone, tells us a great deal that is uncomfortable about the workings of the English mind today. So much of everything we see and hear is 'never quite' anything. Never quite completely dreary, but. . . .

Source: book-review from *New Theatre Magazine*, 1, No. 4 (July 1960), pp. 29–30.

Ruby Cohn   'A Bitter Commentary on the
Human Condition'   (1962)

. . . Although Mick is slang for Irish, it is not clear in *The Caretaker* that
Pinter is again designating the Christian tradition by an Irish name.
Rather, the two brothers jointly seem to symbolise the family
compatibility between a religious heritage and contemporary values.
Thus, it is the elder, conventionally dressed Aston who is a carpenter,
with its evocation of Christ, and it is the leather-jacketed Mick who is
in the building trade and owns a motorised van. It is Mick who
destroys a statue of Buddha, and who has grandiose schemes for
redecorating the house. Aston's projects are humbler; he has been
restored to competence by modern treatments for mental deviates;
before the end of the play, he does manage to tar the roof of the room,
so it no longer leaks. Although Mick is presumably the owner and
Aston the inhabitant of the house, the possession is finally left in
doubt. As Mick explains, 'So what it is, it's a fine legal point, that's
what it is.'

In their attitudes towards the old man, the human derelict, the two
brothers present only surface contrasts. Mick begins by knocking
him down, whereas Aston, instead of allowing him to die in despair,
rescues him, shares his room with him, and opens up hope to him.
Both the brothers name the old man as caretaker, offer him a kind of
scrutiny, which they both subsequently withdraw. Mick turns his
back on the old man for failing to fulfil a role to which he never
aspired, but Aston rejects him for what he is – cantankerous,
self-deluded, and desperate.

Of all Pinter's [early] plays, *The Caretaker* makes the most bitter
commentary on the human condition; instead of allowing an old man
to die beaten, the System insists on tantalising him with faint hope,
thereby immeasurably increasing his final desperate anguish. There
is perhaps a pun contained in the title: the Caretaker is twisted into a
taker on of care, for care is the human destiny.

Pinter's drama savagely indicts a System which sports maudlin
physical comforts, vulgar brand names, and vicious vestiges of a
religious tradition. Pinter's villains descend from motorised vans to
close in on their victims in stuffy, shabby rooms. The System they
represent is as stuffy and shabby; one cannot, as in Osborne's
realistic dramas, marry into it, or sneak into it, or even rave against it
in self-expressive anger. The essence of the Pinter victim is his final
sputtering helplessness.

Although Pinter's God-surrogates are as invisible as Godot, there is no ambiguity about their message. They send henchmen not to bless but to curse, not to redeem but to annihilate. As compared to the long, dull wait for Godot, Pinter's victims are more swiftly stricken with a deadly weapon – the most brilliant and brutal stylisation of contemporary cliché on the English stage today. . . .

SOURCE: extract from 'The World of Harold Pinter', *Tulane Drama Review*, 6 (March 1962), pp. 67–8.

Peter Davison   'The Music Hall Monologue and *The Caretaker*'   (1963)

. . . I begin with two kinds of old monologue, the first being one of Dan Leno's monologues of over sixty years ago. Leno told long, rambling anecdotes, often involving himself and his family, frequently breaking the illusion with mumbled 'asides' (an important characteristic), if one might call such lines 'asides', existing as they do within the framework of direct address. This is how Willson Disher describes his act;[1] note expecially the reference to confessional characteristics. Leno, he says,

wants to tell us his secrets. He must tell us. For the sake of his own peace of mind he wants to explain how he is related to somebody or other who has become involved in a scandal. 'It's like this', he begins, only to realise it is not so, for he has become thoroughly confused over his uncles, cousins, father and grandfathers. Then he pauses with his fingers over his mouth and suddenly croaks, 'There's a postman mixed up in all this'.

This kind of monologue has lasted a long time. Its nature, and the matter of confused relationships are to be found, for example, in Pinter's *The Caretaker* and *The Collection*.[2] Its style is fairly well known and I have, therefore, chosen an extract from a slightly different kind of monologue, one of observation and ironic comment: Dan Leno's *The Robin*.[3] Leno begins by saying he will give an impersonation of a robin, but he digresses to talk about Christmas.

. . . . And then you go home to your Christmas dinner – or other people's Christmas dinners, other people's preferred because there's not so much expense . . . [*grandly*] . . . and there you sit, with your feet under your friend's table, and your eyes on the bottles an' things [*with nostalgic sentimentality*] an' y'have that beautiful feelin' in your heart as y're sittin' an' eatin' – [*sudden deflation*] y'*know* you've got nuthin' to pay for . . . and there you sit, and you think of Christmas.

And just then the little robin comes hoppin' outside the window – hoppin' on his little hop – and you, and you THROW the windows open [*Aside*] weather permittin' of course, an' y're not sittin' there with your neck against it. And there the robin hops along – hops – [*Aside*] I often think it's a pity he hasn't got two more feet to hop on an' give his hoppin' legs a rest. And you say, 'OHH! Merry Christmas', and you throw him a loaf of bread, and he *picks* it up, and *flies* away with it . . . and you say . . . '*This* is Christmas'.

Just then, in comes the beautiful Christmas pudden'. All hot and smokin' with a little bit of holly stickin' on the top – and made of currants and lemons – and bits of string . . . an' all the br-and-y burnin', all round it, all the beautiful brandy burnin'; and you say, 'OH! OHHH!! what a pity the brandy's burnin''. And there you all sit, on the pudden' – yo'll sit down, an' eat of the robin – rob the pudden' – you pudd of the rob . . . Well, that is the reason I want to give you this impersonation of the bird and his song.

[*Pause*]

We will have the male bird on the right and the female on the left . . . or somewhere – she won't be far about – away from him. [*Pause – and then, as if struck by a vital fact which he must tell his audience.*]

The robin of course is a totally different bird to the hedgehog – although they both come out of the forest. But of course the bird, the robin, is the best singer of the two. 'Hm [*as if announcing title*] The Robin Redbreast.

[*Pause*] Well, I don't *know* of a bird that resembles the robin more than the duck. But of course, as a singer – not much, he's not much. Of course, he's very nice, a bit off the chest and the parson's nose, but, as a cage-bird – the duck: No, no good.

[*Firm announcement*] The robin will sing.

[*Long Pause*]

Of course, you can't *hear* the robin, because I forgot to tell you . . . [*a little puzzled*] the robin sings out of sight. But that *is* the robin – I thank you for your kind attention.

Now I hope the directness of the appeal to the audience (and of the effect of the 'aside' within a passage of direct appeal), and the use of deflation and inconsequentiality, are apparent. The play with meaning in this type of monologue (especially the sight-sound relationship) occurs time and again, from Leno, to Flanagan and Allen, to the Goons. Often Leno's humour is far removed from the joke plain and simple, being something much less readily pinned down, as in Leno's description of *The Egg* which Willson Disher quotes:[4]

Of course, there are three kinds of Egg – there is the new-laid Egg (that of course is nearly extinct), then there is the fresh Egg (that is almost the same as the new laid) – but then comes THE Egg. Well, that is the egg I'm talkin' about – that is the Egg that causes the trouble – a little round white thing. You can't tell what it is thinkin' about. You dare not kick it or drop it. It's got no face. You can't get it to laugh. No, you simply look at it and say – 'Egg'.

One is not so very far away from the late Sid Field addressing a golf ball.

In contrast to this kind of monologue, but from the same period of music hall (from 1907, to be precise), I should like to give an example of another kind showing extravagant absurdity and exuberance of language, utilising the malapropism, the non-sequitur, and the tired cliché. In the following example Arthur Roberts has taken the guise of a QC and is defending one Miss Mary Sputkins. The style is vigorous and the key words are spoken with relish, and with a touch of Irishness about them. It is not, incidentally, always quite clear what is the word Roberts intends (e.g., 'perverted' or 'averted' at the end of the third paragraph) owing to the rapidity of his speech and its changes of tone.

May it please your Lordship and Gentlemen of the Jury. In opening the case for the defiant – the defence – I have before me a task of no ordinary difficulty. In the charge sheet it appears that Mary Sputkins is charged under the 33rd section with keeping a licence without a dog. Now M'Lord, the difficulty is, whether or no I am allowed to call rebutting testimony, the law being somewhat *crude* upon the point, as appears in the case of Pecksneeze and Hem'Hm, decided in the House of Lords, whereby it has been held that a person who is a *femme sole*, that is to say an unmarried woman, is not liable under the Innkeeper's Act for any debts that her future husband might contract, in that case notwithstanding.

BUT M'LORD, our contention is according to the terms of the deed – the tenant shall keep the premises in repair, and once every three years paint the outside with three coats of good oil paint.

NOW M'LORD, that being so, I argue that the man had no right to kick the dog, because if the tramcar had kept on the right-hand side of the road, the collision might have been perverted.

Then we have the evidence of the Trinity Pilot who stated, when the ship was leaving harbour, the Captain should have been on the port tack, instead of which, . . . he was on the whiskey tack.

Good God! – it would be simply preposterous, NAY, iniquitous, if such a verdict should be brought in under the pree-mises in which this action has been brought. THEREFORE I say there is no case to go to the jury. If the case *should* go to the jury, then the case must, of a necessity, be returned empty.

. . . and so on.

This kind of monologue was still popular until very recently. The Cockney comedian Arthur English, for example, was a master of incredibly rapidly spoken monologues, full of inconsequentialities. His monologues are, I believe, the antecedents of some of those which Mick has in Pinter's, *The Caretaker*, and of James's account of Hawkins in the same dramatist's play, *The Collection*.

To demonstrate this point I should like to give two extracts from *The Caretaker*. The first one deals particularly with people and their relationships. As given here, in isolation, the passage may seem to be no more than an incongruous digression in music-hall style; however, it is logically related to the concerns, and to the dramatic pattern, of the play as a whole.

MICK: You remind me of my uncle's brother. He was always on the move, that man. Never without his passport. Had an eye for the girls. Very much your build. Bit of an athlete. Long-jump specialist. He had a habit of demonstrating different run-ups in the drawing-room round about Christmas time. Had a penchant for nuts. Couldn't eat enough of them. Peanuts, walnuts, brazil nuts, monkey nuts, wouldn't touch a piece of fruit cake. Had a marvellous stop-watch. Picked it up in Hong Kong. The day after they chucked him out of the Salvation Army. Used to go in number four for Beckenham Reserves. That was before he got his Gold Medal. Had a funny habit of carrying his fiddle on his back. Like a papoose. I think there was a bit of the Red Indian in him. To be honest, I've never made out how he came to be my uncle's brother. I've often thought that maybe it was the other way round. I mean that my uncle was his brother and he was my uncle. But I never called him uncle. As a matter of fact I called him Sid. My mother called him Sid too. It was a funny business. Your splitting image he was. Married a Chinaman and went to Jamaica.

(*Pause*)

I hope you slept well last night.[5]

The second passage from *The Caretaker* makes use of legal jargon, rather after the manner of Arthur Roberts. Again, as in the previous example, the subject matter and technique are relevant to the whole play. Later in *The Caretaker* Davies is to feel, even more pointedly, the malignant 'injustice' of the law, as he feels it when Mick explains Aston's rights to the room.[6]

Mick is telling Davies the terms he will accept for the room and for the upper storey.

MICK: . . . Eight hundred odd for this room or three thousand down for the whole upper storey. On the other hand, if you prefer to approach it the long-term way I know an insurance firm in West Ham'll be pleased to handle the deal for you. No strings attached, open and above board, untarnished record; twenty per cent interest, fifty per cent deposit; down payments, back payments, family allowances, bonus schemes, remission of term for good behaviour, six months lease, yearly examination of the relevant archives, tea laid on, disposal of shares, benefit extension, compensation on cessation, comprehensive indemnity against Riot, Civil Commotion, Labour Disturbances, Storm, Tempest, Thunderbolt, Larceny or Cattle all subject to a daily check and double check. Of course we'd need a signed declaration from your personal medical attendant as assurance that you possess the requisite fitness to carry the can, won't we? Who do you bank with?

(*Pause*)

Who do you bank with?[7]

Another example of the monologue tradition in contemporary drama can be found in *The Birthday Party*. Behind Goldberg's description of his Uncle Barney there seems to hover the spirit of that portly comedian, Maxie Bacon: 'The secret is breathing. Take my tip. It's a well-known fact. Breathe in, breathe out, take a chance, let yourself go, what can you lose?'[8] Finally, there is, the appropriately named Hamm of Beckett's *Endgame*.[9] His attempts to tell a story are notable for their self-comment, for all the world like a man composing and trying out a music-hall monologue. . . .

SOURCE: extract from 'Contemporary Drama and Popular Dramatic Form', a lecture delivered in November 1963, reproduced in *Aspects of Drama and Theatre* (Sydney, 1965), pp. 160–7.

NOTES

[Renumbered and reorganised from the original]

1. M. Willson Disher, *Winkles and Champagne* (London, 1938), p. 31.
2. The extract from p. 31 of *The Caretaker*, quoted below [Mick's discourse on his uncle's brother] contains such a passage, and see also Hawkin's speech on p. 32 of *The Collection*.
3. A recording of this monologue, and of that by Arthur Roberts, has been issued as a long-playing record by the Delta Record Company, Ltd, London (Delta, TQD 3030). I have added some directions (in brackets and italics) to suggest how the Leno extract goes.
4. Disher, op. cit., p. 34.
5. Harold Pinter, *The Caretaker* (London, 1962), p. 31. This passage was spoken rapidly in the manner of Arthur English. All but the last line was given as if it were a monologue, and then, after the pause, changing to the legitimate convention for 'I hope you slept well last night.'
6. See *The Caretaker*, p. 71:
MICK: Yes. I could tell him to go. I mean, I'm the landlord. On the other hand, he's the sitting tenant. Giving him notice, you see, what it is, it's a technical matter, that's what it is. It depends how you regard this room. I mean it depends whether you regard this room as furnished or unfurnished. See what I mean?
DAVIES: No, I don't.
MICK: All this furniture, you see, in here, it's all his, except the beds, of course. So what it is, it's fine legal point, that's what it is.
7. *The Caretaker*, p. 36.
8. Harold Pinter, *The Birthday Party* (London, 1965), p. 27. This passage, to obtain the music-hall effect, requires to be said in the exaggerated Jewish music-hall fashion.
9. Samuel Beckett, *Endgame* (London, 1958), pp. 35–6.

Harold Pinter & Clive Donner 'Filming *The Caretaker*' (1963)

INTERVIEWED BY KENNETH CAVANDER

Harold Pinter's play, *The Caretaker* gave him his widest audience. It has now become his first film. Produced without guarantee of distribution, financed by private subscription, and shot entirely on location at the top of an old house in Hackney, it involved Pinter and his director, Clive Donner, in an exceptionally close and successful collaboration. Donner, editor of *Genevieve* and director of several major films, the latest of which was *Some People*, worked with Pinter from the beginning of the script. In April of this year [1963] they had reached the final stages of editing, and I went to visit them and find out their reactions to what had been, for both of them, a new experience.

CAVANDER: What experiences did you have with the film industry before *The Caretaker* film?

PINTER: Well, I've written an adaptation of a novel. Before I went into *The Caretaker* I'd only done that. I'd never been in a film studio except once as an extra.

CAVANDER: How did the idea of making *The Caretaker* start?

PINTER: Donald Pleasance had a great deal to do with it. But we all had it in mind, and then Donald, Bob Shaw and myself discussed it, and finally Donald got on to Clive about it.

DONNER: Yes, Donald asked me whether I thought a film of *The Caretaker* could be made, and how, and what it would cost. I said I thought a film could be made with a very economical budget, shooting on location, with very little adaptation, very little expansion of the play. As far as the budget was concerned, I said we could make it for £40,000. In fact it cost £30,000.

CAVANDER (to DONNER): Does that mean that in effect the initiative came from the actors and yourself?

DONNER: Yes, in a sense.

CAVANDER: And then what happened?

DONNER: We met Harold for luncheon one day . . .

PINTER: I paid for the lunch.

DONNER: He paid for the lunch. We said, 'We think a film could be made of this.'

PINTER: I was very suspicous.

DONNER: He was very suspicious.

CAVANDER (to PINTER): Had you been approached to make adaptations of your own work before?

PINTER: Yes, but I'd never agreed to anything.

CAVANDER: Why?

PINTER: The circumstances didn't seem right. I thought there were all sorts of things needed for film production which I wasn't prepared to deal with. And I was extremely reluctant to make a film of *The Caretaker* because I thought I couldn't possibly get anything fresh from the subject. I'd been associated with the play, you see, through various productions in London and New York for a couple of years.

CAVANDER: What persuaded you this time?

PINTER: It might have been something about . . . I don't know, the general common sense and relaxation of the people I met. I put up a lot of defence mechanisms about it, and said I could possibly even write the draft of a screenplay, couldn't do anything at all, and then someone said, 'You don't have to do anything' (though it turned out I did) . . . and I let myself be won over. I was behaving rather like a child about it.

DONNER: I think that's slightly unfair to say you've been behaving like a child. I think you were expecting a more conventional approach to the adaptation of the work.

CAVANDER (to PINTER): How did you get over this feeling of having worked through it?

PINTER: Well, I suppose it was because no one said to me, 'This is a film with a capital F.' That would have frightened me off, I think. They simply said, 'This is the idea, this is the work, these are the characters – how can it all be transposed into a film in keeping with what we have, what must be there.' We had long discussions about it and I worked out a kind of draft.

CAVANDER (to DONNER): Did you feel you were making the script from the beginning? Do you know what I mean?

DONNER: Not quite, no.

CAVANDER: Well, I suppose ideally one thinks of the director as working from the beginning, on the conception, and then through to the final screenplay. Ideally. Agreed?

DONNER: Well yes, but it very rarely happens. It's certainly not happened to me. Yet.

CAVANDER: Yes, and here you're faced with a script that is settled – not only settled but has been running for a long time. A *fait accompli*.

DONNER: Oh no, I don't think that's quite true.

CAVANDER: In what ways wasn't it true?

PINTER: Well, Clive and I did work intensively on the script when I really got excited about the idea. We saw it as a film, and we worked on it as a film. We weren't thinking about something that was set in any kind of pattern. There was an obvious overall pattern to the work, but we had to see it and work on it in terms of movement from one thing to another.

DONNER: And you see there's a sort of compulsion in film-makers to 'open out' (whatever that means) subjects that they set out to film. I decided from the beginning that this approach was a blind alley. It seemed to me that within the situation, and within the relationships that developed between the characters there was enough action, enough excitement seen through the eye of a film camera, without imposing conventional film action treatment.

PINTER: It seemed to me that when you have two people standing on the stairs and one asks the other if he would like to be caretaker in this house, and the other bloke, you know, who is work-shy, doesn't want in fact to say no, he doesn't want the job, but at the same time he wants to edge it round . . . Now it seems to me there's an enormous amount of internal conflict within one of the characters and external conflict between them – and it's exciting cinema.

DONNER: The fact that it doesn't cover enormous landscapes and there aren't hordes of horses galloping in one direction and hordes of bison in the other has nothing to do with it. It's a different sort of action, but it's still action. And it's still capable of being encompassed in the cinema.

PINTER: You can say the play has been 'opened out' in the sense that things I'd yearned to do, without knowing it, in writing for the stage, crystallised when I came to think about it as a film. Until then I didn't know that I wanted to do them because I'd accepted the limitations of the stage. For instance, there's a scene in the garden of the house, which is very silent; two silent figures with a third looking on. I think in the film one has been able to hit the relationship of the brothers more clearly than in the play.

DONNER: What I think Harold means when he says that the film has developed on what happened for him in the theatre, with particular reference to the relationship between the brothers, is that the psychological richness of the original play was to a certain extent hampered by the need to project out into a theatre.

PINTER: Yes, I think the actors on the stage are under the delusion that they have to project in a particular way. There's a scene in the film, also in the play when the elder brother asks him if he'd like to be caretaker in the place. On film it's played in terms of great intimacy and I think it's extraordinarily successful. They speak quite normally, it's a quiet scene, and it works. But on stage it didn't ever work like that. The actors get a certain kind of comfort, I think, in the fact that they're so close to the camera.

DONNER: The cinema obviously can deal with that very much more subtly and specifically. I think that the writing is such that *The Caretaker* isn't just a piece of theatre, but it can go further and further and discover more and more facts to the characters, so that rather than repeating what happened in the theatre one can enrich and develop it much more surely.

PINTER: I'm not sure I agree that the cinema will be able to gain in subtlety. I think that when one talks in these terms one thinks of a stage miles away with a vast audience and the characters very small. But I think you can be as subtle on a stage as you can in the film. You just do it in a different way. In this case the director understood what was necessary and what I, the fellow who had written it, meant. Which is a very rare thing. I'd always understood that everything is always bastardised in films, and that they were a real lot of fakes, phonies, charlatans. The whole relationship between the people concerned was something I hadn't quite met in any medium.

CAVANDER: So you had the script. Did you ever consider going through the normal production-distribution channels to make it?

PINTER: Yes, in fact we not only considered it, we were involved in it. We were right up to our necks in a very affable relationship with an American international distribution organisation, but at the last moment they pulled out.

DONNER: We'd also had a great deal of interest from certain sources in this country, but in the end they all got slightly cold feet – very cold feet. Then this American distributor pulled out, leaving us committed to crew, house, and various other expenditure.

CAVANDER: And that's the point where you collected the money by subscription.

DONNER: Well, we either had to dip into our pockets and pay everybody off, and not make the film, or we had to decide to go on and make the film. Peter Hall who'd been involved in the financial support of the stage production had said early on 'If you'd like some support from me on this I'd be happy to give it'. When this particular crisis occurred we took him up on that, and realised there was a possibility of raising the rest of the money, in the same way.

CAVANDER: Do you find that exhilarating as a way of doing things – or suspenseful – or just hell?

PINTER: My feelings were clear. I hated the whole dealing with the American company from the start. I distrusted it, and I was right to distrust it. They proved eminently untrustworthy, and good luck! I think part of their – excuse me, what I am saying? They *must* be untrustworthy otherwise they would cease to be respected . . . So we all sat down in a pub, and we had a marvellous name-dropping session of everyone we were going to write to, all the people who sympathised either with us personally or with the play. We wrote to them, we expressed terms in the letter, and we were over-subscribed. We turned away £60,000. We really thrust through, and what was suddenly clear about it was that each and every one of us wanted to do the film. It was a great moment, that. I was full of disgust and nausea and spleen and whisky, and we could so easily have said 'To hell with the whole thing. What's the point?' I could certainly. It was confirming my darkest suspicion about the film industry. But we didn't . . .

DONNER: And it wasn't only Harold. It was Mike Birkett, and Donald Pleasance and . . .

PINTER: Not only that. If we're going to indulge in a bit of remembrance – I remember so well that the continuity girl who was down there at the time, engaged by our company, such as it was, a very rocky company, she suddenly, sitting in this pub, offered to put in some money.

CAVANDER: How long did it take to collect the total?

PINTER: I think from the time we decided it was about a fortnight.

CAVANDER: So then you were ready to go.

DONNER: Well, during this period we were in fact already rehearsing, and we spent two, three days of our rehearsal time sitting round scratching our heads. So that although we went forward with a certain amount of renewed confidence, once we'd decided on the thing, each time that Michael Birkett came upstairs into the room where we were rehearsing with another telephone message, another telegram saying that Noel Coward or somebody or other had come forward, it was very exciting . . . and frequently stimulating.

CAVANDER: But you got it all before you started shooting?

PINTER: Yes, we had assured promises of all the money before we started shooting.

CAVANDER: Apart from this crisis while you were rehearsing, the thing went more or less as scheduled?

PINTER: Yes, except we lost a few days sitting round eating salt beef sandwiches.

DONNER: If anybody had come forward then, and offered the amount of money that would have made it possible for us to shoot the film in a studio, or in a more lavish way, I wouldn't have taken it.

CAVANDER: Did you ever think you might do it in a studio?

DONNER: No, Never!

PINTER: I wish the actors were here to ask, but I'm sure that for them it was tremendous – I'm sorry to say this, it sounds rather strange, almost as if I'm asking for realism, which I'm not – but I think it did an awful lot for the actors to go up real stairs, open real doors in a house which existed, with a dirty garden and a back wall.

CAVANDER: You were there every minute of the shooting?

PINTER: Not entirely. I arrived late quite often.

DONNER: I think Harold was there most of the time.

PINTER: I don't know whether other script writers are there to the extent I was.

CAVANDER: How did you react to it?

PINTER: As a complete layman to the film medium I found that looking round that room where one had to crouch to see what was going on (the whole film was shot in a kneeling or crouching posture) – I found there was a smell to it. Since then I've been down to a studio, Shepperton, and things are very different. You don't have to crouch, you don't have to kneel, you can absolutely stand up straight, there are lots of lights, the walls open, they float, that's the word, float, and you've got no worries at all. Well, I found the limitations on location, in this house, gave a freshness to the work. I think the actors found that too. They found new answers, answers they hadn't been able to find or at least hadn't within the circumstances been able to find when they were playing it on the stage.

DONNER: And on location like this house I find one is dealing in tones of grey. There are no blacks and whites. The sets, the photography, are seen in terms of grey (rather than in terms of black . . .).

PINTER: What I'm very pleased about myself is that in the film, as opposed to the play, we see a real house and real snow outside, dirty snow, and the streets. We don't see them very often but they're there, the backs of houses and windows, attics in the distance. There is actually sky as well, a dirty one, and these characters move in the context of a real world – as I believe they do. In the play, when people were confronted with just a set, a room and a door, they often assumed it was all taking place in limbo, in a vacuum, and the world outside hardly existed, or had existed at some point but was only half remembered. Now one thing which I think is triumphantly expressed in the film is Clive's concentration on the characters when they are outside the room, outside the house. Not that there aren't others. There are others. There are streets, there is traffic, shadows, shapes about, but he is for me concentrating on the characters as they walk, and while we go into the world outside it is almost as if only these characters exist.

CAVANDER: What struck me just now was your thoroughness in following the film through the editing stages.

PINTER: Well, this editing stage was for me, of course, completely new. It was the first time, and an absolute eye-opener.

CAVANDER: I can see you were enjoying it.

PINTER: It's great. It's great that one can move from one thing to another, or duplicate it, or cut it out, the wreck that can be wreaked in editing.

DONNER: Havoc, you mean.

PINTER: The havoc, yes, the havoc is terrifying.

CAVANDER: But you must have been involved in television productions, and to that extent you must have had some feeling for what happened and what you could do. You know what pictures roughly you're going to use, in about the same way as you know in a film.

PINTER: But it's very primitive. All that's open to you is just a position of sequences, or possibly cuts, but you haven't got the flexibility that you have in films. For instance in this particular play, there was a moment on stage when the two brothers smiled at each other. That was it. One stood on one side of the stage and the other stood on the other, and they smiled briefly.

CAVANDER: That was written into the text?

PINTER: Oh yes. And then one of them existed and that was that. Now, on film, either you're going to hold both things, in other words, the two brothers smiling, then one goes out. But it isn't the same as the stage, you don't get the complex thing which makes it so much of a moment on the stage. The distance, the separation cannot be the same. The balance, the timing, and the rhythm to this, the silent music, as it were, are determined in so many different ways, and I know we both felt, Clive and I, there was something to come there. I said something, I don't know what, and Clive said, 'We want to go from one to the other, one to the other, to the other'. Now the balance of the whole thing is that if you don't go to the other then there's no point made, but if you go from the other back to the first then the point is overmade. The balance, the editing balance, is crucial, as everyone knows, but it needs an eye and a relaxation which the film affords you, and no other medium can. You can sift it, you see, and the sifting is of value. Of course, on the stage, you can say to the girl, 'Go out, this won't do, try another one . . .' and if you make a decision and you're proved wrong you correct it. But in films you're dealing with something that's going to be finished once you make a decision. You cannot go on changing ad infinitum, and you may make a decision and six months later you say, 'That was entirely wrong'.

DONNER: This is very interesting about such a moment as the smile. To a certain extent, in the theatre, one entrusts the satisfactory presentation of this moment entirely to the actors. You expect that they have either consciously or intuitively sensed the way an audience is going with them and the play at a particular moment, and they can infinitely adjust their performance each night, to each audience. Now one of the things that actors feel terribly strongly about in the cinema is that their performances are taken out of their hands. They resent this, and I understand it completely. It seems to me a miserable thing to have to accept, particularly with the sort of actors we have in this film, who are extremely intelligent men, extremely successful, extremely creative. They do it, then they go away to other films, other projects, and leave us with the film to edit in a way that ultimately we have to take a decision on alone. Well, as Harold says, you may decide at this moment that one thing is right, and six months later you see it, and you say, 'I was wrong' – and actors, alas, have to accept this.

PINTER: Surely with this film, all the actors would subscribe to what is being done. Because we weren't asking them merely to go on there and give their performances as such; we were asking to examine how you should give your performance in relation to producing a finished film.

DONNER: To take creative responsibility, which is the aim of all these ventures, I think.

CAVANDER: So now the thing's done. Do you know how, or when, it will come out?

PINTER: Well, not precisely, no. It'll be shown, that's all I know at the moment.

DONNER: There's not much we can say about this, except that I think this piece is not solely an art-house-film, or need not be.

CAVANDER: In other words, you don't want it to be.

DONNER: Well, I don't think it need be, because from my own experience of seeing audiences react to the play, both in London and New York, I know that much wider audiences than would be reached by an art-house release, enjoyed the play. But at the same time I think it would be very wrong to put this film out on ordinary general release – for two reasons. One, because I think the piece, by its nature, demands a concentration, a special attention which even unsophisticated audiences coming in coach tours to the Duchess Theatre in London brought with them – by virtue of the fact that they'd made a special journey to be there. Now, I don't think that people going out to their local cinema will make that same special effort, and I think the piece does require an effort for an audience to appreciate, to be able to enjoy it. And I think the other reason why I would not like a general release is because I think it would be very bad if after all the hooha of a full general release, it failed. Not only for its own sake, but because I think it would then tend to muck up the chances of another film that we or anybody else might make, and which might demand less of its audience than this. I think somewhere between a full general release and limited arthouse release there is a market for *The Caretaker* which I would like to find.

CAVANDER: So what you're trying to do is trace this special audience.

DONNER: Well, I would just like to have it exposed to a wider audience than an art-house audience, but not be lumbered with the full heavy-weight responsibilities of exploitation costs and print costs which a full circuit release implies.

CAVANDER: How do you expect to do this?

DONNER: I think it can be done by cinemas agreeing to show it in certain locations where they know or suspect or are prepared to try and find out that there is an audience prepared to make the effort to come and see this film, and to enjoy it.

CAVANDER (to PINTER): Have you discussed any of this, or doesn't it interest you?

PINTER: Yes, it does interest me. But I think myself the work has been preserved in film, I think it's perfectly true to what I wrote, and I think it's funny. But really I simply feel that whatever happens with it, a lot of people are going to see it, and I can only come down again to the fact that what absolutely amazes me is that there it is. It's been done and as far as I'm concerned it's absolutely on the nail.

CAVANDER: So in a sense the kind of classification and squaring off that is done by the press and formers of public opinion no longer matters.

PINTER: Who cares? We all did it for nothing at all, not money, no conveniences, public conveniences, no facilities, the food was bloody awful, the curry was the same as the steak and kidney pudding, and I think it's been worth doing.

SOURCE: interview-article in *Transatlantic Review*, 13 (June 1963), pp. 17–26.

John Russell Brown   'Gesture and Movement'
(1972)

... The beginning of *The Caretaker* is defined wholly by movement; not a word is spoken in the first episode:

MICK: *is alone in the room, sitting on the bed. He wears a leather jacket.*
Silence.
He slowly looks about the room looking at each object in turn. He looks up at the ceiling, and stares at the bucket. Ceasing, he sits quite still, expressionless, looking out front.
Silence for thirty seconds.

The best way to appreciate what Pinter is requiring from his actor is for the reader to perform the actions for himself. Look at many individual objects '*in turn*'. Do this at first with ordinary speed, and then fulfil the direction to do it 'slowly'. Remember that the process is completed by looking up – at the bucket that '*hangs from the ceiling*'. This conclusion of motion results in silence during which the actor must be '*quite still, expressionless, looking out front*'. Small, purposive gestures, taken 'in turn' as if in accordance with a specific order or routine, lead to less, not greater, physical statement. If the reader gives sufficient time to this enactment, he will realize the actor's necessity of discovering *how* to cease movement so completely: it is a silent change of engagement, requiring a change of purpose and of consciousness. Is Mick satisfied with what he sees, and therefore has nothing to do but wait for something of greater importance? But if so, why is he '*expressionless*'? Is he uninterested in the outcome, or unable to imagine it? Is he consciously choosing to be inexpressive, as a trick or game, or as a training exercise? Does it imply strength or weakness?

Thirty seconds is an appreciable time for the silence to be held, so that when the drama takes a new turn from a direction outside Mick's gaze, it will sharpen attention in the audience:

> *Silence for thirty seconds.*
> *A door bangs. Muffled voices are heard.*
> MICK *turns his head. He stands, moves silently to the door, goes out, and closes the door quietly.*
> *Silence.*
> *Voices are heard again. They draw nearer, and stop. The door opens.* ASTON *and* DAVIES *enter,* ASTON *first,* DAVIES *following, shambling, breathing heavily.*

Mick's privacy is disturbed, but he ackowledges this only by moving his head: he displays almost the smallest possible reaction. In contrast to the door banging outside, he moves '*silently*' and closes the door after him '*quietly*'. In effect, this is an answer to a challenge coming from outside the room. But the audience having followed the sequence of Mick's behaviour, will still wait for a confrontation as he goes out the door. Pinter has prepared this expectation, but he thwarts it, for the stage-direction calls for another '*Silence*', not a greeting. At this point '*Voices are heard again*', coming nearer and then stopping. All eyes will be on the door as it opens: but two entirely new figures now enter. They are physically contrasted, for the second is '*shambling, breathing heavily*'. Neither betrays any sign that they have met the man who has just left.

Perhaps the audience will not consciously ask where Mick has gone, and why, nor who he was, for now their attention is held by the new contrasting pair. The one in the lead is silent like Mick, but showing purposive action as he '*puts the key in his pocket and closes the door*'. The other is not silent, but '*breathing heavily*': he will therefore draw more attention and will be seen to do what Mick had done for the direction concludes: 'DAVIES *looks about the room*'. The repetition is with a difference, for he does *not* look at individual objects '*in turn*'.

By refusing all clearly audible words, by arranging repetitions and contrasts, by encouraging expectation of a meeting and then disappointing it, and, in the figure of Mick who has now left the stage, by requiring unexpected actions, each less expressive or less dynamic than normal, Pinter has forced the audience to look closely. He has repaid them with a questioning involvement that will be the greater and more unsettling with every point they catch.

Having gained visual attention, Pinter now sustains it by words in support. The two figures are heard (as they have been seen) in relationship to the room and to each other:

ASTON: Sit down.
DAVIES: Thanks. (*Looking about*) Uuh . . .
ASTON: Just a minute.
 (ASTON *looks around for a chair, sees one lying on its side by the rolled carpet at the fireplace, and starts to get it out.*)
DAVIES: Sit down? Huh . . . I haven't had a good sit down . . . I haven't had a proper sit down . . . well, I couldn't tell you . . .
ASTON (*placing the chair*): Here you are.
DAVIES: Ten minutes off for a tea-break in the middle of the night in that place and I couldn't find a seat, not one. All them Greeks had it, Poles, Greeks, Blacks, the lot of them, all them aliens had it. And they had me working there . . . they had me working . . .
 (ASTON *sits on the bed, takes out a tobacco tin and papers, and begins to roll himself a cigarette.* DAVIES *watches him.*)
All them Blacks had it, Blacks, Greeks, Poles, the lot of them, that's what, doing me out of a seat, treating me like dirt. When he come at me tonight I told him.
 (*Pause.*)
ASTON: Take a seat.
DAVIES: Yes, but what I got to do first, you see, what I got to do, I got to loosen myself up, you see what I mean? I could have got done in down there. [pp. 7–8]

The suggestion that Davies should 'Sit down' provokes 'Thanks', but also a repetition of his '*Looking about*' together with an inarticulate 'Uuh . . .'. Aston interprets this as looking for a chair and – looking '*around*' with simple purpose – he gets a chair from the various piles of possessions that fill the room. He places it, with 'Here you are', but Davies does not sit down; he talks of the need for a 'sit down', but he does not make the expected movement. Instead, he changes the subject of talk which makes the physical refusal still more noticeable. Aston sits on a bed, making no difficulty of being seated, and at once is silent, concentrating his attention on rolling a cigarette, a physical activity that is small in scale and has a very narrow focus of attention.

In effect, Aston cuts himself off from Davies, but now 'DAVIES *watches him*' and still does not sit, even on the quite specific 'Take a seat'.

Until this moment, Pinter has held attention on Davies's refusal to accept the offered (and desired) comfort, on his unease, and lack of physical purpose beyond suspicion of the room and then of Aston, but he now gives him a decisive physical action, accompanied by a loud but incoherent cry:

> (DAVIES *exclaims loudly, punches downward with closed fist, turns his back to* ASTON *and stares at the wall. Pause.* ASTON *lights a cigarette.*)
> ASTON: You want to roll yourself one of these?
> DAVIES (*turning*): What? No, no, I never smoke a cigarette. (*Pause. He comes forward.*) I'll tell you what, though. I'll have a bit of that tobacco there for my pipe, if you like.
>
> [p. 8]

Within Davies there was, from the beginning of the scene, some kind of aggressive energy which is expressed only in his talk (with short, piled-up rhythm) and in small physical reactions of fear and suspicion. When an inescapable offer of comfort is made, he resists until the last possible moment; but then he recalls the fight that has just taken place, and the need for self-defence, and the violence comes to the surface in the punch and cry, and the turn away from Aston.

Aston's response to the sudden activity is almost as unexpected. He must have been concentrating on rolling his cigarette with such intensive purpose that Davies's violence doen not distract him. (Later in the play he repeatedly takes pride in being good 'with his hands'.) He proceeds to light his cigarette and follows his earlier purpose by making another offer to his visitor. Davies now turns and, after a refusal and a pause, '*comes forward*' with a counter-suggestion and an acceptance.

An actor who needs to give coherence and believability to his part will have prepared for Davies's violent outburst or Aston's concentration on his cigarette. All the earlier movements and gestures will have been made in an incomplete or unbalanced way, so that these developments were implicit in them, through tensions or 'shadow movements' too small to be noticed by any but the most observant and trained in the audience. When the strong gestures come at last, they will thus be credible and inevitable, made with the authority that springs from the expression of a hitherto suppressed truth. This delayed assurance is a part of the performances that will be responded to by the audience, even if they do not consciously notice or identify it.

After the acceptance of the tobacco, Davies and Aston talk more extensively. At one point, Davies '*shambles across the room*'; but even when he comes '*face to face*' with the Buddha sitting incongruously, and thus questioningly, on the gas-stove, he simply '*looks at it and turns*'. Soon he is '*Coming closer*' to Aston again, now in a boasting vein. When he finishes his speech, which seems to demand some sort of response in acknowledgement of Davies's rights, Aston simply says, 'Uh', and then '*crosses down right, to get the electric toaster*' [p. 9]. Nothing in the dialogue explains, or even refers to this action; nor to the unscrewing of the plug, the fetching of another, and the refixing that follows. Aston continues '*poking*' into the plug, through various diversions, until the end of the first episode of the play. When Davies goes to bed and the '*Lights fade out*', Aston is still sitting with the plug and screwdriver in his hand [p. 21]. His only verbal acknowledgement of all this activity is just before the end, when, in answer to Davies's inquiry whether he is getting in bed, he says 'I'm mending this plug' and Davies '*looks at him and then at the gas stove*'.[1] The activity with the toaster is thus given great prominence: the audience is forced to notice it and to observe its importance to Aston. The actor must enact it so that it is a recurring, continuous and, often, overriding concern. The particular posture, the small, 'probing' gestures, and the intensely focused concentration of Aston's attention, will make their verbally unheralded effect. When verbal explanation does come, it will seem insufficient: there is still no answer to why he is mending the plug at this time, with this persistence.

Two kinds of statement are being made here through gesture and movement. One concerns an individual's motivation, the other the relationship between two figures and between them and the room. The statements are co-existent, but not even the individual statements can be fully appreciated from this extract alone. Davies's violence is a preparation for the two occasions when he draws a knife, once in self-defence and once in aggression, both much later in the play. Together these gestures sustain the underlying danger of his apparently pliant and shifty nature. Aston's cigarette-rolling and lighting prepares for his attention to the toaster and its plugs, and together these all look forward to his talk about an electric fire and to his repeated returns to the toaster. This involvment is never wholly explained, but it is significant that it stops once he has rejected Davies from his room the second time and is determined to get 'busy' with the shed in the garden [p. 76]; then he turns his back on both Davies and the toaster in order to look out of the window to the garden where the shed will be built. In some way, the toaster seems to be connected with Aston's interest in Davies, a defence against him and, possibly, consciously or unconsciously, an attack.

In a long speech at the end of Act II, noticeably without action or gesture, Aston speaks of being forced to have shock treatment in a mental hospital. He says that he had had to be quiet for a time after his escape, talking to no one so that he could lay everything 'out in order'. In hospital, he says, they had brought some electrical appliances round to him:

> they looked like big pincers, with wires on, the wires were attached to a little machine. It was electric. They used to hold the man down, and this chief . . . the chief doctor, used to fit the pincers, something like earphones, he used to fit them on either side of the man's skull . . .   [p. 56]

In short, when he was being cared for in hospital, he was treated as he now treats his toaster.

In some way Aston associates his electrical appliance with revenge – 'I've often thought of going back and trying to find the man who did that to me' [p. 57] – and with 'taking care' of Davies. This, perhaps, is why he broke his self-confessed rules, did not 'steer clear of places like that café', and did talk to a stranger, one who was already being attacked. Behind the apparently trivial gestures of the first episode of the play, a conscious or subconscious intention to murder seems to be implied in the small tensions and half-hidden impulses created by the actor to account for his strange actions and to give cohesion to his role. There are other correspondences between this hospital speech and unexplained activity that Aston makes in the presence of Davies: why did he have a sheet and pillow ready for his visitor's bed? Why make him don a white coat as caretaker, one that hung ready by his bed? Why have a glaring light over Davies's bed? Why wake him up and examine his face? All these actions are paralleled by what Aston says, or infers, had happened in the hospital. Through the emphasis of oddity and repetition, and through surprising interplay with words, Aston's silent activity will catch the audience's attention, perhaps without them being able to pinpoint or name them as the source of their apprehension for the safety of Davies and of Aston.

In shorter compass, Mick also has gestures in this first episode that must be given precise meaning by an actor. Only a sense of committal to some unspoken purpose will explain his stealthy exit, his lack of surprise, his stillness. Does he expect Aston to find a victim? Does he 'take care' of his brother, by allowing him to 'take care' of himself by finding an unknown victim? An actor will need to know, for it is far harder, if not impossible, to act such details without some sustaining 'through line' of intention and some cohesive purpose and 'natural effort disposition'. Again, the 'meaning' of these gestures depends on

Mick's role as a whole. In his last appearance in the play, when he has smashed his brother's Buddha, crying 'THAT'S WHAT I WANT!', and has passionately asserted that he has his other worries, he denies interest in the house and Aston:

> I'm not worried about this house. I'm not interested. My brother can worry about it.
> . . . I'm not bothered. I thought I was doing him a favour, letting him live here. He's got
> his own ideas. Let him have them. I'm going to chuck it in.   [p. 74]

Again '*A door bangs*' and in the ensuing silence neither Mick nor Davies moves:

> (ASTON *comes in. He closes the door, moves into the room and faces* MICK. *They look at each other. Both are smiling, faintly.*)

Here is the confrontation missing in the first episode, and together they silently express complicity and satisfaction. Mick is about to speak, but leaves instead; and then:

> (ASTON *leaves the door open, crosses behind* DAVIES, *sees the broken Buddha, and looks at the pieces for a moment. He then goes to his bed, takes off his overcoat, sits, takes the screwdriver and plug and pokes the plug.*)

Significant changes are that Aston leaves the door open, that he ignores the Buddha, which he had been pleased to get 'hold of' [p. 18], moves straight to the plug, and does not bother to speak to either Davies or Mick. The relationships between the brothers are clearly revalued by this resumption of silence and this assumption of independence. Within Mick's first, unsmiling silence there must have been the possibility of this other relationship. If the last one is to be true, some tensions must have been contained in the first, waiting to be resolved; or else tensions must develop, so that, even after his '*passionate*' outburst, Mick is under some constraint as he leaves Aston in possession.

Pinter is aware that physical performance expresses inner conflicts and resolutions. He insists that the verbal drama yield at times to silent passages where the audience is forced to look, and so to perceive impulses and reactions that would be altered out of all recognition or just proportion had they been expressed in words. If this physical language is seldom precise, that is one of its strengths, for many of the deepest and most irresistible human impulses are not easily limited or defined: it is these motivations that Pinter wishes to explore and show in his plays. The inter-play between physical and verbal drama, whether by contrast or correspondence, strengthens expressions of the indefinable, gives it associations and enforces attention.

SOURCE: extract from *Theatre Language: A Study of Arden, Osborne, Pinter and Wesker* (London, 1972), pp. 60–70.

NOTE

1. In the first version of the play (1960), Aston also explained that the plug 'doesn't work' and that he had a 'suspicion' of the 'root of the trouble'; in the second version (1962), five speeches are cut, and Aston's business with the plug is left more vague.

Austin Quigley   'Linguistic Relationships'
(1975)

The stage set for *The Caretaker*, like that for *The Room*, is a shabby, all-purpose room, but there is an important contrast between the two settings: the objects surrounding Rose function clearly in a fixed pattern of life with Bert, but those surrounding Aston seem largely random. The stage is littered with things; boxes, vases, paint buckets, a stepladder, a lawn mower, a shopping trolley, a coal bucket, and a statue of Buddha are strewn around the room. Even apparently functional objects like the kitchen sink and the gas stove are reduced to random stature by their lack of proximity to a water pipe or a gas supply. Far from evoking a highly structured life, this setting suggests not only a lack of such structure but a breakdown of more usual connections. The possibility of discovering or imposing order and pattern on this environment is a constant counterpoint to the efforts of the characters to establish significant structures in their own relationships. The potential links between the characters are as tentative and exploratory as those between the various objects that Aston keeps bringing home; a new object, like a newcomer, provides different possibilities of permutation among what is already at hand.

The play develops from the new alternatives that Davies's arrival provides. Before his arrival there is a relationship between Aston and his brother Mick which centres on the junk-cluttered room. Whatever benefits and liabilities that relationship involves for each of them is set in opposition to the new possibilities that emerge. A third person entering a binary relationship sets up a situation that demands not only new relationships with the newcomer but also an adjustment of the relationship that holds between the original pair. The common ground, the common reality, the common language between three people must inevitably differ from that between the original two. Instead of examining this readjustment largely from the point of view of one of the participants, as in *The Room*, Pinter here gives considerable attention to the needs, hopes, and problems of all three characters.

In widening his focus, Pinter also widens the scope of interrelational complexity. While the characters in *The Room* employ a largely similar range of verbal strategies, the characters in *The Caretaker* are differentiated by diverse linguistic abilities as well as by a diversity of goals. As the play progresses it becomes increasingly clear that the conflicting concerns of the characters are inextricably intertwined with verbal vulnerability and verbal power. The linguistic ability to create and sustain a social identity becomes a focus of thematic concern as the liabilities as well as the benefits of particular abilities gradually emerge.

. . . the duologue provides the basic structural unit of this play. In these duologues, four alternatives are explored as the three characters seek to order their new situation: (1) The three can establish a relationship that includes them all. (2) Aston and Davies can exclude Mick. (3) Mick and Davies can exclude Aston. (4) Mick and Aston can exclude Davies. These alternatives constantly underlie the struggles for control, which are presented in a series *à deux*. An important indication of the progress of a particular binary relationship is the kind of attitude toward the absent member that individuals attempt to establish as a common ground of their relationship. The play falls into fourteen sections when based on these duologues, and the several sections are linked by the fixed locale, the constant presence of Davies, and a series of recurring motifs.[1]

Section 1: Davies and Aston (pp. 7–21)

. . . Throughout Act II and Act III frequent reference is made to whichever member of the trio is absent at any given time. As the new situation presented by Davies's arrival involves an adjustment for all three characters, any adjustment between any pair must affect and be affected by the third person. Thus Pinter makes an effort to get Mick involved in Act I even though it is largely devoted to the embryonic relationship between Davies and Aston. For this reason, Act I begins with Mick briefly alone in the room prior to Davies's and Aston's arrival and ends in mid-scene with Mick once more onstage. While Mick says nothing at the opening of the play, his appearance adds an important perspective to the succeeding events. He spends some moments gazing slowly round the junk-littered room 'looking at each object in turn' [p. 7]. And this, of course, leads the audience to do the same. His rapid exit upon hearing the approach of voices leaves his link with the house and its occupants unspecified but established – a type of link which is reflected in the clutter onstage and which becomes characteristic of the play as a whole.

The Davies/Aston relationship immediately picks up on this motif as the characters enter together and begin to converse. While such joint activity is frequently evidence of a degree of common ground it soon becomes apparent that in this case such common ground is, at best, minimal. But more important, it also becomes apparent that the degree of concern that this generates is markedly different for each of the two characters. Though the fact of a link between the two characters seems to be mutually agreed upon, the nature of that link remains highly tentative, and Davies seems much less able to cope with this uncertainty than is Aston. In this discrepancy we encounter the first manifestation of the difficulties that the play ultimately focuses upon.

The Davies/Aston relationship begins with Aston apparently in command of the situation as both host and rescuer of the itinerant Davies. His calm, quiet acceptance of the uneasy guest seems a natural posture of superiority, and Davies at first accepts it as such. As both guest and rescued, Davies, in contrast to Aston, is noisy, repetitive and insecure. The evident aim of his early initiatives is to locate a potential common ground and preferably one that will lessen his degree of dependency in the relationship. Ironically, his insecurity is increased by the very means that he adopts to diminish it. The fact that it is he, and not Aston, who feels compelled to talk undermines his position at the same time that his verbal maneuvers seek to strengthen it.

DAVIES: Sit down? Huh . . . I haven't had a good sit down . . . I haven't had a proper sit down . . . well, I couldn't tell you . . .
ASTON (*placing the chair*): Here you are.
DAVIES: Ten minutes off for a tea-break in the middle of the night in that place and I couldn't find a seat, not one. All them Greeks had it, Poles, Greeks, Blacks, the lot of them, all them aliens had it. And they had me working there. . . . All them Blacks had it, Blacks, Greeks, Poles, the lot of them, that's what, doing me out of a seat, treating me like dirt. When he come at me tonight I told him.
    (*Pause.*)
ASTON: Take a seat.   [pp. 7–8]

That Davies should invoke in rapid succession a sense of injury, a major prejudice, and a defiant self-reliance gives us a quick resumé of the potential roles he might adopt relative to Aston. That Aston ignores all three, providing neither sympathy for the first, reinforcement for the second, nor admiration for the third gives us an immediate indication of the likelihood of their success.

Aston's seeming refusal to encourage any of Davies's tentative roles provides Davies with major problems. In the face of Aston's taciturnity he is forced to thresh around desperately for some means of altering the situation. It soon becomes apparent that his large supply of words is not matched by a similar supply of verbal strategies. As the conversation progresses he simply resorts to repeated use of the tactics implicit in his first speech. Appeals to Aston's sympathy and to his prejudices recur repeatedly, though Davies is smart enough to defend himself against becoming a victim of the kinds of prejudice to which he feels himself vulnerable:

All them toe-rags, mate, got the manners of pigs. I might have been on the road a few years but you can take it from me I'm clean. I keep myself up. That's why I left my wife. Fortnight after I married her, no, not so much as that, no more than a week, I took the lid off a saucepan, you know what was in it? A pile of her underclothing, unwashed. The pan for vegetables, it was. The vegetable pan. That's when I left her and I haven't seen her since. [p. 9]

As he finishes speaking he finds himself to face to face with a 'statue of Buddha standing on the gas stove'. The mutual incompatibility of the stone face and that of the tramp comments directly on the success of these efforts to manipulate Aston's attitudes and concerns. The silent inscrutable Buddha, incongruously perched on the gas stove, is as much beyond Davies's comprehension as the taciturn Aston surrounded by the diverse objects collected in his room.

Davies's other category of approaches involves attempts to assert a degree of independence from Aston. But his efforts to create an image of self-reliance are even less successful than his previous moves and not entirely compatible with them. His appeals for sympathy for his age and health mingle uneasily with assertions that he intends revenge for his misuse at the café: 'I'll get him. One night I'll get him. When I find myself around that direction' [p. 10]. The strength of this commitment is clearly undermined by Davies's vague reference to when it will occur and by his admission that this would not be his primary reason for going there.

In spite of these repeated failures, Davies's stock of variations on his maneuvers is not yet exhausted. Indeed, he has yet to play his trump card. Unsuccessful as the heroic survivor of the café incident, unsung as the virtuous rejector of an unhygienic wife, and unsympathised with as a downtrodden, exploited old man, he invokes a new image of one on the verge of self-sufficiency and success. The tack is circuitous, involving shoes, the weather, a false name, and papers that will 'prove everything' [p. 20]. But, in essence, the theme is that of a journey to Sidcup which will solve all problems and structure his life anew. Once the journey is made all difficulties will disappear, and Davies will once more be a man to be reckoned with:

> DAVIES: If only I could get down to Sidcup! I've been waiting for the weather to break. He's got my papers, this man I left them with, it's got it all down there, I could prove everything.
> ASTON: How long's he had them?
> DAVIES: What?
> ASTON: How long's he had them?
> DAVIES: Oh, must be . . . it was in the war . . . must be . . . about near on fifteen year ago.
> *(He suddenly becomes aware of the bucket and looks up.)*   [pp. 20–1]

But this maneuver, too, is thwarted by Aston's reactions to it. Clearly, Davies does not match his emphasis on the importance of the journey with a similar commitment to getting there. The time lag he admits to makes nonsense of the value he places on the journey, and Aston's puzzlement is evident. Once again the haphazard dialogue is matched revealingly with an item of junk that is eminently visible but obliquely connected to its surroundings.

At this point, Aston's contribution to the 'conversation' seems rather unfriendly, to say the least. Whatever Davies does to try to improve the connection between himself and Aston is neutralised by his inability to elicit from Aston the responses he needs. To Davies it seems that Aston's posture of quiet superiority is a consistent strategic imperviousness to his needs and wiles. But Aston's behavior seems peculiarly inconsistent. His apparent unconcern for Davies's psychological needs is sharply contrasted with an evident concern for his physical needs. Aston's initial generosity toward Davies in the café is extended by offers of cigarettes, shoes and money, and by a willingness to go and retrieve Davies's belongings for him. This inconsistency, this apparent lack of connection between two aspects of Aston's behavior, is another manifestation of juxtaposed but unclearly linked data in the play. But its effect on the relationship is by no means unclear; this inconsistency disorients Davies and maintains his subservience as effectively as Mick's later inconsistent conversation. As this section progresses, however, it gradually becomes apparent that Aston's efforts (unlike Mick's) are not deliberately aimed at this goal. Indeed, it is very difficult at this point to perceive a deliberate aim in any of Aston's behavior. It does seem clear, however, that he does not share Davies's urgent need for a verbally explicit rapport.

The problem the audience has in understanding Aston is obviously shared by Davies. Sensing the failure of his efforts to impose on Aston any of the relationship roles he has in mind, Davies eventually switches to trying to draw out of Aston information that might guide him to more successful maneuvers. Feeding him topics dealing with the room and its contents, Davies once more finds himself making little headway:

DAVIES: You got any more rooms then, have you?
ASTON: Where?
DAVIES: I mean, along the landing here . . . up the landing there.
ASTON: They're out of commission.
DAVIES: Get away.
ASTON: They need a lot of doing to.
    (*Slight pause.*)
DAVIES: What about downstairs?
ASTON: That's closed up. Needs seeing to . . . The floors . . .
    (*Pause.*)   [pp. 11–12]

Aston's unwillingness to discuss any of these more neutral topics suggests that his reluctance to converse with Davies is motivated by something more than mere resistance to Davies's wiles; the reluctance seems to proceed from a general antipathy toward any kind of conversation. But, paradoxically, he is not entirely unwilling to talk. While evasive about the house and his legal relationship to it, he does venture the information that he 'might build' a shed in the back garden. This willingness to talk is further indicated by a sudden longer statement on the drinking of Guinness – a topic that he discusses with a seriousness that does little to calm the puzzled, uneasy Davies:

    (*Pause.*)
I went into the pub the other day. Ordered a Guinness. They gave it to me in a thick mug. I sat down but I couldn't drink it. I can't drink Guinness from a thick mug. I only like it out of a thin glass.[2] I had a few sips but I couldn't finish it.   [p. 19]

This relates to nothing previously discussed, and whatever significance it has for Aston is not shared by Davies, who resorts to a quick change of subject.

The short speech is undoubtedly odd, but the kind of oddity it represents provides the first clear indication of the basic difficulty confronting the pair. If Davies fails to respond to or follow up on this topic because he is unable to locate its significance, perhaps this is also the reason for Aston's similar reactions to Davies's conversation topics. The speech itself, while specifying nothing precisely, undermines Davies's operating assumption that Aston's taciturnity is simply a manifestation of superiority and disinterest. Such an assumption has already been brought into question by Aston's non-verbal generosity to Davies, and this speech suggests that Aston, in spite of his general silence, also has a need to talk. The section ends with Aston, as he has done extensively during this opening scene, devoting his attention to a faulty plug on an old electric toaster. His persistent concern for this faulty connection characterises the activity of the opening section: potential links between the characters remain uncertain because the means of establishing appropriate connections has gone awry.

DAVIES: I used to know a bootmaker in Acton. He was a good mate to me.
    (*Pause.*)
You know what that bastard monk said to me?
    (*Pause.*)
How many more Blacks you got around here then? [p. 14]

. . .

SOURCE: extracts from ch. IV of *The Pinter Problem* (Princeton, N.J., 1975), pp. 113–15, 115–22.

NOTES

[Reorganised and renumbered from the original]

1. [Ed.] Quigley examines each of these sections in turn. In the space available in the excerpting here it is possible to include discussion only of the first section.
2. The Grove Press edition of 1965 of *The Caretaker* misprints 'thin' as 'tin' in this speech, p. 19.

Ronald Knowles   The 'Point' of Laughter
(1979)

The initial reviews of Harold Pinter's *The Caretaker* generally followed a pattern: the brilliance of the actors was celebrated and the questions of influence, primarily Beckett's, were linked to discussions of the relationship between the comic and serious elements in the play. Interpretations of the 'meaning' varied from the literal to the fully allegorical, by way of generalised abstract tags. Subsequent academic criticism, deriving from textual study rather than stage performance, has nearly always followed the serio-tragical-symbolical-abstract line – what we might call Modern Man in Search of His Insurance Cards, or, I Stink Therefore I Am. The comedy of *The Caretaker* is not a dispensable palliative. To discuss 'meaning' without taking this into account is to distort the play as a whole and devalue its achievement. The combination of the comic and the serious, laughter and silence, is often deeply disturbing for an audience: but only in confronting it can we begin to understand the play.

For one member of the audience, at least, the relationship between the comic and the serious elements was unacceptable. Leonard Russell, the *Sunday Times* book reviewer, recorded his impressions of a performance at the Duchess Theatre in an open letter to Harold Pinter:

I will go so far as to admit that I found it a strangely menacing and disturbing evening. It was also a highly puzzling evening; and here I refer not to the play but to the behaviour of the audience. On the evening I was present a large majority had no doubt at all that your special contribution to the theatre is to take a heart-breaking theme and treat it farcically. Gales of happy, persistent, and, it seemed to me, totally indiscriminate laughter greeted a play which I take to be, for all its funny moments, a tragic reading of life. May I ask this question – are you yourself happy with the atmosphere of rollicking good fun? (*Sunday Times*, 14 Aug, 1960, p. 21)

Pinter's reply, printed with this, is of such crucial importance for an understanding of the play, that I give it in full:

Your question is not an easy one to answer. Certainly I laughed myself while writing *The Caretaker*, but not all the time, not 'indiscriminately'. An element of the absurd is, I think, one of the features of the play, but at the same time I did not intend it to be merely a laughable farce. If there hadn't been other issues at stake the play would not have been written. Audience reaction can't be regulated, and no one would want it to be; nor is it easy to analyse. But where the comic and tragic (for want of a better word) are closely interwoven, certain members of an audience will always give emphasis to the comic as opposed to the other, for by so doing they rationalise the other out of existence. On most evenings at the Duchess there is a sensible balance of laughter and silence. Where, though, this indiscriminate mirth is found, I feel it represents a cheerful patronage of the characters on the part of the merrymakers, and thus participation is avoided. This laughter is in fact a mode of precaution, a smoke-screen, a refusal to accept what is happening as recognisable (which I think it is) and instead to view the actors (a) as actors always and not as characters and (b) as chimpanzees. From this kind of uneasy jollification I must, of course, dissociate myself, though I do think you were unfortunate in your choice of evening. As far as I'm concerned, *The Caretaker* is funny, up to a point. Beyond that point it ceases to be funny, and it was because of that point that I wrote it.

Pinter's letter is an essential starting point for discussion of the play. Adequate criticism must be based on a recognition of both the comic and 'tragic' elements compounded in the parallel process of stage performance and audience response. Our emotional reaction of laughter or silence complements what happens on stage. Both actors and audience create a structure of feeling that the play has in its 'living moment', as Pinter puts it.[1] The 'point' where *The Caretaker* 'ceases to be funny' must be found within the movement of the play itself and within the emotional complex of our 'participation'. In order to do so, I want to focus not so much on the physical structure which is relatively straightforward but rather on the structure of feeling, the emotional rhythm of laughter and silence which culminates in the arrested tension of both.[2] Rather than follow the tendency to generalise from paraphrase and thereby lose the essential drama, I wish to examine certain passages in order to bring out the deeply sensitive psychological insight that lies behind Pinter's plain statement.

When the curtain rises, Mick shares the activity of the audience. 'He slowly looks about the room looking at each object in turn. He looks up at the ceiling, and stares at the bucket'.[3] Then he brazenly separates himself from the audience. 'Ceasing, he sits quite still, expressionless, looking out front. Silence for thirty seconds'. Mick then leaves upon hearing 'muffled voices'. This silent enigma is in dramatic contrast to the end of the play. At the outset Mick, in effect, rejects the audience by walking offstage after a protracted silence, while at the close it is Davies who is left onstage rejected by the audience in so far as we recognise that he must go. But this formal, inverted symmetry is recognised retrospectively. Mick's silence and departure stays as a qualm, leaving a question behind the laughter that is immediate.

Aston's opening invitation to Davies to 'sit down' is manifestly frustrated by the evident disorder of the attic. As Aston sorts out a chair, Davies breaks into the first of so many complaints: 'Sit down? Huh . . . I haven't had a good sit down . . . I haven't had a proper sit down . . . well, I couldn't tell you . . . Ten minutes off for a tea-break in the middle of the night in that place and I couldn't find a seat, not one. All them Greeks had it, Poles, Greeks, Blacks, the lot of them, all them aliens had it. And they had me working there . . . they had me working . . . All them Blacks had it, Blacks, Greeks, Poles, the lot of them, that's what, doing me out of a seat, treating me like dirt. When he come at me tonight I told him' [pp. 7–8]. Davies's categorical discriminations ('sit down . . . good sit down . . . proper sit down') express the degree of deprivation that he feels he has suffered. His present gratitude is deflected and finally demolished by recrimination directed at the immediate past. An aggrieved sense of active and collective discourtesy by default is magnified to a major injustice; it is as if the merely adventitious revealed the latent injustice of victimisation as a permanent condition of the world. As so often in comedy a mundane occurrence is given an unwarrantedly inflated significance. Davies's bigotry, aggravated by constitutional self-righteous defensiveness, evidently distorts whatever really happened, and as a consequence we laugh rather than sympathise. The insistent repetitions inadvertently suggest that, on the one hand, it is both the multi-racial conditions of work *and work itself* that has pained Davies, and on the other that his appeal is in part determined by a bit of tobacco coming his way: as Aston *begins to roll himself a cigarette.* Davies *watches him* [p. 8]. This initial comedy continues to develop in the ever widening gap between the intentions of Davies's speech and its effect on the audience.

Even before he speaks Davies's tramp-like appearance has prompted a certain predisposition in the audience. Socially, tramps are at an 'inferior' extreme, and their condition precludes a normative response by definition. Reactions to tramps are nearly always compounded of fear, distaste, embarrassment, seeming indifference, or a degree of sympathy arising from unconscious self-reproach at our own well-being. Whatever feeling predominates depends upon the tramp's behaviour on a scale from abasement to aggression. Abasement invites individual, summary charity as a token of Society's larger responsibility for victims of circumstance. Aggression (like Davies's), though frightening on actual encounter, ultimately prompts laughter in the dramatic representation of self-determined viciousness. The transformation of the actual into the dramatic, the street into the theatre, the individual into audience, brings with it the laughter of relief.

Before taking a seat, winded by climbing the stairs, Davies must loosen himself up. He *exclaims loudly, punches downward with closed fist* crying 'I could have got done in down there' [p. 8]. There is no blood and Davies's evidently exaggerated claim is undermined even further by comic colloquialism. The stance of retrospective pugilism suggests a purely mimetic valour. It is clear that the combination of self-assertion and self-deception creates for Davies a fiction to live by. But although the imperatives of his existence have confounded fiction and fact, the distinction is evident to the audience throughout. Aston immediately offers Davies a roll-up but he replies: 'What? No, no, I never smoke a cigarette. . . . I'll tell you what, though, I'll have bit of that tobacco there for my pipe, if you like . . . That's kind of you, mister. Just enough to fill my pipe, that's all. I had a tin, only . . . only a while ago. But it was knocked off. It was knocked off on the Great West Road'. [p. 8]. Davies's refusal of the roll-up is reinforced by a categorical statement similar to the earlier example which expresses both the certainty of negative choice and yet an alternative possibility in the suggestion of a latent discrimination. His initial question – 'What?' – is a response to Aston's putative motive and means; Davies is rejecting what he feels may be charity but offering to accept Aston's tobacco in terms of his own positive preference for the more socially acceptable pipe, all the time leaving the actual decision to Aston. Davies's acknowledged indebtedness is modified by the subsequent etiquette. His self-conscious moderation forestalls any charge of excess, establishing his action as a-gentlemanly custom rather than revealing a condition of permanent dependence. The closing anecdote is intended to alter the action of giving and receiving into a form of indirect restitution. A similar rationalisation takes place later in the act when Davies accepts 'a few bob' from Aston: 'Thank you, thank you, good luck. I just happen to find myself a bit short. You see, I got nothing for all that week's work I did last week. That's the position, that's what it is[2] [p. 19]. Though retrospective criticism of this nature articulates the ironies of Davies's gesture and utterance, the immediacy of the audience's experience registers this emotively, responding to the comic moment which is immediately fulfilled when Aston fails to corroborate Davies's revision of his misfortune. 'You heard me tell him, didn't you?' Davies asks. Aston replies 'I saw him have a go at you', forcing him to attempt to draw sympathy by reference to age, 'Go at me? You wouldn't grumble. The filthy skate, an old man like me'. But here Davies's aggressive demotic ironically pre-empts the response he seeks, while the claim that breathlessly follows – 'I've had dinner with the best' – incites the broadest laughter with its blatant improbability. Aston, with a neutral imperturbability that promotes our laughter even further, refuses to comply and calmly repeats himself, 'Yes, I saw him have a go at you'. Davies's only recourse is to recall his personal standards to bolster his present judgments: 'All them toe-rags, mate, got the manners of pigs. I might have been on the road a few years but you can take it from me I'm clean. I keep myself up. That's why I left my wife. Fortnight after I married her, no, not so much as that, no more than a week, I took the lid off a saucepan, you know what was in it? A pile of her underclothing, unwashed. The pan for vegetables, it was. The vegetable pan. That's when I left her and I haven't seen her since'. [p. 9]. Davies has no apparent sense that such demonstrative probity is so farcically disproportionate that it cancels what it claims. Following

Davies's earlier revision of events, this exaggeration suggests that what we hear is a ludicrous distortion of whatever may have happened. The indiscriminately vulgar language of the opening – 'All them toe-rags, mate, got the manners of pigs' – burlesques the posture of arbiter of decorum which it protests. Immediately following this, Davies describes the row in the café. While claiming 'proper respect' due to 'an old man', if a few years younger he would break in half 'that Scotch git'. All the socially regulative values Davies claims – dignity, respect, propriety, decorum – are confounded by the language and gesture of a caricatured ethic more appropriate to an anti-social 'wild animal', as Mick later describes him. In short Davies's comic character is founded on a total travesty of the mode of being to which he aspires. The pathos of his deprivation is made comic with the citation of a public lavatory attendant as a promoter of personal hygiene. Vast significance is given to the quotidian – 'Shoes? It's life and death to me, man'. Davies's scale of values inverts the normative values of the audience, accustomed to more abstract priorities, which remain unquestioned since Davies's cannot be taken seriously. We 'reason not the need' when it is rendered in comic picaresque.

Elaborating on his need for footwear, Davies launches into the celebrated tale of the quest to the Luton monastery. A 'bastard monk', the representative of a holy order, warns the suppliant, 'If you don't piss off . . . I'll kick you all the way to the gate'. As Davies expands on his misfortunes, mounting audience laughter accompanies each incident, culminating in applause at the close of the story. And with applause action is temporarily suspended. For a few crucial seconds the actor is divorced from the character as the audience celebrates a comic performance. The reality of whatever happened in Luton is subverted by characteristically jaundiced aggression which is transferred to the monk, diametrically evoking laughter rather than sympathy. Thereafter, Davies as a credible being struggles not only with Aston and Mick, but with the theatrically formalised predisposition of the audience, a predisposition to see Davies as a type, a brilliantly embodied 'act', at best a tramp, but hardly an individual. Shortly after the Luton story, the anecdote of Sidcup and the 'papers' consolidates this.

Davies insists that the Sidcup papers 'prove who I am . . . They tell you who I am' [p. 20]. But we know he will never collect those chimerical documents of fifteen years ago. Lack of shoes, or bad weather, or something else will always intervene. His reassumption of a past bureaucratic identity could not alter what he is. It is being a tramp which has shaped his body and soul, and not the fact that he is called Bernard Jenkins rather than Mac Davies. Every utterance and every gesture he makes denote a class rather than an individual; dialect subsumes idiolect. Davies is finally no more than his language and appearance – and this is how Mick encounters him at the end of the first act.

It is as if throughout most of Act I Mick has been listening in, since he shows an uncanny insight into Davies's character. In this sense Mick is almost a representative of the audience, knowing, sardonically, as much as they know. On the other hand Mick knows his Davieses as he knows his London, but he expresses it indirectly in terms of Aston's behaviour:

MICK: He doesn't like work.
    (*Pause*)
DAVIES: Go on!
MICK: No, he just doesn't like work, that's his trouble.
DAVIES: Is that a fact?
MICK: It's a terrible thing to have to say about your own brother.
DAVIES: Ay.
MICK: He's just shy of it. Very shy of it.
DAVIES: I know that sort.
MICK: You know the type? [p. 48]

At the end of Act I Mick immediately recognises Davies's work-shy 'type', and his first words, 'What's the game?' are really the later statement, 'I know what you want' [p. 59], put in the form of a question.

It has been shown by Peter Davison [see his discussion, in this Part Three of our selection, above – Ed.] that Mick's first two speeches derive in form from the traditional music-hall monologue. As such, along with something like the bag-passing game, they border on the farcical. But there is more to them than this. In laughing at the combination of the ludicrous, the grotesque and the improbable, the audience joins Mick in laughing at Davies. In other words, Mick provides the relief of a new comic perspective which enlists the audience on its side. At this point the verbal slapstick seems almost innocuous:

You remind me of my uncle's brother. He was always on the move, that man. Never without his passport. Had an eye for the girls. Very much your build. Bit of an athlete. Long-jump specialist. He had a habit of demonstrating different run-ups in the drawing-room round about Christmas time. Had a penchant for nuts. That's what it was. Nothing else but a penchant. Couldn't eat enough of them. Peanuts, walnuts, brazil nuts, monkey nuts, wouldn't touch a piece of fruit cake. Had a marvellous stop-watch. Picked it up in Hong Kong. The day after they chucked him out of the Salvation Army. Used to go in number four for Beckenham Reserves. That was before he got his Gold Medal. Had a funny habit of carrying his fiddle on his back. Like a papoose. I think there was a bit of the Red Indian in him. To be honest, I've never made out how he came to be my uncle's brother. I've often thought that maybe it was the other way round. I mean that my uncle was his brother and maybe he was my uncle. But I never called him uncle. As a matter of fact I called him Sid. My mother called him Sid too. It was a funny business. Your spitting image he was. Married a Chinaman and went to Jamaica'. [p. 31]

In spite of its seeming inconsequentiality this speech manifestly says a lot about Davies, Mick and Aston on a naturalistic and psychological level. Mick's sardonic delivery expresses at once both discursive doubt and impatience with the conversation game, and a sadistic playfulness. The verbal barrage parallels the earlier arm-twisting: verbal intimidation follows physical domination. Mick is equally dexterous at both. What Mick is really saying behind the formal obliquity of his narrative is this – I recognise your sort, a tramp ('always on the move'), with your story of 'papers' ('never without his passport'), your ridiculous physical posturing ('Bit of an athlete'), thrown out of a monastery ('they chucked him out of the Salvation Army') of questionable background ('a bit of the Red Indian in him'), now mixed up with my brother ('I've never made out how he came to be my uncle's brother'), why don't you clear off ('Married a Chinaman and went to Jamaica'). But at the same time Mick is deflecting a suppressed view of his own brother that is forced into his mind by the fact of Davies's presence: my brother ('You remind me of my uncle's brother') has picked up this nut ('Had a penchant for nuts'), he must be nutty as a fruit cake ('wouldn't touch a piece of fruit cake'). Mick's feelings only emerge eventually by way of his surrogate, Davies, whose exclamation 'He's nutty!' enables Mick to savour the suppressed, emotionally forbidden, word: 'Nutty? Who's nutty? (*Pause*) Did you call my brother nutty? My brother' [p. 73].

Mick's second speech is also something more than an exercise in intimidation. It is a comically indirect way of elaborating on what is implicit: the foreignness of Davies. The indigenous Mick ironically compares the indigent Davies with a fellow Londoner. Mick's irony is sharpened by his reflection on the sense of difference felt by a working-class North Londoner for those from south of the Thames: 'When I got to know him I found out he was brought up in Putney. That didn't make any difference to me' [p. 32]. The 'bloke', after all, 'was born in the Caledonian Road, just before you get to the Nag's Head'. Mick's North London references are to *neighbouring* localities linked by bus routes at the centre of which is the 'bloke's old mum . . . still living at the Angel'. Mick evokes neighbourhood, pub and home – the self-advertisement of a particular kind of Londoner recognising an outsider and reminding him of the fact.

By contrast Davies's lonely wandering existence is reflected by sporadic, peripheral references to places outside of London proper (Sidcup, Luton, Watford, Wembley) and to past friends: 'I used to know a bootmaker in Acton. He was a good mate to me'. Whereas Mick's two speeches are littered with familial terms (uncle, brother, mother, cousin), Davies's anecdotes suggest that over the years, in all of London between Luton and Sidcup, only two encounters have ever led to friendship – and both friendships of a dubious kind. The style and delivery of Mick's speeches suggest the amateur comedian at home in pub, club or family; Davies is only a solitary tramp stranded somewhere on the Great West Road or the North Circular, an anomaly. But all these serious undertones are checked by a sense of game. Mick's interrogation of Davies is deliberately punctured by straight music-hall cross-talk:

MICK: That's my bed.
DAVIES: What about that, then?
MICK: That's my mother's bed.
DAVIES: Well she wasn't in it last night!   [p. 35]

Even when Mick rounds on Davies in this third long speech 'You're stinking the place out. You're an old robber, there's no getting away from it. You're an old skate . . .' [p. 35] – the serious force of his charges is tempered, firstly by his appropriation of Davies's language ('filthy skate', [p. 9]) and secondly, by an extended parody of the conditions of tenancy and purchase. Between an outline of costs and recommendation of Aston as decorator, Mick threatens 'Otherwise I've got a van outside, I can run you to the police station in five minutes, have you in for trespassing, loitering with intent, daylight robbery, filching, thieving and stinking the place out' [pp. 35–6]. Amusing to the audience, this exaggeration is frightening to Davies since the language parallels his own exaggerated sense of persecution. The ludicrous magnification of the obligations, commitments and penalties of legal responsibility in buying a house is a humorous reminder to the audience of an often exhaustingly protracted business, but to Davies it is a manifestation of a bureaucratic world that excludes him. Mick makes the point in his repeated final question 'Who do you bank with?' This complex verbal humour is accentuated by the visual comedy. Throughout the act Davies has been on stage without his trousers, in his long pants, and Mick emphasises the fact by flicking Davies's trousers in his face – 'several times'. This is then followed, almost immediately, by one of the oldest ploys in the slapstick repertoire, the bag-passing game with its knockabout sequence reversal. Threat and menace are conflated in Mick's speeches and the bag-passing game is almost wholly funny (but not merely funny, since the game symbolises the way in which Davies himself passes from brother to brother). Then, with the terrifying attack in darkness and the succeeding revelation that it is Mick merely 'spring cleaning' with an electrolux, violence and laughter are powerfully juxtaposed.

Thus Pinter exploits different kinds of comedy in a cumulative and structured way: comedy of character is established in Act I and then extended by music-hall monologue and broad farce in Act II. Comedy of language, gesture and action is then allowed to build up to the moment when it is dramatically arrested by Aston's long, painful account of treatment in a mental hospital, and the events leading up to it. Aston's speech has always been recognised as a major moment in the movement of the play, but its full significance has not been adequately discussed.

John Russell Brown has pointed out the correspondences between Aston's hospital treatment and his present behaviour. [See excerpt in this Part Three of our selection, above – Ed.] He underwent electrical treatment and now fiddles obsessively with electrical equipment: he has a white coat, a pillow and a sheet at the ready; the uncovered light bulb glares down; he stares smilingly over Davies in bed. Brown also points out that Aston did go back to places like the café and did talk to strangers again – namely Davies – and suggests that the impetus for this was two-fold. Aston is haunted by revenge and somehow sees his own role as a 'caretaker' of Davies. These are all important points, but need to be taken further.

Aston refers to the 'piles of papers' he was shown as medical evidence: Davies refers to the 'piles of papers' kept in the attic. Aston says that the window of his hospital room was barred: the indications are that the attic window was kept open even before Davies's malodorous entry. Aston spent five hours sawing at the bars, and is now preoccupied with saws, ostensibly to carry out the building work. He recognises that in café and factory he 'talked too much', and his long speech is a chilling reminder that he still does.

What does all this add up to? Surely the commonly accepted notion of Aston's 'charity' in taking in Davies is called in question here. Rather than a disinterested act deriving from an impulse or conviction of moral duty (and thus a token of his social rehabilitation) it is part of the irreparable damage brought about by his sufferings. Aston's 'charity' is a way of simultaneously vindicating himself and impugning those who have harmed him. Davies is there in the attic because of Aston's psychology, not because of his ethics: Aston sees Davies as a version of himself.

Aston's recollections of the glass of Guinness and the lady in the café indicate his continuing disorientation. Both these speeches occur after pauses and have no relation to what precedes them, and both contrast forcefully with Aston's previous reticence. As conversational gambits they are disastrously bizarre; it is almost as if part of an interior monologue has suddenly come to the surface. The preoccupations of Aston and Davies are psychological treadmills imprisoning each in his mutually exclusive world. For Aston to work on the house he needs to clear the garden for a shed. To build the shed he needs wood. Saws are needed for the wood, a sawbench is needed for sawing, a shed is needed for a sawbench, a cleared garden is needed for the shed. Davies, to sort himself out needs his papers at Sidcup. To get to Sidcup he needs good shoes, to get good shoes he needs money, to get money he needs his papers to sort himself out . . .

Both minds have been numbed by the different experiences of being on the road and being in a mental hospital: both are reduced to a preoccupation with the physical function of hands and feet. With Aston's speech the laughter ceases. Its pathos is deepened by the laughter that has preceded it. And there is no 'caretaker' for them. The audience is silenced and confounded as the darkness grows.

As Act III opens, and before anything is said, Davies is seen in a comic tableau, pipe in hand and incongruously garbed in a smoking jacket. Here, after the strain of confronting the nature of Aston's being, we are at last allowed the relief of laughter. But when Davies speaks, although his concerns seem much the same (the gas stove, blacks, shoes etc.) his continual references to Aston compromise and complicate our response. At this point a subjective coefficient of guilt rises in us, deriving in part from our former complicity with Mick (now more evidently working on his strategy of expulsion) and in part from laughing at Aston's expense. Whereas earlier Davies seemed self-determining and thus responsible for what he is, he now seems more like a plaything being used by Mick for certain questionable ends.

The serious and the comic are now much more forcefully counterpointed. Mick's dry-mock is still there ('You must come up and have a drink sometime. Listen to some Tchaikovsky' [p. 64]) and Davies's procrastination, although now invidiously ungrateful, is still lightened to pure comedy ('The only way to keep a pair of shoes on, if you haven't got no laces, is to tighten the foot, see?' [p. 65]). But Davies's response to Mick's evocation of a penthouse 'palace' – 'What about me?' – gives voice to the inevitable question at the heart of the situation. Mick's 'All this junk here, its no good to anyone' [p. 61], is much less casual than it seems. Davies as, part of the 'junk', will obviously have to go, and we recognise it.

Mick obliquely incites Davies's verbal attack on Aston by giving
voice to what the tramp has felt from the outset. Davies's real feelings
in surveying the attic are compromised by the fact that Aston has
rescued him. As a consequence Davies says the opposite of what he
feels:

DAVIES: This your room?
ASTON: Yes.
DAVIES: You got a good bit of stuff here.
ASTON: Yes.
DAVIES: Must be worth a few bob, this . . . put it all together.
    (*Pause*)
    There's enough of it.
ASTON: There's a good bit of it, all right.
DAVIES: You sleep here, do you?
ASTON: Yes.
DAVIES: What, in that?   [p. 11]

Similarly, Mick's pointed summary not only places Davies as part of
the rubbish and simultaneously predisposes him to attack Aston, but
gives utterance to that protracted stare at the opening of the play: 'All
this junk here, it's no good to anyone. It's just a lot of old iron, that's
all. Clobber . . .' [p. 61].

Davies echoes this in his viciously prolonged attack on Aston as an
irresponsible lunatic, '. . . all this junk I got to sleep with . . . this lousy
filthy hole' [p. 67]. Davies's contemptible vilification is emotionally
complex for an audience. If it confirms our opinion of Davies's
opportunist nastiness and strengthens our impulse to reject him as
wholly objectionable, at the same time it provides almost a release for
our strained protective feelings towards Aston. The opening lines of
the speech [pp. 66—7] continue Davies's exaggerated sense of comic
victimisation made ludicrous by disproportionate expectation: 'It's
getting so freezing in here I have to keep my trousers on to go to bed. I
never done that before in my life. But that's what I got to do here. Just
because you won't put in any bleeding heating!' We may derive a
temporary sense of relief in what follows by intellectually assessing
the circularity of Davies's charge – Aston is lunatic because he is
irresponsible and irresponsible because he is a lunatic – and even
maintain our distance when Davies claims the friendship and kindred
opinion of Mick. But this relief is completely shattered as Davies
sadistically baits Aston with the prospect of renewed electrical
treatment. As the emotion rises both in Davies and the audience it is,
paradoxically, both undercut and heightened by localised London
slang: 'They'd take one look at all this junk I got to sleep with they'd
know you were a creamer'. Davies charges Aston with what, in all

probability, has been levelled at him, 'a creamer'. It is almost funny as an unexpected synonym for the more current 'nutcase', but at the same time more insidiously mocking for Aston, since Davies uses the highly specific *argot* of Aston's own background. Yet even at this point we are tempted to laugh as Davies's expression gets more and more Welsh in self-righteous anger: 'You want me to do all the dirty work all up and down them stairs just so I can sleep in this lousy filthy hole every night? Not me, boy. Not for you, boy.' But the idioms that provoke laughter also arrest it: 'You're up the creek! You're half off!' Our awareness of the possibility of this being true checks our natural tendency to respond humorously to figurative exaggeration. Davies's subsequent question 'Who ever saw you slip me a few bob?' simultaneously recalls Aston's kindness in doing just that, and predisposes the audience to take up a defensive position, on Aston's behalf, against Davies's final callousness – 'I never been inside a nuthouse!' Even here, the colloquially derisive reduction makes us want to laugh, as we have laughed at the peremptory idiom of Mick's attack on Davies. But as Davies draws his knife an ominous silence supervenes. This tableau recalls Davies's ineptitude in threatening Mick earlier, and Aston finally breaks the tension with a delayed understatement that is totally deflating: 'I think it's about time you found somewhere else. I don't think we're hitting it off!'

This is precisely what Mick has been worming towards. He could have thrown Davies out whenever he liked, but he has waited two weeks for Aston to see through Davies's character. Mick has promoted the exposure in order that Aston will see and feel as he does. The usual interpretation of Mick and Aston's relationship – that there is an unspoken bond of brotherly love between them – is really rather naive and sentimental. Mick smashes the Buddha to pieces out of a frustrated rage that derives from his suppressed acknowledgement of the truth of Davies's previous accusation ('He's nutty'), and his subsequent passionate outburst is a wilful attempt to see Aston's condition in terms of his failure to decorate the house, rather than in terms of what lies beneath it. To have thrown Davies out would have been a tacit admission that Aston was a lunatic to have brought him there in the first place. (Perhaps Davies wasn't the first?)

In other words, Mick's obligation to his brother is formal rather than affective. Mick's character – tough, sardonic, worldly-wise – is similar to that of the people in the café and the factory who found Aston 'funny' and were instrumental in having him put away. Like his mother, and the doctor, Mick wants Aston to 'live like the others' [p. 55]. He understands Davies so well because they both have a kind of bureaucratic view of the world. They both see human activity in terms of status conferred by institutions that regulate society (social security, solicitors, etc.). Whereas the Buddha for Aston was an example of something 'well made', for Mick it embodies all that he cannot face in his brother – the inscrutable, the passive, and the alien. But, in tarring over the roof Aston is learning *to take care of himself*, in Mick's terms. At the opening of the play the suspended bucket focusses for Mick his brother's condition as he understands it, and their only exchange in Act II concerns the problem of tarring over the leaking roof. As Act III opens, Davies contemplates Aston's silence in terms of his single activity of doing the job (ironically this anticipates his own expulsion). This small task signalises that Aston will comply with Mick's view of things, a complicity dramatised by the 'faint smile' they exchange towards the close. Mick smiles in recognition of what he sees as his rightness in paying off Davies, and Aston smiles back conceding the fact – his last words to Davies were 'Get your stuff'.

Davies must go, however plangent his appeal: 'What am I going to do? . . . Where am I going to go?' [pp. 77–8]. The pauses between each utterance are lengthened into the *long silence* of the final stage direction. Aston *turns back to the window, remains still, his back to him, at the window*, but we are faced with Davies's concrete questioning presence. We are forced here to confront not only what laughter has created but also what laughter has suppressed. The repetitions of Davies's language echo those moments of comedy which are now stifled by the spectre of destitution. Davies's need for material items has created moments of high comedy, but the serious moral implications of such subsistence culminate in these questions. The material, social and cultural privileges that presuppose our presence in the theatre are indices of the totality of Davies's deprivation. Throughout the play Davies has been the object of the solidarity of laughter, but now the audience itself is exposed in its own silence before him. The possibilities of food, shelter and warmth are now to be replaced by the possibilities of hunger, cold and exposure, intimations of which have been present all along ('I could have died on the road', Davies says at one point. Was this the substance of his nightmares?). The harsh regimen of the doss-house has been evoked earlier in Davies's hurried attempt to forestall what he knows must happen as the rule of each daybreak: 'Don't you want me to get out . . .?' [p. 24].

The points where the laughter spasmodically ceases are obvious enough in the rhythm of the play. These dramatic moments correspond psychologically to the point in each of us where conflicting impulses and vestigial atavism and ostensible civility meet. We experience, in *The Caretaker*, the Hobbesian triumph of superior laughter over inferior object and ludicrousness transforms the socially embarrassing. But beneath this is the self-protective impulse to remove what is psychologically painful. Just as children laugh at (and thus exorcise) the sight of physical deformity, so we react to Davies's warped morality – all the time expecting him to ask for our compassion. But Davies remains intransigent; he does not offer us the adult compromise of compassion. In our laughter there stirs an uneasy atavism which grows in proportion as Davies's nastiness increases. We cannot finally accept Davies on his own terms – as he is. He has to be either 'killed off' by our laughter, or transformed by the tragic dignity of self-awareness. Our emotional expectations are in part shaped by dramatic convention. Davies must be either contemptible or pitiful; a comic vice exposed in laughter, or, by token of some redemptive self-insight, an ultimately tragic figure. But he is actually neither, and this is what is almost too painful. In the theatre adult emotions are customarily channelled into a comforting species of self-protective compassion. Pinter refuses to provide this. Initially Pinter felt that there would have to be a death at the end of the play,[4] but it is clear that this would have only provided another kind of emotional release – and evasion. Pinter not only dropped this notion but, in revision, chose to stress the ineluctable concrete actuality of Davies there before us[5]: resistant to allegory, abstraction, and moral formula. Here, in the *long silence*, no longer so much an audience as a disparate assembly of individuals which includes Davies, we are forced to confront the limits of our human response, the edges of emotional vulnerability, the barriers of social ordinance that join and divide us all. This is our 'participation', and this is where the 'point' of laughter and silence, as Pinter's letter reminds us, both begins and ends.

SOURCE: '*The Caretaker* and the 'Point' of Laughter', *Journal of Beckett Studies*, 5 (Autumn 1979), pp. 83–97.

NOTES

[Reorganised and renumbered from the original]

    1. Interview with John Sherwood, BBC European Service (3/3/1960).
    2. Cf. Bernard F. Dukore *Where Laughter Stops: Pinter's Tragicomedy* (Columbia, Mo., London, 1976), particularly pp. 25–31.
    3. Second edition, revised (London, 1962). All references to this edition unless otherwise stated.
    4. The point arose in several early interviews, firstly with Kenneth Tynan (BBC Home Service, 28/10/1960) '. . . the original idea when writing [*The Caretaker*] was that I was going to end the play with a violent death of the tramp . . . It suddenly struck me that it wasn't necessary.'

5. Pinter deleted several of the final exchanges between Davies and Aston, added pauses, and delayed Aston's moving to the window and turning his back, thereby emphasising Davies's isolation and rejection. Cf. *The Caretaker* (London, 1960), pp. 79–82.

T. C. Worsley 'Immensely Funny, Disturbing and Moving' (1960)

REVIEW OF FIRST LONDON PRODUCTION, ARTS THEATRE

With this new play – not to be missed at the Arts Theatre – Mr Harold Pinter has moved up a step from extraordinary promise to extraordinary achievement. *The Caretaker* is both a wonderful piece of theatre, immensely funny, rich in observation, and below that level a disturbing and moving experience.

It has only three characters: all are brilliantly acted. But Mr Donald Pleasance, in the longest and ripest part of the three, gives what must now stake a claim as the finest acting performance to be seen in London. It is, quite simply, perfection.

Mr Pinter has been accused in the past – and rightly – of failure to communicate. We have all recognised his gifts, but have been baffled by his use of them. And here, too, we may start by worrying ourselves into disenjoyment by fearing that we are missing meanings.

Relax! Certainly we seem to be in the Godot country – this dingy, downstairs room with its iron bedsteads, its antediluvian gas cooker, its scattered accumulation of useless junk. Then to complete the parallel, the slow, monosyllabic, dull, respectable-looking young man who inhabits it brings in a tramp, a garrulous, bent, scratchy old piece of flotsam he has met in a café, and offers him the spare bed.

The parallels continue in a kind of a way. The old creature is waiting for his Godot, is always on the point of getting himself sorted out. If only he could get some shoes, if only the weather would break, he would be on his way to – Sidcup. That's his Eldorado. That's where his papers are, and what are you without your papers? But look at his shoes, look at the rain! How *can* he get to Sidcup?

So we are in the Beckett climate, but not in the Beckett fog where everything means something else. We can take the play straight – to start with, anyhow. Mr Pinter's vision begins with the dispossessed and the disconnected. The characters who set him off are those whose connection with the world hangs by a thread. (And since all of us at times feel this about ourselves – even the most stable-seeming have their moments of disconnection in the nightmare hours – his plays, even at their most comic moments, prick beneath one's skin.)

The three characters here are extreme cases, of course. Aston, the owner of the room, has been in a mental hospital and had shock treatment, it comes out in a stumbled monologue which Mr Peter Woodthorpe delivers with a fine, groping pathos. And this accounts for his slowness and silence.

His younger brother, Mick, is a builder: he owns the tumbledown house and lets his brother live in it. He is going to do it up one day; and his grandiose plans for this are culled from the glossy advertisements. And Aston is going to help him, one day, when he gets round to building that shed in the garden which will be his workshop.

But the house won't be done up, any more than Davies, the tramp, will get to sorting himself out at Sidcup. The hold each of them has on life is too tenuous, a weak cotton thread of never-to-be fulfilled intentions. And hence the pent-up violence in each of them which keeps erupting into impotent gestures of attack.

But, by trying to catch something of the underneath atmosphere of the play, I am, I realise, only succeeding in making it sound like a lot of other gloomy plays that have been around in the last four years. And it isn't at all like that. Its surface is hilariously funny. The audience for three-quarters of the time is kept in fits of laughter. And the only way for you to see why is to go yourself to watch Mr Donald Pleasence as this battered bit of old driftwood refusing to lie down and die.

Several years ago I had the pleasure of proclaiming Mr Pleasence a potentially great actor in a very different kind of performance – in a Pirandello play, also at the Arts. Since then I had feared that the typecasters had got him for good and all. For the TV and the Films and the commercial managers do terrible things to their raw material: they choose them a Proscrustean bed of a size to fit their most obvious qualities and then squeeze them or stretch them to fit it. And I have sadly watched this process doing its best to ruin Mr Pleasence as an actor.

But, praise be, he has emerged quite unscathed. He has been given a part here that gives his talent full scope, and he has matched it with every resource of art and skill. The character is brought out with a richness of comic detail impossible to describe. Every movement of every part of him is carefully calculated to add another touch to a portrait, complete, whole, and devastatingly true. The truth is of primary importance for the play – for the truth that lies at the heart of all great comic performances is the kernel of pathos. The very tenacity with which, shiftily and cunningly, this broken remnant clings to his slender thread of life, makes his rejection by the two brothers all but unbearable.

Mr Alan Bates and Mr Peter Woodthorpe, two of our most talented young actors, are the brothers, and each is exact. Mr Donald McWhinnie's production is unobtrusively helpful, and Mr Brian Currah's set is appropriately dingy.

This is just the sort of play that the Arts Theatre Club should be putting on, and that the Arts Theatre audiences should be queueing to see.

SOURCE: review article in *Financial Times* (28/4/1960).

Charles Marowitz (1960) 'A Kind of Masterpiece'

REVIEW OF FIRST LONDON PRODUCTION

In the same way that the works of Shakespeare affirmed the innovations of Christopher Marlowe, the plays of Harold Pinter solidify the gains of Samuel Beckett. This, let me say fleetly, is not the commencement of a watered-down paean of faint praise. Pinter is not, as some would make him out to be, a British purveyor of Irish-French originals. The mark of Beckett on Pinter is dominantly stylistic; as for the subject matter, it may have a Beckettian tang to it, but the recipe is original. If there is similarity in the works of these two writers it is more the result of mutual outlook and common concepts than of a transference of personal characteristics. When Marlowe and Shakespeare looked out the window, they saw the Chain of Being; when Beckett and Pinter look out, they see the cosmic void.

This whole critic-engendered nonsense of 'influences' has tended to obscure the fact that *The Caretaker*, Pinter's latest play, is a national masterpiece. And it is the dynamic presence of nationalism in the play which makes it such a masterpiece. This is a British play about a British sub-society rendered in the tart language of the regions from which the three characters hail. The meat of *The Caretaker* is certainly translatable, but the delicious little spicings that glisten all over it (dazzlingly colloquial authenticities carried to hilarious extremes) can be appreciated nowhere else but in England.

On the day *The Caretaker* was completed I was talking with Harold
Pinter, and when pressured into saying something about the play's
ideas he said: 'It's about love'. When I left the theatre I found it
difficult to reconcile the author's words with the play I had seen, but
when I equated 'love' with 'need', a certain pattern fell into place. Of
course *The Caretaker* is no more about love than *Hamlet* is about
revenge. Being a great play it is about everything, but the spray of
universalities issue from a small spout which does seem to concern
itself mainly with people trying desperately to connect with other
people. It is pointless to explore narrative in a play by Harold Pinter,
for narrative is only the gong which sends out the countless
reverberations which make up the true tone of his works, but briefly:
the play deals with a murky tramp-figure who is taken into a house
which belongs to two brothers: one, a faintly stirring zombie-type who
broaches the possibility of the tramp's becoming caretaker; the other
a glib sadist whose relationship with his brother is shrouded in
tantalising shadows. The line of the play consists of the tramp's
movement toward one brother and then the next, his painful rejection
by both, and his ultimate ejection from the premises. (An ending
which sings on a dozen different levels and which, without Pinter's
pressured context, could be the corny denouement in any one of fifty
melodramas from the 1900s.)

The production is faultless. Director Donald McWhinnie is a sly
BBC Third Programme-man who knows precisely how to alternate the
words with the silences in order for one to illuminate the other.

There are a few arbitrary shock-tactics – like a spell-binding speech
about lobotomy which seems too clinical and dragged-in to blend
with the poetic texture around it, but Peter Woodthorpe's rendition of
it is so chilling, one doesn't question it till afterwards.

The play-proper is an elaborate network of ambiguity stretched
tight over a simple little story. Although it is searingly accurate in its
diction and characterisation, it is too organised and surreal in effect to
be called naturalistic. If Pinter uses tape-recorders to achieve such
verisimilitude, he also edits his tapes poetically to avoid stale
reproductions of life. It is painful and frustrating to coin definitions
about the play. It is a kind of masterpiece, and will suffer the terrible
consequences which critics inflict on all such works.

SOURCE: review article in the *Village Voice* (New York); reproduced in *Confessions of a
Counterfeit Critic* (London, 1973), pp. 47–9.

John Russell Taylor   'Admirable Revival'
(1981)

REVIEW OF KENNETH IVES'S PRODUCTION, NATIONAL THEATRE

. . . it was fascinating to look back on the NT's admirable revival of
[Pinter's] first big success, *The Caretaker.* How would it hold up?
Would it be staled by familiarity? Would it look like a period piece?
Would it need deliberate reinterpretation, or sustain it? Well, perhaps
other people were not asking all these silly questions, but I was, since
though I have had frequently to refer to the text through the years, I
have never seen it on stage since that memorable first production.
And I have to say that I was very impressed by its staying power, its
ability to change and grow with different readings, while yet
remaining essentially the same. For one thing, it has always been in
my mind's eye a very intimate, claustrophic play. But the wide stage
of the Lyttelton allowed, if it did not force, Eileen Diss's set to spread
out into something which might possibly, with work done on it, turn
into a desirable residence. At the same time, the intensity of the
human relations among the three characters remains unimpaired.
Especially in the new readings by Jonathan Pryce (Mick), Kenneth
Cranham (Aston) and Warren Mitchell (Davies): different indeed
from the readings of the original cast, but equally authoritative.
Kenneth Ives seems in his direction to have settled on the view of the
play as the story of Mick's attempt to re-establish contact with his
brother, using any means at his disposal. Davies therefore becomes a
useful tool, because it is he who has somehow managed to revive, in
however rudimentary a form, Aston's desire to make contact with the
world outside. Mick's attitude to him, in Jonathan Pryce's dazzling
performance, is malevolent (fuelled perhaps by jealousy) but also
motivated by a desire to explore his potentialities as a way of getting
to Aston, and the speech in which Mick outlines his plans for the
future of the house loses much of its irony but gains in congruence
with the rest of the play: it is not just a brilliant set-piece, but a
moment in which Mick genuinely reveals his own vulnerability.
Kenneth Cranham plays Aston as something much nearer a human
inkblot test, seldom indicating any emotion of his own, even in the big
speech about his hospital treatment. He remains largely the
battleground between Mick and Davies; which is just as it should be,
since most of the drama is between these two characters, jockeying

for position and seeing which can use which the more effectively. Warren Mitchell is fine, whether cringing and fawning or blustering and bullying when he overestimates his influence on Aston and overplays his hand. . . .

SOURCE: extract from review article on new productions in London, *Drama* (2nd quarter, 1981).

PART FOUR

The Homecoming

Irving Wardle The Territorial Struggle
(1971)

. . . *The Homecoming*, when it first appeared, took one by surprise because it seemed so much coarser and less musical than his previous work. But all Pinter had done was to remove the conventional mask and show the naked animal. The play, as a result, has to be understood in territorial terms or not at all.

The little society that takes shape in the first scenes resembles the type of animal organisation which Robert Ardrey calls the 'noyau': a central stronghold whose members go out to work off their excess energies on the frontiers, living with their neighbours in a 'dear-enemy' relationship. It is a family of predators, and as things stand to begin with, it is clear that a power contest is going on. Max, the old bull, is losing ground to his two sons Lenny and Joey; for the time being, most of their activity is directed outside the family – Lenny's into acquiring other properties as a pimp and Joey's into boxing. In the meantime Max still nominally retains his right as proprietor, even though he is reduced from his former dignity as a hunter (an ex-butcher, he talks about 'going all over the country to find meat') to acting as the family cook. (Immediately we are on thin ice. Pinter always destroys things by explicit reference; nobody's word is to be trusted. But as nobody challenges Max's statements about his past, it's fair to take them as more than a mere strategic fantasy.) On the margin is Max's younger brother Sam, the weakling of the pack, a hired-car chauffeur who owns nothing of his own and likes to paw enviously at other people's possessions, such as Max's dead wife. He tries to make himself useful in the kitchen, but Max takes this as a territorial invasion, and his favourite way of displaying his proprietary authority is by threatening to throw Sam – the only member of the family he can be sure of beating – out of the house.

Within these first scenes, two prevailing motives are established, one conservative and the other aggressive. I cannot improve on Ardey's definition of them. 'Through the holding of territory, we defend what social status we have achieved; by challenging our neighbour, we attempt to better ourselves.' The territorial side is clear enough; it is manifest in the characters' setting and physical actions. Being static, it rarely furnishes any dramatic impulse. The impetus comes much more from the status contest, each member of the pack trying to enlarge his domain at the expense of those around him.

Much of the dialogue in *The Homecoming* is devoted to status battles, and one can instantly recognise it from the quality of the language which modulates, as it were, into italics. Characters depart from their normal idiom so as to lay claim to experiences of which they seem only to have read in newspapers. Lenny has only to be deciding which horse to back to provoke Max into claiming a lifetime's experience of the track and long-standing friendships with the Ascot set. The same thing happens again and again. Joey's boxing brings out the same emulation. And when Teddy the philosopher arrives, Lenny, the most predatory of the group, tries to level with him by asking, 'Do you detect a certain logical incoherence in the central affirmations of Christian theism?' To which Teddy returns the perfect territorial reply, 'That question doesn't fall within my province.'

Teddy is a complete outsider; if we have any doubts on that score, they are dispelled when Lenny tells him he belongs to the family unit. Any reassurance from that mouth is bound to be untrue! And his behaviour inside the house literally illustrates the ethological comparison between proprietary and intrusive behaviour. Off his home ground Teddy hardly exists; he is a wraith compared with the others. There is no reason to doubt what he says about life in America, but it comes off his lips with so little confidence that it sounds like lies. 'It's a great life, at the University . . . you know. . . . We've got a lovely house . . . we've got all . . . we've got everything we want. It's a very stimulating environment.' On the threshold with Ruth he delivers a pep talk about the family, telling her not to be nervous. But Ruth is not in the least nervous. Teddy is talking for himself and projecting his own fears onto her.

Ruth is the play's pivot (as one might suspect in Pinter from a character who says so little), and she supports two territorial assertions: that when a female passes out of a male's stamping ground, she cancels her bond with him; and that her love goes to the male who owns the best piece of property.

The play's title refers to her, not to Teddy. It is no homecoming for him; whereas she (even distrusting her probably untrustworthy statement that she was born nearby) is instantly on home ground. Teddy, however, has a legitimate claim to belonging there, which she has not. And the main action of the piece shows her taking possession of the territory while Teddy is being dispossessed.

Ruth is equally impervious to insult and flattery. She takes in the situation – a houseful of males who have not had a woman living on the premises since the mother died – and moves straight towards her target. The two dominant males, Lenny and Max, both initially respond to her with a show of violence – Lenny by telling the story of the girl he almost murdered; Max by physically assaulting Joey and Sam so as to prove himself, in her eyes, as the king stag. Ruth's response in the first case is to answer Lenny's violence with an aggressive sexual challenge; and in the second, to take Max's brawl in her stride as a fitting tribute to what she has to offer.

By this time Teddy has already been edged out of the combat. His behaviour changes from feeble protest to the tactic (discussed in Desmond Morris's *The Naked Ape*) of going limp in the aggressor's arms and even lending what energy he has to the opposing side. The clue to the Teddy–Ruth relationship is in their contrasted imagery of cleanliness and dirt. America for Teddy is a land of swimming pools, early morning sunlight, and quiet sedentary work. In London, he says, there is nowhere to bathe: 'It's like a urinal. A filthy urinal!' This is the view of a cerebral creature whose change of country amounts to an amputation of his animal inheritance. For Ruth, America is a desert populated only by insects; it is not an environment that supports animal life. The dirt and aggression of the London house provide the environment she needs. It's summed up in Max's speech: 'I've never had a whore under this roof before. Ever since your mother died.' It sounds like a joke line; but Ruth would see nothing inappropriate in it and could well take it as a compliment.

From this reading, *The Homecoming* emerges as a very ironic play. Ruth's relations with the family consist of extended bargaining: she has sex to offer, they have the territory, and in the end they strike a deal. In conventional terms she seems to get the worse of it; exchanging her status as a well-to-do wife and mother for life as a prostitute with four men to satisfy free of charge in her spare time. But in territorial terms, the position is reversed. The female is the sexual specialist, and the exercise of that function robs her of nothing. Sexually she retains the whip hand – a point which Pinter emphasises in the last scene when the apparently victorious Max falls on his knees begging for attention from her. She is the queen bee, not the captive. Her own tactics are absolutely clear. She wants to translate sexual power into real estate, and she does so by specifying precisely the property she desires – the number of rooms, services, domestic assistance, wardrobe – and putting the whole thing in contractual terms. What we see, in other words, is a ritualised tournament in which the two instincts of sexual desire and territorial aspiration fight it out under the scrutiny of an emasculated observer on the sidelines. There is no doubt that territory is the winner.

Source: extract from essay in J. Lahr (ed), *A Casebook on 'The Homecoming'* (New York, 1971), pp. 40–4.

Martin Esslin   'A Case For *The Homecoming*'
(1970/1982)

... *The Homecoming* shocks its audiences not only by the casual and matter-of-fact way in which sex and prostitution are discussed in it, but also, and even more, by the apparently inexplicable motivations of its main characters: why should a woman, the mother of three children and the wife of an American college professor, calmly accept an offer to have herself set up as a prostitute; how could a husband not only consent to such an arrangement but actually put the proposition to his wife? Is the author merely out to shock for the sake of shock? Is the whole story not totally incredible? Alternatively, those who admired the play's obvious theatrical effectiveness, with its sudden surprises and unexpected turns, defended it as being a cluster of symbolic images and poetic metaphors which should therefore not be subjected to excessive scrutiny on counts of verisimilitude and realistic credibility.

It is my conviction that *The Homecoming*, while being a poetic image of a basic human situation, can also stand up to the most meticulous examination as a piece of realistic theatre, and that, indeed, its achievement is the perfect fusion of extreme realism with the quality of an archetypal dream image of wish fulfilment.

Let us first examine the validity of the play as a realistic and perfectly explicable series of events as they could, in fact, happen to a family living in the circumstances outlined and clearly indicated by the author. The sequence of events portrayed in *The Homecoming* is inexplicable only in terms of a convention of drama in which the past history of the characters and their motivations must be clearly outlined in the exposition. As Pinter regards this convention not only as contrary to strict realism (people don't explain each others' past lives and motivations, which are already well known to them) but also somewhat presumptuous (as it postulates an omniscient author), he does not supply a neatly worked out set of backgrounds and motivations; yet all the information is given in the most natural manner in the course of the play.

For example: there can be little doubt that Max was a butcher by trade, or that his friend MacGregor also started out as a butcher in the shop of Max's father. But that does not mean that Max and MacGregor could not also, and in addition, have been engaged in less savoury occupations, that in fact they might have been members of the London half-world of pimps and gangsters. In the very first scene, Max reminisces about MacGregor and himself:

Huhh! We were two of the worst hated men in the West End of London. I tell you, I still got the scars. We'd walk into a place, the whole room'd stand up, they'd make way to let us pass. You never heard such silence.   [p. 8]

At that point in the play the audience will tend to take this as empty boasting from an old man, but in the light of subsequent events it may well seem to contain at least part of the truth. And what would have been more natural than that Lenny should have followed a family tradition by taking up the profession of a Soho pimp? His story about the beating up of a diseased prostitute establishes his profession fairly early in the play. Moreover, in this story there is a hint that chauffeurs, like Sam, are an integral part of an organisation like Lenny's:

Don't worry about the chauffeur. The chauffeur would never have spoken. He was an old friend of the family.   [p. 31]

Hence it becomes likely that Sam, who now works for a respectable hire-car firm, might, in his youth, have been a driver for prostitutes run by Max and MacGregor. His insistence to Max that he was always looking after Max's wife, Jessie, when driving her about the West End, may well indicate that indeed Jessie herself might have been one of the prostitutes involved. And this in turn would explain Lenny's bitter outburst when he asks his father about the circumstances of his conception. It would also explain Max's ambivalence about the mother of his children, whom he praises to the sky at one point and then calls a slutbitch. Even Max's statement that Jessie taught the boys all the morality they know would then become ironically double-edged: certainly Lenny and Joey have the morality of pimps and rapists which they may well have been taught by a prostitute. Even Max's indignant outburst when he first meets Ruth and immediately assumes that she is a tart has a double meaning:

I've never had a whore under this roof before. *Ever since your mother died.* My word of honour.   [p. 42; my italics]

Which might well mean that Teddy's mother *had* been a whore.

In a family which had been living from prostitution for decades, Max's and Lenny's final proposition to Ruth would therefore be the most natural thing in the world. No wonder that it is made quite casually, and received quite casually also by Teddy, the son who became an intellectual and ran away from home precisely because he did not like the family's way of life, but nevertheless is wholly conversant with it.

So much for the husband's complacency. But what of the wife's equally casual acceptance of the offer? It is made quite clear by Ruth that when Teddy met and married her she was a nude photographic model – and this is widely known as a euphemism for a prostitute. The country house she so lovingly recalls as the scene for her nude posing by the lake and where there were drinks and a cold buffet sounds like the scene of orgies rather than a place for photography. If Ruth therefore had been a prostitute or near-prostitute when she first met Teddy (and she protests when Max praises her charm: 'I was . . . different . . . when I met Teddy . . . first') and if both Lenny on first meeting her – he does not pay any attention to her assertion that she is married to Teddy – and Max immediately recognise her as a tart, then surely it is quite possible that she does not like the life of a college professor's wife – she describes America as an arid desert infested by insects, an unmistakable image of her boredom in uncongenial surroundings – and that, indeed, her marriage to Teddy is on the point of breakdown. This would be a very believable motivation for the sudden and unannounced trip to Venice: just the kind of last minute attempt at a second honeymoon to save the marriage one would expect. The likelihood is that this trip did not produce the desired result. Ruth's refusal to go up to the bedroom with Teddy on her first arrival in the house could be seen in the light of her reluctance to be exposed to what might have become a tedious or unsatisfactory sexual relationship. No doubt in the narrow world of a university campus somewhere in Texas Teddy's marital crisis might have given rise to embarrassing gossip, perhaps there might even have been rumours about Ruth's previous life. What would therefore be more natural than that Teddy, having come to the conclusion that his marriage has broken down and that Ruth cannot be turned into a respectable college professor's lady, should regard the prospect of her not returning home with him with a certain amount of equanimity, even relief? Hence his eagerness to reassure Ruth that he and the boys might well be able to manage without her.

So much then for the credibility of the events of *The Homecoming* on a realistic level: once we realise that the family depicted is one which has always been living on the fringes of the respectable, normal world, that Ruth, although a college professor's wife, might well also have been a prostitute in the past, the actions and reactions of all the characters fall into place.

But, as do most of Pinter's plays, *The Homecoming* also exists on another level: its real, its realistic, action is a metaphor of human desires and aspirations, a myth, a dream image, a projection of archetypal fears and wishes. Just as the events in the *Oedipus* of Sophocles, or in *King Lear*, are both valid on a level of real, particular human beings, but can also be seen as dreams, nightmares of guilt and human suffering, *The Homecoming* also transcends the realistic level to become just such an archetypal image. And indeed it deals with the themes both of *Oedipus* and *Lear*: the desolation of old age and the sons' desire for the sexual conquest of the mother.

That there is a very strong antagonism between the two younger sons, who live with Max, and their father is made clear from the very start of the play. In the first few minutes Lenny abuses his father in the rudest possible language: 'Why don't you shut up, you daft prat?' And when Joey demands his evening meal from his father, Max complains:

They walk in here every time of the day and night like bloody animals. *Go and find yourself a mother.*   [My italics]

The absence of a mother, and the personality of the dead mother, Jessie, pervades the play. Max's inadequacy – or supposed inadequacy – as a cook is the most telling symbol of this state of affairs. But it is also made clear that at least one of the two younger sons, Lenny, also sees the mother as a sexual object. When he interrogates his father about the moment of his own conception, the act of sexual intercourse that gave him life, he is above all thinking of his own mother in that erotic context. And his violent hatred of his father is clearly also motivated by the suffering it causes him to imagine his mother in his father's embraces – in other words in that particular scene Lenny is a Hamlet figure.

Lenny and Joey closely resemble those other brothers, Mick and Aston in *The Caretaker* (who are also engaged in a conflict with a father figure); like Mick and Aston, Lenny and Joey are complementary: Lenny slick and fast, Joey slow and strong, and they act as one: Lenny arouses Ruth and then hands her, without a murmur, to Joey. In fact, these two could be seen as different aspects of one personality: Lenny embodying the younger son's cunning and cleverness, Joey his strength and sexual potency. Similarly Max, the father, and Teddy, the elder brother could be seen as two aspects of the father figure: Max embodies the father's senility and ill temper, Teddy his superior wisdom (hence Lenny's needling of his philosophy). At the end of the play Max and Teddy have been defeated, Lenny and Joey are victorious. And what was the bone of contention between the two sides in the conflict? Ruth.

It is surely no coincidence that Ruth, Teddy's wife, like Jessie, Max's wife, has three sons. The point is specifically underlined by Max. As the elder brother's – a father substitute's – wife, Ruth is a mother figure, she is a reincarnation of Jessie. Max's violent reaction on first meeting Ruth could then be seen as the outcome of his sudden confrontation with the image of his dead wife. (I've never had a whore under this roof before. Ever since your mother died.')

At the end of the play Ruth again rules the household. This is the 'homecoming' of the title. It is not Teddy who has come back home – after all he left after one day – but the mother who has returned.

The mother whom the son desires in his infancy at the moment of the first awakening of his sexuality, is not an old woman but a young one. It is *her* image which still dominates his dreams when he is grown up. Ruth, the mother of three boys whose ages must range from five to three, therefore represents the dreams of Lenny and Joey in that period of their lives. The final image of *The Homecoming* therefore is the culmination of their Oedipal dreams: their mother, young and beautiful, has become available to them as a sexual partner, as a 'whore', while the defeated father grovels on the floor pleading for some scraps of her sexual favours. This wish-fulfilment dream is the exact reversal of the real situation that faces a young son: the father in proud possession and the son rejected, oppressed, dominated.

From the sons' point of view therefore, *The Homecoming* is a dream image of the fulfilment of all Oedipal wishes, the sexual conquest of the mother, the utter humiliation of the father. From the father's point of view the play is the terrifying nightmare of the sons' revenge.

The very ease with which Ruth is persuaded to take up a life of prostitution and to become a readily available sexual partner for Joey and Lenny seems, if the play is seen as a dreamlike myth, the most natural thing of all; it is merely the characteristic way in which wishes miraculously come true in dreams. Even the way in which Lenny encounters Ruth in the middle of the night when she has turned up from nowhere bears all the characteristic features of the manner in which dreams develop from a consciousness of lying in bed and imagining what one would most desire to happen. Lenny's two long stories which he tells Ruth at this first encounter and which deal with his brutal treatment of women fall into place as a child's attempts to convince himself that he is strong enough and big enough to impress and conquer a grown woman like his mother. Ruth however, in the episode with the glass of water, has no difficulty in asserting her immediate and effortless superiority.

Like Sarah in *The Lover*, like Sally in *Night School*, like Stella in *The Collection*, Ruth is both mother and whore. A whore is the most passive of women, the one who can be treated as a sexual object without any consideration of her own feelings or desires. The more helpless a male, the more he will tend to dream of women as obedient slaves – prostitutes. Hence the stern, unapproachable mother image must, in the sexual dreams of a child, tend to turn into the image of the whore. And that is why both Jessie and Ruth are both mother and whore.

If the view that *The Homecoming* is a wish-fulfilment dream seen, primarily, from the viewpoint of the young son is correct, then the character of Ruth *must* be a passive one: she is the object of male desires and, being an image in a dream, yields to these desires without putting up any resistance. Yet the play must also function on the realistic level; and here Pinter's success in making Ruth a credible character even when seen as a real person and not just the passive object of archetypal desires, is a virtuoso achievement.

For Ruth sees herself – has resigned herself to be seen – as a passive object of desire. That is the significance of her speech about herself as a moving object in response to the discussion about the real nature of a table. Having failed in her marriage, Ruth is in a state of existential despair, a deep accidie, which is both fully understandable and completely motivates her behaviour. She has tried to fight her own nature and she has been defeated by it. Now she yields to it, and surrenders beyond caring.

The character of Sam, on the other hand, embodies the family's self-awareness about the true nature of the mother, Jessie, and the man who was her pimp, MacGregor – who indeed, on a deeper level, merely represents Max's own activity as an underworld character – Max, in fact, when he was like Lenny. Thus Sam is the family's conscience, its super-ego; hence it is only natural that he collapses at the moment when the situation about which he has felt ashamed and guilty all his life is restored.

The subject matter of *The Homecoming* appears in various guises in a number of Pinter's previous plays. In *The Birthday Party* a son figure is brutally torn from a near-incestuous relationship with a loving mother figure – and the chief agent of this traumatic experience, Goldberg, has much in common with the father figure of Max. In *The Caretaker* two sons expel a father figure (and again the old tramp Davies has much in common with Max's garrulousness and irascibility, while Mick and Aston are very close to Lenny and Joey). In *Night School* a son (Walter) is fighting with a father figure (Solto) for the possession of a girl who is half schoolteacher (mother) and half night-club hostess (whore). In *The Lover* the hero dreams of his wife (who is a mother) as a whore. But it is in *The Homecoming* the Oedipal theme emerges most fully and most explicitly. It is as though it had gradually risen to the surface as Pinter gained the self-confidence and formal skill which enabled him to meet it head-on rather than merely obliquely.

The universality of the archetypal situation dealt with in *The Homecoming* on the other hand, and its immense relevance, however deep down in their subconscious, to theatre audiences everywhere, seems to me also to provide the explanation for the powerful impact of the play in spite of an initial reaction of incomprehension and puzzlement over its apparent surface 'implausibility'. However much audiences may reject the play on the rational level, they ultimately respond in the depth of their subconscious. Hence the abundance of discussion and probing about *The Homecoming*. . . .

SOURCE: extract from *Pinter the Playwright* (London, 1982), pp. 153–61 – previously published as *The Peopled World* (1970).

Simon Trussler   'A Case Against *The Homecoming*'   (1973)

. . . *The Homecoming* piles effect upon effect in a way that is reminiscent of vintage melodrama; and it demands rather the same kind of conditioned but extremely limited response. It is full of pavlovian dramatic devices, which trigger off an audience's instinctive reactions so as to induce, as required, a sense of menace, of sexual reconnoitring, or just of some ill-defined 'significance'.

Not that Pinter would wish his play to assert any significance beyond itself – yet the only clue to what might have given it coherence and significance *within* itself, spelt out with unwonted explicitness in this speech of Ruth's, is more tantalising for the kind of play it promises than the play it is supposed to predicate:

Look at me. I . . . move my leg. That's all it is. But I wear . . . underwear . . . which moves with me . . . it captures your attention. Perhaps you misinterpret. The action is simple. It's a leg . . . moving. My lips move. Why don't you restrict . . . your observations to that? Perhaps the fact that they move is more significant . . . than the words which come through them. You must bear that . . . possibility . . . in mind.
[pp. 52–3]

What is one to make of this? Again, as an isolative, attention-distracting stunner it is fine: it surrounds Ruth with an aura of smooth, soothing sexuality – and it also *changes the subject* after Lenny has threatened to bog the action down in one of his attempts to taunt Teddy into swopping quasi-philosophical speculation.

Here, he has been pondering the old solipsistic favourite about the nature and solidity of a table:

LENNY: Take a table, take it. All right, I say, *take* it, *take* a table, but once you've taken it, what you going to do with it? Once you've got hold of it, where you going to take it?
MAX: You'd probably sell it.
LENNY: You wouldn't get much for it.
JOEY: Chop it up for firewood. [p. 52]

Now one critic has solemnly argued that this dispute signals Lenny's impotence (he *takes* the table but doesn't know what to do with it), Max's mercenary-mindedness, and Joey's castration complex – after all, he 'didn't get all the way' in his adventure upstairs with Ruth [p. 66]. Her interruption of the sterile argument could well, one feels, be Pinter crying out to such critics. For Ruth seems to be imploring her listeners not to try to complicate or simplify – not to *rationalise* in any manner at all: and the speech stands, washed by a slowly ebbing wave of silence, as a statement of her own quintessence and of the play's methodology. And yet, isn't it as blatant a simplification, derived from as banal a metaphysic, as those it is refuting? Ruth is using words – a carefully, compellingly poised self-definition – to deny the relevance of words. The movement of her lips is more significant than what she is saying: and yet this *is* what she is saying. *The Homecoming* certainly works best (perhaps can only work at all) as a kind of sexual mime with accompanying word-music: but words are *not* music, and their meaning, or lack of meaning, modifies the action and one's own response to it – most notably, in this very speech of Ruth's.

The speech is pivotal not only to the philosophic rationale of the play, but to the characterisation of Ruth. It is from this moment that Ruth's reversion to her origins becomes irrevocable. Before, she has been perfectly in control of herself and of those who attempt to terrorise her, at an intellectual rather than an instinctive level. Her first meeting with Lenny (though *why* it takes the offhand shape it does, as if these two total strangers were picking up the threads of an earlier acquaintance, is never at all clear) shows how consummately well she can *use* words when she wishes – whether the words are her own or, by holding her peace, she is letting Lenny lose himself in a verbal maze of his own making. Lenny's conversational style is similar to Mick's in *The Caretaker* – a confusion of carefully misplaced connectives – but his opponent has her own, more economic method of verbal warfare. Calling Lenny's bluff, by neither encouraging nor quite repelling his sexual advances, Ruth forces him into long, rambling anecdotes which put off the moment when a gesture must be made, a gambit followed through: and so Lenny launches into a long story about a girl who began 'taking liberties with me', but who was 'falling apart with the pox' [p. 30], and next into a tale about an old lady who wanted his help moving a mangle [pp. 32–3].

Both anecdotes end in acts of violence – towards, that is, the whore of the first story, and the mother-figure of the second. Ruth takes no notice of the aggression thus harmlessly sublimated, and deigns to join in the verbal fisticuffs only when Lenny stops feinting and threatens a direct attack. He wants to take away a glass of water he has earlier brought her, an act of taking as purposeless as the gesture of giving:

RUTH: I haven't quite finished.
LENNY: You've consumed quite enough, in my opinion.
RUTH: No, I haven't.
LENNY: Quite sufficient, in my own opinion.
RUTH: Not in mine, Leonard.
    (*Pause*)
LENNY: Don't call me that, please.
RUTH: Why not?
LENNY: That's the name my mother gave me.
    (*Pause*)
  Just give me the glass.
RUTH: No.
    (*Pause*)
LENNY: I'll take it, then.
RUTH: If you take the glass . . . I'll take you.   [pp. 33–4]

Lenny blusters on for a bit, but he is now clearly on the defensive. Ruth's superiority and sexuality are established. But at what cost? One responds to Ruth's triumph with a reflex-action of admiration: but it is for a dramatist's manipulative skill, not a woman's wiles. Ruth's temper and her tactics are alike unmotivated: their effect comes before their cause. As one so often feels in *The Homecoming*, the writing is becoming automatic – even that familiar pinteresque device of the rejected name being pressed into service to anticipate the future role of Ruth as whore and mother-figure.

Lenny's first move of all against Ruth has actually reverted to the slight-ache motif – a tick in his bedroom that's been keeping him awake.

I mean there are lots of things which tick in the night, don't you find that? All sorts of objects, which, in the day, you wouldn't call anything else but commonplace. They give

you no trouble. But in the night any given one of a number of them is liable to start
letting out a bit of tick.   [p. 28]

Now this tale of a tick, and the dramatic purpose underlying it, has
become, for me at least, so recognisably a pinteresque tic – here, just
about halfway between Mick's purposive nonsense, and the earlier
Len's sense of the threateningly inanimate in *The Dwarfs* – that it sets
off a different sort of slight ache altogether: a nagging doubt, which
increases as the play proceeds, that Pinter's purely technical expertise
has taken over, and made such theatrical interest as remains a matter
of imposing a formula upon a form.

However, at least the ineffably physical Ruth will have served some
purpose if she remains a final, definitive version of all her prototype-
sisters. Lulu in *The Birthday Party* was her relatively harmless, even
homely embryo. The girl who picked up poor Albert in *A Night Out*
was one of the less overweening members of the sorority, sheltering
behind her protective pretence of a past as a continuity girl and
a present as the refined mother of a girl at boarding school. Sally in
Night School, on the other hand, was doing very nicely in her chosen
line, adopting her schoolteaching disguise merely for the convenience
of renting her digs. These were the respectable-minded whores: but
Flora in *A Slight Ache*, Stella in *The Collection* and Sarah in *The Lover*
had their respectability for real, and for them it was only the symbolic,
actual or fantasised taking of a lover that could create that sense of
their own wholeness which Pinter's younger and sexier women have
always felt to be dependent upon their sustaining the dual roles of wife
and whore. Ruth is at once daughter to them all, and mother-superior
to their high-class bawdy house.

This sense of the duality of the female psyche has been one of
Pinter's least productive preoccupations; but here it is at least purged
by being taken to excess. Ruth thus becomes even less malleable *on
stage* than any of Pinter's earlier amateur or professional prostitutes –
partly because here the prostitution is pivotal, partly because Ruth
does have an inkling of an individual identity, which might have been
developed and felt more fully had it not been overlaid by her
representative role. For her, one begins to sense, living and being is an
end in itself, and the immediacy of experience is all that matters. Her
actions have significance in what they embody, not in what they
signify – just as she claims that her words matter only because her lips
are in movement. There's nothing very original about this simplified
form of existential coming-to-terms with oneself, but it might have
made Ruth less of a ready-made character. As it is, her existence
cannot precede her essence: because as the *quintessence* of pinteresque

womanhood, her freedom of action is hemmed in by her dramatic heredity.

In particular, this causes her change-of-heart at the peripetea of the action to seem sudden and lacking in conviction, unbalancing the whole play. Her scene alone with Teddy, during which this change first becomes perceptible, is stilted and uncomfortable – and whereas she had before been perfectly aware of Lenny's fantasising about how he would 'probably have gone through Venice' if he'd been old enough to fight in the Italian campaign [p. 30], and although she had then gauged its sexually off-putting purpose and made use of it, now she truckles to the empty fantasy, and even feebly joins in.

> TEDDY: You liked Venice, didn't you? It was lovely, wasn't it? You had a good week. I mean . . . I took you there. I can speak Italian.
> RUTH: But if I'd been a nurse in the Italian campaign I would have been there before.
> [p. 55]

This is terribly, quite tangibly wrong: it should be, almost, a moment of epiphany for Ruth, but the quality of the transmitted experience is bathetic. She 'closes her eyes' as Teddy departs. Lenny appears, and she indulges in a remembrance of her modelling past – much more rhapsodic, this, but as directionless and somehow *padded* as before, so that Teddy has to return with the suitcases to generate renewed activity.

Ruth dances with Lenny, kisses him, and lapses off-handedly into a sort of mini-orgy with the two brothers, Joey embracing and Lenny caressing her inert body – whilst Max simultaneously swops friendly commonplaces with Teddy. Tremendously difficult to stage, the episode is gratuitously sensual yet strangely sexless – as ostensibly abandoned as Max's sudden outburst of violence at the end of the first act, yet so arbitrary and empty of emotion as to be almost abstract in its quality. And least of all does the scene show Ruth living in the movement of her body: like the half-time whore she is, she is as impassive in a man's embrace as her husband is in observing it.

Thus, while Max is laying about Joey and Sam, and again while Ruth is laying about with Joey and Lenny, Teddy stands, regarding and regardless, a lump of stage suet. What is Teddy? An embodiment of impotent liberal humanism? Or the foredoomed poor fish of the family? Or just the intellectual academic incapable of action? He, like Ruth, gets a self-explanatory speech, and one draws upon it in desperation:

> There's no point in my sending you my works. You'd be lost. It's nothing to do with the question of intelligence. It's a way of being able to look at the world. It's a question of how far you can operate on things and not in things. I mean it's a question of your

capacity to ally the two, to relate the two, to balance the two. To see, to be able to *see*!
I'm the one who can see. That's why I can write my critical works. Might do you good
. . . have a look at them . . . see how certain people can view . . . things . . . how certain
people can maintain . . . intellectual equilibrium. Intellectual equilibrium. You're just
objects. You just . . . move about. I can observe it. I can see what you do. It's the same
as I do. But you're lost in it. You won't get me being . . . I won't be lost in it.   [pp. 61–2]

So there it is – Teddy's *apologia pro inertia sua*, and very grateful one
must be for it. Indeed, had the play been a kind of clinical observation
from this non-participant's point-of-view, cinematically angled and
fined-down, it might have made more sense. But as a work for the
stage, in which an audience sees the whole family miniaturised, and
through a fixed, far-off focus, in their disproportionately huge house,
Teddy shrinks into the most dwarf-like of them all.

It's just as possible, for that matter, to fit this eldest son into the
pattern of the play by thinking of him as a sort of contemporised
Oedipus, who's been sleeping with his mother-substitute but loses her
to the father he hasn't got the guts to kill. The trouble is that this is just
one of a multitude of possible interpretations – and the number of
possibilities derives not from a density to be profitably yet never
definitively disentangled, but from a yawning probability gap to be
filled in as best it can.

True, Teddy – holding up his intellectual equilibrium, no doubt –
tells Ruth that he "can manage very easily at home . . . until you come
back' [p. 75], but the play, unlike Pinter's richest and most rewarding
works, fades out of existence after its final curtain. It is full of
ambiguous episodes which are there rather to fill out than to enrich
the action – the business of Teddy's quite out-of-character theft of
Lenny's cheese-roll [pp. 63–5], for example, or of Sam's *tête-à-tête* with
his nephew, during which he confides that Teddy was 'always the
main object' of his mother's love [p. 63]. More pervasively, the point
of Uncle Sam's involvement in the action remains a mystery. He
certainly provides some welcome moments of light relief with his
elaborate discourses on the art of being a good chauffeur [pp. 13–16],
or with his compulsive routine of washing-up that so infuriates Max
[pp. 38–40]. But as soon as Sam starts getting significant, he is either
inexplicable – as at the moment of his collapse – or all too explicable,
as in his function as the Teddy of an earlier generation, unable to
escape the family clutches.

Max even anticipates Sam's providing for the household's sexual
needs as Teddy is about to do:

When you find the right girl, Sam, let your family know, don't forget, we'll give you a
number one send-off, I promise you. You can bring her to live here, she can keep us all
happy. We'd take it in turns to give her a walk round the park.   [p. 15]

But the dramatic irony is worse-concealed even than the threat – and is piled on thicker still a few exchanges later, when Max tells his family to go 'and find yourself a mother' [p. 16]. In any case, when Sam's big moment arrives nobody seems to care a damn, either for confession or confessor. Max, by all accounts, has never doubted that his wife was a whore, whether or not with MacGregor: but Jessie, in spite of his incessant passing references to her, no more comes alive than her latter-day counterpart.

Neither, for that matter, does Max. He is a sort of instant character, easily etched in by the violence of his language – which consists largely in readily-rung changes on his repertoire of curses – and by his totally erratic behaviour: but he is never purposeful, even in his inconsistency. His role gets considerable dramatic emphasis – it is with an impression of Max that the play both begins and ends. Yet his opening scene is one part exposition to two parts compinterised characterisation, and his grand climacteric is one of the uneasiest scenes in a play full of uneasy scenes, as, falling on his knees, whimpering and moaning, he crawls past the prone body of his brother, and approaches Ruth:

> I'm not an old man.
>   (*He looks up at her.*)
> Do you hear me?
>   (*He raises his face to her.*)
> Kiss me.
>   (*She continues to touch Joey's head, lightly. Lenny stands, watching.*)   [pp. 81–2]

And the curtain falls. Again, the sheer grotesqueness of it all engages the attention – but only instantaneously, and without *connecting* the scene to what has gone before, let alone to any conceivable emotional reality outside the play itself. In between times, Max has merely been benevolent or bellicose, affectionate or aggressive, clever or thick-headed – yet always, one senses, as it suits Pinter's purpose, not Max's mood.

The play's shocks are thus almost exclusively the cheap thrills of non-recognition. Consider more closely Ruth's sudden inversion of Lenny's threat, already quoted – 'If you take the glass . . . I'll take you' [p. 34]. The retort is neat, nicely balanced verbally, and it makes a good theatrical moment. Yet it could as well be Flora talking to the Matchseller for all its contextual relevance or particularity. Similarly, Max's tale of his knack of handling racehorses might have been spun by any one of half-a-dozen of Pinter's earlier characters, and been more relevant and insightful than it is here [pp. 9–10]. During Lenny's rebuke of Teddy over the cheese-roll incident comes, however, the most disturbing example in the play of Pinter's loss of touch, and groping for a gratuitous laugh – a thing he has very rarely had to resort to, so surely does he usually let the laughs arise easily and incidentally out of what a character can't help but say anyway.

> Dad's getting on now, he's not as young as he used to be, but the thought of three cheeky kids looking up and calling him Grandad is probably the greatest pleasure he's got left before he dies. In fact it'll probably kill him.   [p. 65][1]

This is pushing things just a bit too far – a straining after effect that one notices again and again in the play, because it is little else *but* a succession of isolated effects.

   The Homecoming is, in short, a modishly intellectualised melodrama, its violence modulated by its vagueness, its emotional stereotyping disguised by carefully planted oddities of juxtaposition and expression. To suspend disbelief in this play is to call a temporary halt to one's humanity. Pinter had written other bad plays, and had got fixated by his own bad habits before this: but *The Homecoming* is his only work by which I have felt myself actually soiled and diminished. If a work is pornographic because it toys with the most easily manipulated human emotions – those of sex and (more especially) violence – without pausing to relate cause and effect, then *The Homecoming* can even be said to fall into such a category. One has only to think of such a roughly contemporary work as Edward Bond's *Saved* to realise that what may be pornographically objectionable depends not on the number of blows struck, curses or girls propositioned per page – because for Bond's characters even at their most callous one can feel compassion, and sense human causality. For the characters of *The Homecoming* I, at least, can feel nothing, other than an occasional shock of surprise or disgust: and even these shocks are subject to a law of rapidly diminishing returns. Here, Pinter's enterprise is sick, and each thing melts in mere, unmotivated oppugnancy.

SOURCE: extract from *The Plays of Harold Pinter* (London, 1973), pp. 123–4.

NOTE

1. [Ed.] This passage is omitted from the second edition of the play.

Andrew Kennedy   'Ritualised Language'
(1975)

... In *The Homecoming* ... there is a shift away from the human –
artistic balance of *The Caretaker* – to greater ingenuity in the 'shaping',
with a language at once more violent and more mannered. A black
family ritual – the initiation of the new mother-whore, with all due
ambivalence – provides the climax for the meeting between hosts and
homecomers; and the action – more indirect, more fragmented, and
more dependent on gradual clue-assemblage than the earlier plays –
is almost entirely verbal. True, one character, Ruth, warns her stage
audience that her lips move and 'Perhaps the fact that they move is
more significant . . . than the words which come through them' [pp.
52–3]. But words are used to underscore those lips, and for the rest,
every character is a speech-maker. Pinter himself has implied that
there is less 'writing' (in the sense of wordy or gratuitous writing) in
this play than in *The Birthday Party* or *The Caretaker*, saying that it is the
only play that comes 'near to a structural entity which satisfies me'.[1]
But we may add that this 'structural entity' goes with a highly
elaborate texture woven out of the dehumanising abuses of speech.

The ritualised language of the family lies at the centre of the play,
and it is arranged in broadly juxtaposed patterns of ceremony and its
violation.[2] It can best be seen in Max's schizoid-seeming shifts from
the language of celebration to verbal defecation (and the other way
round). There is something like a key-change at the end of Act I when
Max suddenly switches from the abuse of Ruth as a whore ('We've
had a smelly scrubber in my house all night. We've had a stinking
pox-ridden slut in my house all night'.) to the mother-ceremony
('You a mother? . . . How many you got?') and then to the
father-ceremony: 'You want to kiss your old father? Want a cuddle
with your old father? . . . You still love your old Dad, eh? . . . He still
loves his father!' The repetition, the rhythmic intensity – as much as
the change from bawdy to baby-talk – alerts us. By the opening of Act
II the contraries become quite clear. Max's long, decorative speech
(that rare thing, a subtle, comic pastiche) intensifies the ceremony:
'Well, it's a long time since the whole family was together, eh? If only
your mother was alive . . .'

The speech (too long to quote in full) draws on a whole thesaurus of
sentimental clichés in its evocation of 'fine grown-up lads', 'a lovely
daughter-in-law', grandchildren who – if only they were present and

Jessie, the first mother-figure, were alive – would be 'petted', 'cooed over', 'fussed over', 'tickled'. The mother-figure herself taught the 'boys' 'every single bit of the moral code they live by', she was 'the backbone of this family . . . with a will of iron, a heart of gold and a mind', to be attended in her lifetime with tribal ceremonies:

> she put her feet up on the pouffe and I said to her, Jessie, I think our ship is going to come home, I'm going to treat you to a couple of items, I'm going to buy you a dress in corded blue silk, heavily encrusted in pearls, and for casual wear, a pair of pantaloons in lilac flowered taffeta. Then I gave her a drop of cherry brandy. I remember the boys came down, in their pyjamas, all their hair shining, their faces pink, it was before they knelt down at our feet, Jessie's and mine. I tell you, it was like Christmas.   [p. 46]

The counter-images follow at once, in the just as elaborately patterned, and comically violent, speech abusing his brother Sam and the whole 'crippled family, three bastard sons, a slut-bitch of a wife', with retroactive curses. There follows an immediate switch-back to the celebration of the homecoming pair – as if they were newly wed and in need of paternal blessing – in an almost orientally ornate tone (beginning 'But you're my own flesh and blood . . .'). Such sudden switches not only make up a whole scene but clarify the 'shaping' in the play; and they foreshadow Max's final great contraries, the wish to expel and then incorporate the new mother-whore.[3]

A.: Where's the whore? Still in bed? She'll make us all animals.
B.: But you . . . Ruth . . . you're not only lovely and beautiful, but you're kin. You're kith. You belong here.

The point to stress here is that these rites of transformation are enacted entirely through *naming*, through a switch in the evocative range, as if using language magically. This resembles the way Othello transforms Desdemona's room into a brothel by going through the 'appropriate' gestures and naming [*Othello*, IV ii 24–96]. But in *The Homecoming* the to-and-fro shifts of language cumulatively create a playful mood, a series of *as if* situations or simulated transformations, including the central transformation of the home into a family brothel. The effect is that of 'op art': rapidly flickering style signals which yield this or that pattern, depending on the angle of vision. It is only in retrospect that the spectator or reader can see that each of those shifts in language has been as precisely coded as traffic signals – green into red and so on – and it is only then that the 'shaping', and with it the meaning of the play, is seen.

This account underlines the virtuosity – and the mannerism, once more – in the structure and texture of the dialogue. And there are other aspects of the dialogue that support this reading. First, the excessive use of pastiche not so much in Max's speeches just discussed, as in Lenny's. There are too many of these, and it is only late in the play that we are able to make the connection between the pimp and the style-monger. Then we see the point of these appropriately centreless pastiches: the facility in assuming any tone, in using words seductively, as in the three 'stories' of his initial encounter with Ruth in Act I [pp. 27–34], or in the manner of a glossy ad, as in the taunting of Ted in Act II [pp. 63–4]. Secondly, conventional comedy-of-manner lines seem to be over-distributed. Max's manic slips of the tongue ('I gave birth to three grown men' [p. 40]) and comic antithesis ('I've never had a whore under this roof before. Ever since your mother died' – [p. 42]) match his ornate ceremony speeches; and Lenny's elaborate inquiry into the facts of his conception [p. 36], may be justified as father-baiting; but even a deliberately low-toned and barely articulate character like Joey becomes a goonish phrase-maker on sexual intercourse, ringing speculative changes on 'going the whole hog' (rising to 'Now and again . . . you can be happy . . . without going any hog at all').

Cumulatively, such effects tilt the play too far towards parody and away from empathy or the shock of recognition. There is a 'too-muchness' on the surface. This may be the price of an over-conscious ingenuity in the post-naturalist idiom of the play, where the links between the overall shape and the detail of the dialogue are deliberately teasing and tenuous.

The compensating achievement of the play is the subtly worked out counterpoint which brings different kinds of dehumanised speech into collusion. The grossly perverted vernacular of Max and Lenny is balanced by the homogenised academic jargon of Teddy, which goes with an attitude ('It's a question of how far you can operate on things'), and provides a stylistic clue (the only one we get) to his at once clinically detached and voyeurish connivance at his wife's imagined prostitution. Between these two patterns hovers Ruth, whose gradual transformation is shown through the transformation in her language: from the slow, desultory marital conversation of her arrival, to the seductive innuendos and the fragmented story of her modelling in the two key encounters with Lenny, and then, at the end of the play, switching to the farcically clear-cut mercenary jargon of her professional terms, a mark of triumphant self-assertion. In the final effect, the play language of a comedy of manners is weighted by the cumulative imagery of flesh: Max's butcher-talk, Lenny's pimp-talk. Their scatological invective saturates the play with an almost Jacobean exposure to corruption of the body, and its vocal organ – the tongue.[4] And after such exposure Pinter is flexible enough to end the play with what comes over as an authentic human voice: 'I'm not an old man. Do you hear? Kiss me.' moans Max, crawling on the floor as his verbal fantasies collapse. . . .

SOURCE: extract from *Six Dramatists in Search of a Language* (London, 1975), pp. 184–8).

NOTES

[Reorganised and renumbered from the original]

1. *Paris Review*, no. 39, p. 26.
2. See also Kelly Morris: 'Within the Format of Excessive Decorum, the Idiom is Aggression: *The Homecoming*', *Tulane Drama Review* (Winter 1966), p. 186.
3. The ensuing quotes: pp. 68 and 75 respectively. For a full discussion of the theme of Ruth as queen-bee, mother and whore, see Hugh Nelson, '*The Homecoming*: Kith and Kin' in J. Russell Brown (ed.), *Modern British Dramatists* (Englewood Cliffs, N.J., 1968), pp. 145–63.
4. Hugh Nelson draws a parallel between *The Homecoming* and *Troilus and Cressida* (op. cit., pp. 157–60); and Ronald Hayman, *Harold Pinter* (London, 1975), p. 67, says about the play: 'In mood, it's rather like a *Troilus and Cressida* taken over entirely by Thersites and Pandarus'. Perhaps the language of the play, 'coming from below', releases one of Wilson Knight's 'Dionysian' powers: 'some dialect that has not been attenuated by modern sophistication' – though the sophistication is there in the shaping. (See Wilson Knight, 'The Kitchen Sink', *Encounter* [Dec. 1963], pp. 48ff., written before *The Homecoming* appeared.) One can understand why Pinter objects to 'this scheme afoot on the part of many "liberal-minded" persons to open up obscene language to general commerce. It should be the dark secret language of the underworld'. (*Paris Review*, no. 39, p. 34.) Pinter's attitude to 'the dark secret language' is thus the opposite of what D. H. Lawrence wanted.

Bernard F. Dukore   'Different Viewpoints in the Play'   (1982)

. . . (The) characters in *The Homecoming* vie for positions of power, don protective masks, and both flippantly and abrasively mock each other.

To an all-male household – Max, a former butcher, his chauffeur brother Sam, and his sons Lenny and Joey, a pimp and a part-time boxer – the oldest son Teddy returns after six years in America, where he teaches philosophy, with his wife Ruth – a surprise to the family who did not know he had married or that he has three sons. At the end of the play the family proposes that Ruth stay, service them, and become a prostitute. After blurting out that Max's late wife Jessie committed adultery with his best friend, Sam collapses. Teddy leaves for America. Ruth remains.

In Act I the titular homecoming is Teddy's ('I was born here' [p. 22]; in Act II Ruth's ('I was born quite near here' [p. 53]. Even Act I hints at her homecoming. When she leaves for a solitary walk, Teddy gives her his key, which suggests possession. The title indicates a return not only to a house, but also to a state of being; a set of relationships, attitudes, and values; an ineluctable condition: 'Nothing's changed', in Teddy's words, 'Still the same' [p. 22].

The play disorients. A butcher cooks what one of his sons calls dog food. A young fighter is knocked down by his old father. A philosopher refuses to philosophise. A chauffeur is unable to drive. A pimp takes orders from his whore. The whore does not go all the way with a man. Words disorient, as when Lenny says of Teddy, 'And my goodness we are proud of him here, I can tell you. Doctor of Philosophy and all that . . . leaves quite an impression' [p. 31]. The first phrase appropriate to an old woman not a young man, the triteness of the phrase that ends the first sentence, 'and all that' belittling the advanced degree – these disorient, thereby conveying the impression that what is said is not what is meant.

During the opening dialogue Lenny reads the facing section of a newspaper while Max asks for scissors and a cigarette. Although Max wants them, what underlies his requests is a demand for acknowledgement and attention. Lenny's indifference to his reminiscences, questions, insults and threats indicates that the exchange is commonplace. Usually Lenny says nothing, a suggestion of his superior status (indeed, if he were not dominant, Max would not behave as he does). When Lenny speaks, it is often to assert a prerogative or to silence Max. When he initiates a subject (horseracing), it is to re-establish his status by contradicting Max, and when Max continues on it, Lenny's only response is to request a change of subject. Lenny takes the mickey out of Max who understands what Lenny is doing. When Max loses his temper and threatens to hit Lenny with his walking stick, Lenny mocks him by talking in a childlike manner. Beneath and through the dialogue they struggle for power – demanding recognition of status and self.

After the audience has seen Teddy's family, Teddy brings Ruth to the house. Before she meets them he describes them, first his father: 'I think you'll like him very much. Honestly.' From what we have seen, the statement is without foundation and Teddy's final adverb, designed to reassure Ruth, has a disconcerting effect on us, suggesting that he deliberately misleads. This suggestion intensifies when he describes them all as 'very warm people, really. Very warm. They're my family. They're not ogres' [p. 23]. More imprecise than incongruous, the description is not technically a lie since warm means both affectionate (his suggestion) and passionate or heated (as they are in their hostilities); but, as before, Teddy misleads. If the reiterated 'very warm' or the overemphatic 'really' insufficiently indicates as much, then 'not ogres' should, for the family resembles ogres more than not ogres. The play confirms Teddy's deviousness. Before he married he did not introduce Ruth to his likeable father or very warm family who are not ogres, did not invite them to the wedding or even mention it (let alone his three sons), and he waits six years to surprise them with the news of his marriage. Alert to her husband's linguistic stratagems, Ruth refuses to reply. Since he waits a full page before he makes the second statement, he seems alert to her stratagems. Perhaps the devious Teddy did not introduce her to his family when they married but does so now because he expects to happen later what he expected to happen then. If this is the reason for his homecoming, a subtext helping to create the theatrical dynamics of this ambiguous play, it could underlie Pinter's statement (to John Lahr) 'that if ever there was a villain in the play, Teddy was it' and the identical words of Peter Hall and Paul Rogers (Max in Hall's production), that Teddy is 'the biggest bastard of the lot'.[1]

Ruth's encounter with Lenny, a struggle for domination, further reveals her proficiency at dealing with verbal stratagems. After she declines his offer of a refreshment, he says they do not have an alcoholic drink in the house. She does not respond, even with surprise, to his insult. Aware of his technique, she does not reveal hers. Trying another tactic, he says that she 'must be connected with' his brother. 'I'm his wife', she states [p. 28]. Immediately he changes the subject – another insult, to which, as before, she does not respond. Nor does she react to his sexual provocation, which denies her status as his brother's wife: 'Isn't it funny? I've got my pyjamas on and you're fully dressed.' Maliciously taunting her, he suggests she has left her husband (he feigns surprise that both are in Europe), he speaks as if she were his brother's mistress ('What, you sort of live with him over there, do you?'), and he insinuates that the only European sights she saw were bedroom walls ('On a visit to Europe, eh? Seen much of it?'). Replying not to the underlying mockery but to the words on the surface, Ruth denies him satisfaction and control. When he twice asks if he might hold her hand, she twice, unruffled, asks why. By refusing to respond in terms he dictates, she controls the situation. If his story about hitting and kicking a syphilitic woman who propositioned him shocks or worries her, she does not show it but disconcertingly

192 BERNARD F. DUKORE (1982)

intimates, by asking him how he knew the woman was diseased, that his violence does not concern her. More subtly she insults him. When he says he has often wished he were as insensitive as Teddy, she asks, 'Have you?' [p. 31]. At the end of the scene she bullies him with the same property he used to try to bully her: a glass of water that, unasked, he gave her to drink. Now she refuses to surrender it. When he threatens to take it, she threatens to take him. Earlier he told her not to call him Leonard because it is the name his mother gave him – implying that she is not good enough to use it. Now she dominates by disregarding his order, and she demeaningly puts him in the position of a child, inviting him to sit on her lap while he sips, then while she pours water into his mouth, and commanding him to lie on the floor while she pours it down his throat. Victoriously she laughs, drinks the water, smiles, and leaves. He shouts after her. Whereas his taunts fail to crack her cool demeanour, hers succeed in cracking his.

Max insults her further. After calling her a tart, a slut, a scrubber, a whore, a slopbucket, a bedpan, and a disease, and after striking two men, he commands her to come to him, maliciously calling her 'Miss'. Instead of leaving she maintains her mask and calmly approaches him – picking up a gauntlet without acknowledging that she does so. 'You a mother?' 'Yes.' 'How many you got?' 'Three.' (*He turns to* TEDDY.) 'All yours, Ted?' [p. 43]. Still she does not crack. This is the warmth Teddy promised, these the 'not ogres'.

Insults pervade the play, as do verbal violence (including a threat to chop someone's spine off and stories of beating women) and physical violence (Max hits Joey in the stomach and strikes Sam on the head with his stick). Although the power struggles are derisive and vicious, how strong are the characters? Peter Hall's 1965 production stressed menace and savagery. Kevin Billington's 1978 revival emphasised vulnerability and humanity. In Hall's interpretation a character's taunts charged the atmosphere with imminent violence or psychic destruction. In Billington's the weakness behind the mockery and the falseness of the bravado were so apparent, the challenger seemed to hope he would not have to make good his threat. In Hall's production Max's collapse after his brutal assault was a resting place while he gathered his considerable forces for the next struggle. In Billington's the momentary outburst took a greater toll on the weak old man, whose renewal required more effort.

Different viewpoints determine different performances. Lenny mocks his brother's profession. Apparently Teddy is an effete victim whom Lenny successfully taunts. Inquiring about his 'Doctorship of Philosophy', Lenny asks what he teaches. Is Teddy's reply – 'Philosophy' – straightforward or does he effectively mock the mocker? When Lenny, questioning him about the known and the unknown, calls it 'ridiculous to propose that what we *know* merits reverence', he implies that his brother, whom he knows, deserves no respect. Is Teddy caught short or does he coolly respond to the surface of the question, not the subtext? Since such questions are outside his province, he says, he is not the person to ask. Employing pseudo-philosophical locutions, Lenny presses his brother, who tries to maintain an air of calm detachment, but does he succeed? Perhaps Teddy is direct and effective (his statements are simple and clear), Lenny evasive and slow to reach the point ('Well, look at it this way' is a typical opening gambit) [p. 52]; but the actor playing Teddy might appear uncomfortable and the actor playing Lenny might speak his opening phrase maliciously.

After Teddy has packed his and Ruth's suitcases to return to America, Max proposes that she stay to service them. With a smile, Teddy suggests otherwise. Ignoring him, Max urges everyone to contribute to her maintenance. Still calm, Teddy refuses. Lenny suggests she earn her keep as a prostitute. When Max mockingly asks Teddy about her performance in bed, he responds as coolly as if the question concerned cornflakes. He remains detached when he hints to Ruth of his family's proposal and says nothing when they specify what they expect of her. Calmly Ruth negotiates terms. The power is hers, for no one else has the supply and everyone else has the demand. As Pinter says, 'She's misinterpreted deliberately and used by this family. But eventually she comes back at them with a whip. She says "if you want to play this game I can play it as well as you".'[2] According to Paul Rogers and John Normington (Sam in Hall's production), the outrageous setting-up of Ruth is an improvisation for the benefit of Teddy and Ruth and the astonishment of each other. When she takes them seriously, perhaps setting them up, they are hoist by their own petard.[3] Only one character drops his mask of detachment, Sam, who blurts out that Jessie cuckolded Max and then falls to the floor. The accusation fails to disturb Max, whose only response is to call Sam's imagination diseased, and the collapse merely incommodes Teddy, who must find another ride to the airport. Sam's behaviour highlights the fact that no one else betrays emotion. With studied calm, Teddy bids the men goodbye and accepts a photograph of Max for his grandchildren. With equal calculation, he does not speak to his wife. When she sluttishly tells him not to become a stranger, thereby mocking him, he leaves without a word, thereby mocking her.

Although the play is savage, it is comic too – often at the same time. Incongruity combines with derision when Max peers at Ruth's face as she lies beneath Joey, then tells her husband she is 'a woman of quality' [p. 60]. Lighter mockery underlies comic tautology, as in Lenny's response to Sam's statement that he took an American to the airport: 'Had to catch a plane there, did he?' [p. 12]. Comic repetition is part of power struggles, as in an exchange between Ruth and Teddy: 'Can I sit down?' 'Of course.' 'I'm tired.' 'Then sit down' [p. 20]. The unexpected literalisation of a figure of speech underscores a power struggle: 'Shall I go up and see if my room's still there?' 'It can't have moved' [p. 20].

Verbally Pinter connects sequences of *The Homecoming*. In Act I Lenny talks of having perhaps been a soldier in the Italian campaign during World War II; in Act II Ruth mentions having perhaps been a nurse in that campaign. In Act I Max taunts Sam about taking a wife and bringing her home, where she can make them all happy; in Act II he and Lenny propose this to Teddy and his wife. Before Sam's second act accusation, he hints in the first act that Jessie may have been what Ruth might become, a prostitute. He calls Jessie charming, but he adds an unusual reservation: 'All the same, she was your wife.' His driving her about town gave him 'some of the most delightful evenings I've ever had', he remembers with nostalgia and vindictiveness. Although he does not call her a prostitute, Max's response indicates disturbance at Sam's pleasure: '(*softly, closing his eyes*) Christ' [p. 16]. Max's seemingly unfavourable comparison of Ruth with Jessie actually demonstrates that he regards both women the same way. After Teddy exclaims that Ruth is his wife, Max pauses – suggestive of careful consideration – and then links, as he apparently contrasts, the women: 'I've never had a whore under this roof before. Ever since your mother died' [p. 42].

Parallel actions abound. Each act ends with Max asking for affection – first from Teddy, then from Ruth. In Act I Teddy brings Ruth to his former home; in Act II he leaves her there. When Lenny meets her, he asks what she might want; at the end she gives specifications. Joey's first action concerning her is a refusal to throw her out; at the end she pats his head. When Max first sees her, he ignores her; at the end she does not respond to him. In the first scene Max admits he is getting old; in the last he denies it.

Visually past exists in present. The set shows that '*The back wall, which contained the door, has been removed. A square arch shape remains. Beyond it, the hall*' [p. 6]. When Teddy and Ruth enter, he calls her attention to the arch. John Bury's set for Peter Hall's production was selectively realistic, not naturalistic. The staircase, much larger than an actual one, ascended above the proscenium arch. The setting was stark, suggestive of coldness, hostility, a house wherein no affection could exist. By contrast Eileen Diss's setting for Kevin Billington's production was naturalistic. She even showed the second storey, with characters entering and leaving bedrooms. Savagery and violence, her set suggested, are not strange but exist in a home-like environment, familiar to the audience. Without words Pinter conveys attitudes. After Ruth leaves, Teddy goes to the window at stage right and peers out, watching her. Lenny enters from upstage left and stands there. Teddy turns to see him. The meaning of their words conveys little. The stage picture conveys a great deal: although the brothers have not seen each other for six years, they do not move for almost two pages but regard each other from opposite sides of the stage. Throughout they neither embrace nor shake hands. Moreover this scene occurs after Teddy tells Ruth his family is very warm; it comments ironically on that statement and reveals the brothers' relationship – scrutinising and testing, as if before a fight. When Teddy picks up his and Ruth's suitcases, Lenny offers to give him a hand but does not move. Only after Teddy has gone into the hall and Lenny turned out the light does he follow his brother to ask if he wants anything. By then the question is clearly *pro forma*.

In the second scene between Ruth and Lenny she makes an overture to him (asking what he thinks of her shoes), in contrast to his overtures in their first scene. In the University of Calgary production Richard Hornby suggestively visualised this by placing Ruth on a sofa and Lenny on a foot-stool facing her. Thus, says Hornby, Ruth showed him not only her shoe but also a bit of her leg. 'Lenny, as he said, "They're very nice", let his eyes travel from her feet up her legs, so that it was not quite clear to which he was referring. Continuing to turn her foot and look at it, Ruth delivered her next line, "No, I can't get the ones I want over there", with a kind of *over*casualness.' By slightly over-emphasising 'them' Lenny agreed that footwear was not all she could not get in America. As she concurred their eyes made contact for the first time, confirming that they recognised the subject was more than shoes. Yet 'it was all done in a simple and understanding manner'.[4]

The final stage picture portrays the ambiguous note on which the play ends. Previously Ruth preferred not to finalise the proposed agreement but to negotitate details later. At the end of the play she sits enthroned, with Joey's head in her lap and Max on his knees before her in supplication. Lenny stands apart, mutely and perhaps obediently watching. Possibly Ruth will control the men rather than be controlled by them, but Lenny's silence – maintained, like Ruth's, since bidding Teddy goodbye – may indicate his control, and standing is usually a stronger stage position that sitting or kneeling, particularly here, where Lenny is upstage of and at a distance from the cluster of mistress and attendants. Whatever one may infer from her victory over him in their first scene together is balanced by her taking the initiative in their second. Because Ruth has yet to work out the final terms with a man whose profession is pimp, the play's end – notwithstanding his previous agreement to her demands – is ambiguous.

In their frequently vicious struggles of power, no character is clearly victorious. Does Teddy intend at the start to let the nature of his family take its course and claim Ruth? If so, or if not, he does not leave the London house unscarred. Is Ruth at the end in the position of Queen Bee? If so, she may for specified periods of time become a worker who supports the drones.

SOURCE: extract from *Harold Pinter*, Modern Dramatists series (London and Basingstoke, 1982), pp. 75–84

NOTES

[Reorganised and renumbered from the original]

1. Peter Hall, 'A Director's Approach', in John Lahr (ed.) *A Casebook on Harold Pinter's 'The Homecoming'* (New York, 1971), p. 20; Paul Rogers, 'An Actor's Approach', ibid., p. 169.
2. Henry Hawes, 'Probing Pinter's Play', *Saturday Review*, 50 (8/4/1967), p. 58.
3. Rogers, p. 165; John Normington, 'An Actor's Approach', ibid., pp. 140–1.
4. Richard Hornby, *Script into Performance* (Austin, Texas, 1977), pp. 179–80.

Philip Hope-Wallace   'Feeling Cheated'
(1965)

REVIEW OF FIRST LONDON PRODUCTION, ALDWYCH

At first and even into the second, sadder half, the relentless ribaldry and poker-faced outrageousness of Harold Pinter's new enigmatic parable (*The Homecoming* at the Aldwych) was relished by the first night audience – or most of them. Gleeful squeals of joy greeted the unvarnished home-truths exchanged by Cockney brothers in a widower's home, welcoming back a brother from America and his ex-model suburban British wife with a view to inducing her to go on the streets and keep them in comfort. But by the end I sensed some disappointment and shared it. The thing is perfectly turned, but to what end?

No doubt that is the wrong question to ask. These Pinter pieces, variously amusing according to taste and often fraught with that fashionable commodity, menace, are not really 'about' anything. This play is not 'about' a moral exposé as is Lenormand's *Les Ratés* for example. The pieces are quadrilles, stylishly danced, or like the arabesques and whorls in paint to be seen on the easels of *avante garde* art dealers: superbly executed doodles.

Boredom can set in fairly early with the rationalist. I enjoy myself the outrageousness and am quite happy with the baffling message of motiveless evil lurking in wait. But to me (and to me only it may be) Mr Pinter reverses the chief pleasure in the theatre: which is to sit with fellow humans (the audience) either fully in-the-know or in keen curiosity as to the general state of affairs and then to see the players, probably not in full knowledge or in misguided expectation make a mess of or redeem events through their 'own' devices and character. In Pinter the thing is the other way up. It is *we* who are in total ignorance: the actors who are exchanging wreathed smiles and knowing nods of complicity.

Why, for instance, does the chauffeur uncle have a heart attack? He was such a nice fellow and his boring anecdotes and self-regarding patter are beautifully managed by John Normington. Was it because he didn't have the courage to stand out against the arrangement whereby his niece-in-law was to be set up in prostitution? Arguably Paul Rogers the hectoring old widower also has a heart attack but doesn't die. His whine 'I'm not an old man' addressed to the enigmatic and only too willing daughter-in-law (Vivien Merchant, all poise and polish) finally brings down the curtain.

Most enigmatic of all is Michael Bryant's Teddy (the home-comer) who remains a complete blank and makes off to America again without protest or visible sign of relief at being rid of a tiresome wife. Ian Holm, with enormous gusto and volume, bounces us into feelings of interest for Lenny, the cock sparrow brother with the most enterprise. Peter Hall produces with a splendid sense of what can be got out of the veiled innuendo and non sequitur. The result is often very comic in a wry way. The grey and black horror of a living room designed by John Bury is not the least of the ingredients. But it leaves us feeling cheated.

Source: review article, *Guardian* (4/6/1965).

John Elsom   'Family Ties'   (1978)

REVIEW OF KEVIN BILLINGTON'S PRODUCTION, GARRICK

Kevin Billington has now directed three early Pinter plays; and, in each case, he has refused to dwell upon what used to be regarded as Pinter's distinctive style – the long ambiguous pauses, the hints of distant menace, 'the weasel under the cocktail cabinet'. If there is a weasel in a Billington production, he is on the dining-room table, snarling and biting quite openly. Pinter, at one time, was placed among the Absurdists, with Beckett (who certainly influenced him) and Ionesco; but Billington treats his work as being basically that of a naturalistic dramatist. *The Homecoming* emerges as a tough, powerful play, not puzzling at all except to those who are taken by surprise by the battle between the sexes.

The question arises as to whether we were simply incapable during the early 1960s of taking Pinter's plays at their face value or whether a kind of 'art for art's sake' intervened, changing the shocks just into effective moments, the power into mere conjuring, the substance into decoration. At one time, for example, Ruth's choice in *The Homecoming* seemed bizarre. She decides to abandon her home in the States, her children and her dull but painstaking husband, Teddy, and to accept an offer from Teddy's all-male, craving and brutal family in North London to become a London whore with a three-roomed flat near Greek Street and all the equipment thrown in. Why does she do it?

In Billington's production, it is clear from the moment that Gemma Jones's Ruth comes in that she is suffering from a bad attack of domestic blues, which Oliver Cotton's Teddy, with all his self-doubts and worries about what his father will think, cannot allay. Teddy is struggling to rise above the human condition. He lives in a desert, studying philosophy by a small swimming-pool; and that is all he is fit for. Ruth longs for the sexual battle in which Teddy takes no part. He is an onlooker, a pacifist; and so when Ruth meets Lenny, Teddy's brother and opposite, cool and tough, with a string of call-girls to support his lifestyle, she finds the challenge for which she has been waiting. Michael Kitchen as Lenny gives a performance to remember, dryly ironic and dangerous; and the first scene between them, over two glasses of water and Miss Jones's legs, is charged with such sexual tension that you could light Paul Raymond's Revue-bar empire by it.

From that moment, the play builds up logically as Ruth becomes Queen Bee, taking on Joey (Roger Lloyd Pack), the subnormal boxing brother, and Max (Timothy West), the sweating, hard-hitting and swearing ex-butcher, who has previously been mother and father to his three sons. Ruth's arrival completes the household: she has brought 'home' to them. Their male needs are also what she requires, and thus they have brought home to her; and if Pinter's vision of home, with its greedy exploitation of mutual frustrations, does not tally with more conventional images of domesticity, that is where the shock and originality of his play lies. It may be a savage and, in some respects, unpleasant work; but it is one of the few postwar plays to demand another, and different, London production within so short a space of time.

SOURCE: review article, *Listener* (11/5/1978), p. 611.

SELECT BIBLIOGRAPHY

TEXTS

In addition to the single-volume editions of the plays employed in this Casebook, *The Birthday Party* is published in *Plays: One* (London, 1976, New York, 1977). The other plays in this volume are *The Room*, *The Dumb Waiter*, *A Slight Ache*, *A Night Out*.

The Caretaker is published in *Plays Two* (London and New York 1977). The other plays in this volume are *The Collection*, *The Lover*, *Night School*, *The Dwarfs*.

The Homecoming is published in *Plays Three* (London and New York 1978). The other plays in this volume are *Tea Party*, *The Basement*, *Landscape*, *Silence*.

Plays Four (London and New York 1981) includes *Old Times*, *No Man's Land*, *Betrayal*, *Monologue*, *Family Voices*.

BIBLIOGRAPHIES

The fullest bibliography is Steven H. Gale, *Harold Pinter: An Annotated Bibliography* (Boston, Mass, 1978). See also R. Imhof, *Pinter: A Bibliography* (T. Q. Publications, London, 1975).

BOOKS

Useful books on Pinter other than those already mentioned include Guido Almansi and Simon Henderson, *Harold Pinter* (London and New York, 1983); Michael Anderson, *Anger and Detachment: A Study of Arden, Osborne and Pinter* (London, 1976); William Baker and Stephen Ely Tabachnick, *Harold Pinter* (Edinburgh, 1973); Steven H. Gale, *Butter's Going Up: A Critical Analysis of Harold Pinter's Work* (Durham, N.C., 1977); Arthur Ganz (ed.), *Pinter: A Collection of Critical Essays* (Englewood Cliffs, N.J., 1972); Ronald Hayman, *Harold Pinter* (London, 1975); A. P. Hinchliffe, *Harold Pinter* (New York, 1967); James R. Hollis, *Harold Pinter: The Poetics of Silence* (Carbondale, Ill., 1970); John and Anthea Lahr (eds), *A Casebook on Harold Pinter's 'The Homecoming'* (New York, 1971; new edn, 1974); John Russell Taylor, *Harold Pinter* (London, 1969); David T. Thompson, *Harold Pinter: The Player's Playwright* (London, 1985).

ARTICLES

Further articles of interest include 'Harold Pinter: The Deceptive Poet', in Gareth Lloyd Evans, *The Language of Modern Drama* (London, 1977); Charles A. Carpenter, 'Victims of Duty? The Critics, Absurdity and *The Homecoming*', *Modern Drama*, xxv

(1982), pp. 489–95; Noel King, 'Pinter's Progress', *Modern Drama*, xxiii (1980), pp. 246–57; H. Nelson, '*The Homecoming*: Kith and Kin', in J. Russell Brown (ed.), *Modern British Dramatists* (Englewood Cliffs, N.J., 1968); Eric Salmon, 'Harold Pinter's Ear', *Modern Drama*, xvii (1974), pp. 363–75; Peter Thomson, 'Harold Pinter: A Retrospect', *Critical Quarterly*, xx (1978), pp. 21–8.

NOTES ON CONTRIBUTORS

NIGEL ALEXANDER is Professor of Drama at Queen Mary College, University of London. His publications include editions, articles and papers on Elizabethan and Modern Drama and *Poison, Play and Duel in Hamlet* (1971).

GUIDO ALMANSI is Professor of English and Comparative Literature at the University of East Anglia. His publications include books on parody, on narrative technique in the *Decameron*, on the aesthetics of obscene literature, on Boccaccio and Shakespeare. One of his most recent publications (with Simon Henderson) is the volume on Harold Pinter in Methuen's Contemporary Writers series.

JOHN ARDEN is one of Britain's leading dramatists. His essays on the theatre and its public, *To Present the Pretence*, were published in 1978.

JOHN RUSSELL BROWN was Professor of English Literature at the University of Sussex until his appointments to teaching and theatre-director posts in America. He has written many books on Elizabethan and Modern Drama including *Effective Theatre* (1969), *Shakespeare's Dramatic Style* (1970), *Free Shakespeare* (1974) and *Discovering Shakespeare* (1981).

RUBY COHN is Professor of Comparative Drama in the University of California, at Davis. She is author of *Currents in Contemporary Drama* (1969), *Back to Beckett* (1973), *Modern Shakespeare Offshoots* (1975) and the volume *New American Dramatists 1960–1980*, in the Macmillan Modern Dramatists series.

PETER DAVISON has held professorial posts at St David's University College, Lampeter and the University of Kent. His books include *Popular Appeal in English Drama to 1850* (1982) and *Contemporary Drama and the Popular Dramatic Tradition in England* (1982). He is presently editing the complete works of George Orwell, and is editor of the Casebook on Sheridan's Comedies.

CLIVE DONNER is a British director working in films and television. His films include *What's New Pussycat* (1965) and *The Secret Place* (1956).

BERNARD F. DUKORE was formerly Professor of Drama and Theatre, the University of Hawaii; he has recently taken a professorial position in the University of Virginia. His publications include *Drama and Revolution* (1971) and *Bernard Shaw, Playwright* (1973).

JOHN ELSOM is drama critic of the *Listener* and author of several books on the British stage, including *History of the National Theatre* (1978).

MARTIN ESSLIN was for many years Head of Radio Drama for the BBC. His book *The Theatre of the Absurd* (1961) has become a seminal work in contemporary drama studies. Among his further publications are *An Anatomy of Drama* (1977) and *Mediations: Essays on Brecht, Beckett and the Media* (1980).

SIR PETER HALL is Artistic Director of the National Theatre on London's South Bank. In 1961 he founded the Royal Shakespeare Company.

PHILIP HOPE-WALLACE (1911–79) was drama and opera critic for the *Manchester Guardian* (subsequently retitled *Guardian*).

ANDREW K. KENNEDY is Senior Lecturer in English at the University of Bergen and an Associate of Clare Hall, Cambridge where he was a visiting Fellow from 1979–80. His most recent book, *Dramatic Dialogue: The Duologue of Personal, Encounter*, was published in 1983.

RONALD KNOWLES is Lecturer in English at the University of Reading.

CHARLES MAROWITZ, theatre-director, is a former editor of *Encore*.

AUSTIN QUIGLEY is Professor of English in the University of Virginia and a member of the editorial board of *Modern Drama*.

JOHN RUSSELL TAYLOR was for several years film critic of *The Times* and currently contributes art criticism to it. He is the editor of the Casebook on *Look Back in Anger*.

SIMON TRUSSLER is a distinguished writer on modern theatre and was founding editor of the influential periodical *Theatre Quarterly*. He has published books on a number of modern playwrights, including John Osborne and John Whiting, and has edited a collection of eighteenth-century drama, *Burlesque Plays of the Eighteenth Century* (1969). He has recently launched *New Theatre Quarterly*.

IRVING WARDLE is drama critic for *The Times*. His book, *The Theatres of George Devine*, was published in 1978.

T. C. WORSLEY (1907–77) was drama critic for the *New Statesman* and later for the *Financial Times*. His collection of reviews, *The Fugitive Art*, was published in 1952.

KATHARINE J. WORTH is Professor of Drama and Theatre studies at Royal Holloway College, University of London. Her books include *The Irish Drama of Europe from Yeats to Beckett* (1978) and *Beckett the Shape Changer* (1975).

ACKNOWLEDGEMENTS

The editor and publishers wish to thank the following, who have given permission for the use of copyright material: Nigel Alexander, extracts from 'Past, Present and Pinter', in *Essays and Studies* (1974) by permission of the English Association; Guido Almansi, extracts from 'Harold Pinter's Idiom of Lies', in *Stratford-upon-Avon Studies*, No. 19: *Contemporary English Drama*, General Editors Malcolm Bradbury and David Palmer (1981), by permission of Edward Arnold (Publishers) Ltd; John Arden, article on Harold Pinter in *New Theatre Magazine*, 1, No. 4 (1960), by permission of the author; John Russell Brown, extracts from *Theatre Language: A Study of Arden, Osborne, Pinter and Wesker* (1972), reprinted by permission of Penguin Books Ltd; Ruby Cohn, extracts from 'The World of Harold Pinter', in *Tulane Drama Review*, No. 6 (1962) by permission of the author; Peter Davison, extract from 'Contemporary Drama and Popular Dramatic Form', in *Aspects of Drama and Theatre* (Sydney University Press, 1965), by permission of the author and the Kathleen Robinson Committee; Bernard F. Dukore, extracts from 'The Birthday Party' and 'The Homecoming' in *Harold Pinter* (Macmillan Modern Dramatists, 1982) by permission of the author; John Elsom, review of 'The Homecoming' in *The Listener* (11.5.78) by permission of the author; Martin Esslin, extract from *Pinter the Playwright* (Methuen, London, 1982) by permission of Associated Book Publishers (UK) Ltd; Peter Hall, extracts from 'Directing Pinter', an interview with Catherine Itzin and Simon Trussler, *Theatre Quarterly*, IV, No. 16 (1974/75), by permission of the author; Andrew Kennedy, extracts from *Six Dramatists in Search of a Language* (1975) by permission of the author and Cambridge University Press; Ronald Knowles, extracts from ' "The Caretaker" and "The Point of Laughter" ', in *Journal of Beckett Studies*, No. 5 (1975), by permission of John Calder (Publishers) Ltd; Charles Marowitz, review of *The Caretaker* in *The Village Voice*, New York; reprinted in *Confessions of a Counterfeit Critic* (Methuen, 1973), by permission of Associated Book Publishers (UK) Ltd; Harold Pinter, letter, *The Birthday Party*: A letter to Peter Wood (30.5.58) in *Drama* (1981) by permission of, and published by, the British Theatre Association; and poem, 'A View of the Party', in *Harold Pinter: Poems and Prose* (Methuen, London, 1978) by permission of Associated Book Publishers (UK) Ltd; Austin E. Quigley, extract from *The Pinter Problem* (1975) by permission of Princeton University Press; John Russell Taylor, extract from article, 'The Caretaker', in *Drama* (1981) by permission of Drama (British Theatre Association); Simon Trussler, extract from *The Plays of Harold Pinter: An Assessment* (Victor Gollancz Ltd 1973) by permission of the author; Philip Hope Wallace, review of *The Homecoming* by permission of the *Guardian* (issue 4.6.65); Irving Wardle, 'A Rare Pleasure', review of *The Birthday Party* in *Encore* (1958), reprinted in

The Encore Reader (Methuen, 1965), by permission of the author; extract from 'The Territorial Struggle', in *A Casebook on 'The Homecoming'*, John Lahr (ed.), by permission of Grove Press, New York (1971), and review of *The Birthday Party* in *The Times* (9.1.75) by permission of Times Newspapers Ltd; Katharine J. Worth, extracts from *Revolutions in Modern English Drama* (Bell, London, 1972) by permission of Bell & Hyman Ltd; T. C. Worsley, review of *The Caretaker* in *Financial Times* (28.4.60) by permission of the Financial Times Ltd.

Every effort has been made to trace all the copyright holders but if any have been inadvertently overlooked the publishers will be pleased to make the necessary arrangement at the first opportunity.

INDEX

Page numbers in **bold** type denote essays or extracts in this casebook.